MICHAEL PATRICK TRYON

ISBN: 978-1-963565-08-9 (Paperback)

Library of Congress Control Number: 2024907338

Printed in the United States of America

Published by

info@thequippyquill.com
(302) 295-2278

CONTENTS

To my family

She crossed oceans, deserts, mountains,
Heart aches, snowstorms, picnics gone bad,
Sun drenched beaches, blows on the bay,
The lives of three men, Forty-nine years of marriage,
My heart, my life, my wife, my Janice.

California born, Bermuda baby,
Winter Water Wonderland childhood,
California college, the gift of life
The gift of love, the gift of Lai.

He popped into the world and left too soon.
A daddy, a wife, a very cold life.
Won't give up on the Bears, Wolverines still first.

For Susan, I still can't say goodbye.
Your light still shines on my heart.

Don't go chasing dreams
Pick the right one when it comes along
Dreams can be illusive
Hang on
Once in every lifetime, a dream comes true

Michael Patrick Tryon

Tiffany of Tryon

A description of silk, transparent though be
A description of her she would not agree
What's up with the frogs?

Her smile so bright, like the light in her eye
A mother, a daughter, a lady at neigh
What's up with the frogs?

Her willpower firm with a conquers heart
A woman's intuition, fighting hard from the start
What's up with the frogs?

Her vanity steadfast, along with her plan
We love her, we need her, we who are clan
What's up with the frogs?

Her gift to her cousin, few words could express
Beloved by her uncles, even under duress
What's up with the frogs?

Our lives could be dull, but your spunk is on fire
Your humor, your charm, and that for which you aspire
What's up with the frogs?

CHAPTER 1

Henry Rotyn

*H*enry stared out his window into the northern sky and waited for another falling star. He struggled to keep his eyes open. The moon was not visible from his side of the house, and the stars were brighter from his perspective.

The streetlight at the end of the block peeped at him through the trees. The irksome sparkle irritated his eyes. Henry adjusted his pillow so that the edge of it blocked the flickering glare.

He fantasized about his vacation and tossed restlessly, unable to quell his avid joy. He tried to sleep, but the heat from the summer day was trapped in his bedroom. His window was wide open, but his screen might just as well have been a wall because there was no breeze. His sheets and pillowcase felt damp and sticky in the suffocating July night air.

Imaginative reveries flashed through his young mind off and on as he dozed. His anticipation and excitement grew with every passing hour—fishing, camping, swimming, and canoeing on the river with his best friend Bobby. Henry adored Bobby's two sisters. Brandy was four years older and athletic, but Henry was mesmerized by her beauty. Barby, Bobby's twin sister, was Henry's age—a schoolmate—and she was a real girl who radiated feminine daintiness. He stood in awe of Brandy and enjoyed a close friendship with Barby.

The night's heat and his imagination continued to hinder his rest. Finally, during the waning hours of darkness, a gentle breeze filtered through his screen, the heat dissipated, and a dank chill filled his room. His young mind yielded, and his body succumbed to a night of restful sleep and deep dreams.

Henry often experienced recurring dreams. In them, he relived experiences he could not change and had no control over. But more than that, he wrestled with himself until some compromise settled real and imagined wrongs.

On the night before his big camping trip, his dreams rambled irrationally. He liked his last name, Rotyn, but he would never forget the blemished event in the third grade. He passed gas and evacuated an entire classroom. The inept gesture was loud and stunk. Someone connected his last name with the incident; hence, Rotyn became rotten. At the beginning of every school year, he went through the same teasing for at least a few days. Henry insisted on pronouncing his last name row-tin, but the rotten would come out as soon as someone saw it spelled and tried to pronounce it.

He turned fourteen in January. This would be his last summer vacation before entering high school. Adults presented transitioning from childhood to teenager as a monumental and formidable responsibility. Henry did not think it was a big deal. His transition from twelve to thirteen was not unique. He did not think high school would be any different. He had good manners and thought of himself as trustworthy and responsible. He had an inner confidence that his life would amount to something.

People often complimented him for being mature for his age. Henry favored his version of why he appeared older as most probable; he attributed his maturity to his hair. He had thick, long blonde hair. His mother did not cut his hair until he was six years old. Even then, it was just a trim. Every morning, his mom ran her fingers through his hair, informing him that it was admirable for a man to wear his hair long, especially if he had such beautiful, thick hair. She often shared with him how each man must be willing to stand up for what he believes. She taught him that his personality will flourish when a person develops character, courage, integrity, and virtue. A man with those qualities would accumulate many loyal friends and lifelong companions to bring happiness and contentment into his world. She usually completed her loving collusion with the motherly appeal. Please do not let anyone cut your magnificent hair; it would break my heart."

When Henry listened carefully, he often overheard girls talking about him. Many of the girls in his class whispered when he walked by. His girlfriend, Barby, said they thought he was cute and loved his hair. A few girls commented that his hair looked more likable than most girls. Some even asked him for tips on how he managed it.

Friends and relatives claimed he had his mother's looks. He had her large cerulean blue eyes and light blonde hair. However, his other facial features resembled his father's heavy, wild eyebrows, long, thick eyelashes, a long face, a thin nose, a handsome largemouth, and a strong chin. He had sandy-colored freckles and a dimple on each cheek when he smiled.

Henry was full of dynamic energy. His normal inclination was not sitting still; his mother said he had ants in his pants. He was always on the move doing something, anything but sitting still.

Henry turned over and heard leaves rustle in the breeze. Climbing trees in the summertime, especially when the wind blew hard, was one of his favorite pastimes. The old maple in his front yard was easy to climb. The trunk split three ways. One angled over the front lawn, one angled out over the road, and the third rose straight, although it, too, veered off toward the driveway toward the top. He liked to climb the center trunk up to the last fork. The branch was still ten inches thick; it created a nice perch. The top of the tree swayed and created the elusive image of a pirate in his crow's nest crossing a mighty ocean. The tree was sound, sturdy, and trustworthy. The wind made him feel alive; his skin tingled with excitement. Henry often pretended the wind was his enemy. He spent many summer afternoons conquering the wind in his tree.

If the wind did not blow, Henry would run fast and cause the air to blow over his face. Henry often dreamt he was running; running felt good until his lungs burned. There was a scenic trail along the Millpond; many people in town used it. It was an old dirt trail with willow trees hanging over it. It rose and fell as it traversed the edge of the West Side of the Millpond. It was Henry's favorite place to run.

Henry was extremely close to his mother; she was the most fantastic person he knew. She worked at Barneyville High School and was incredibly involved with the students, even though she was not a teacher. All the kids liked Mrs. Rotyn. She was exceedingly kind, and she instilled confidence in the children. She always took the time to listen to them, no matter how busy she was. One of Henry's friends told him that she made him feel good.

His mother was a single ice-skating dance champion in high school. Henry's Father was also an excellent ice skater. His Father and mother skated together and were ice-dancing partners. She still skated, but less often than Henry. She was a short, petite woman and had a great figure. Strange men whistled at her all the time. Henry's Dad got a quirky smile if he was around, but he never said much.

His Father did not skate anymore because he was disabled. He had black lung disease. He worked as a pattern maker in a foundry that made cast iron car parts. Henry's Father was twenty years older than his mother. He was a rigorous man, but Henry loved him very much. Most kids argued with their parents, but Henry did not. Henry still remembered the night his father told his son that his Father was going to die. He did not like to talk about his Father's impending death.

His Dad worked hard to provide for Henry and his mom. Henry's Dad said they were not well-to-do, but he also said they would never be indigent.

Henry's Dad was in the Marines; his nature was to be a "no bull" kind of guy, but he had always been an excellent father to Henry.

It was tough for Henry to see him now. He only weighed about one hundred and twenty pounds. His Father lost sixty pounds in less than six months. Before the disease set in, he was a powerful man.

The house Henry lived in was an old brick two-story. It was a square house with vines running up the four corners. The early American architecture provided a fine home for the Rotyns and was a step above the usual construction of other homes in the small town. The ten-room house was ancient but weathered even the worst storms well. The house did not have a mortgage; Henry remembered how happy his parents had paid it off last winter.

Barneyville was a small town; it was in a valley between two rivers, the Kalamazoo and St. Joseph. Two State highways intersected its city limits, M60 and M99. Its archrival in high school sports, Litchfield, lay to the west, Albion to the north, and Jackson to the east. There were about 1,500 residents, and most of the houses were old. The downtown was four blocks long. All the buildings were old brick two-story with fake fronts on top that made them look like three-story buildings. Henry loved Barneyville, his hometown.

Rivers were intriguing to Henry; hidden under swirling waters were many secrets. Henry had notable experience uncovering the mysteries associated with both rivers. Remarkably, the only time the rivers were crystal clear occurred after the ice came off the waterways.

The phenomenon occurred during the sucker season. Henry and his dad floated down the river in a flat bottom dinghy with a gas lantern shining deep into the clear water. On cold March nights, the lantern illuminated the bottom and exposed potholes, stumps, stones, muddy bottoms, gravel, and natural and artificial stone bottoms.

Suckers were bottom feeders. Every spring, they ran in schools upriver into tributaries and creeks. They lay on the river bottom sucking food with their thick, soft lips. Henry and his dad used broad seven-prong spears on twelve-foot poles to spear the fish. Fifty or more of the bottom feeders would meet their doom on a good night. They never ate fish but sold suckers for fertilizer or hog food. Henry never made much money at it, but like his dad said, "It was a hell of a lot of fun."

The Kalamazoo River feeds the Millpond in Barneyville, on the north side of town.

The St. Joseph River was on the South Side of town. It was a better fishing river and had many holes, great for swimming. The Kalamazoo and St. Joseph were slow-moving black water rivers other than in early spring.

Henry dreamt about camping for seven days on the Au Sable, Michigan's most famous trout river. He knew of the reputation of the Au Sable. People said its waters flowed at a speedy fifteen miles an hour, constantly stinging cold but crystal clear. After Grayling, the river was only eighteen inches deep for twenty-five miles. The Guinness Book of World Records lists it as the 4th cleanest river on earth.

Henry loved being outdoors. If it rained hard, the wind blew unusually strong, or the snow was deep, he would be out in it seeking whatever thrill he could encounter.

He never missed the TV program "Michigan Outdoors". Every Tuesday night, fisherman and hunters from all over the state displayed their catches. But what Henry liked most were the stories.

The upcoming vacation is Henry's opportunity to create a few stories. He so looked forward to this trip. It was going to be his first experience on a natural river. Sure, St. Joseph and the Kalamazoo were well-known rivers, but they were in a different league than the Au Sable.

Henry had spent a lot of time at other people's homes in the past year. His Dad was often gone for a week or more. He received treatment at the VA Medical Center in Ann Arbor. Henry's Mom usually took him and stayed there with him.

Mrs. Schott was a lovely lady. She was an older woman, about seventy-five. She lived next door on his street. Henry sat and listened as Mrs. Schott told stories about life back in New England, where she lived most of her life. She was married to a man who built submarines for the Navy. He died many years ago.

Henry had great virtue, and President Kennedy used that word a lot; Henry liked the sound of goodness. Henry had a keen sense of right and wrong; that disposition helped keep him focused on innocence, honor, and integrity. All those words were part of virtue.

Henry practiced cleanliness most of the time; he spent at least ten minutes in the bathroom practicing good hygiene every morning.

Henry struggled with a burgeoning desire to look at girls. Many of his peers felt it was abnormal folly to pursue fairer sex. But he often found himself admiring the sleekness of the feminine neck or the contours of the female body. His Father spoke with him on several occasions about sex, but Henry did not understand. Henry considered his lack of understanding of sex an abnormality. The mystery about sex continued, and at times, it bothered him grievously. Sometimes, his peers talked about sex. Henry managed to appear all-knowing, but its many hidden aspects puzzled him.

Henry felt uneasy when he was around girls his age, except Barby. He felt more comfortable around girls in high school. The high school girls thought he was cute and often told him so.

Henry's neighbors across the street owned a car dealership in Battle Creek. Henry's Dad said the Kraneger's had money. Mr. Kraneger was his Father's fishing buddy until his Father became ill.

Henry never went camping with the Kranegers before. They always went on beautiful vacations. Their son Bobby was Henry's best friend. Bobby often told Henry about their fun on their holidays, and this year, Henry could barely restrain his excitement.

His alarm clock sounded, and Henry awoke dreary and languid. He sat on the side of his bed and tried to wake up. Slowly, an anxious, giddy feeling came over him. He leaped out of bed and hopped around his room in an imaginary private celebration.

CHAPTER 2

The Kraneger Family

*H*enry heard a knock at the door. His mother was busy in the kitchen, so Henry ran to see who was there. It was Mr. Kraneger. He stood in the doorway smiling, "Hello, Mr. Kraneger. Would you like to come in, sir?" Henry held out his hand. Mr. Kraneger always shook hands. Henry figured it was because he was a businessman.

Mr. Kraneger was a tall man, and what hair he had left around the crown of his head was black with curly clumps frizzled neatly around the ears. A gray shade was beginning to appear along with his temples and earlobes. He had large green eyes with puffy bags under them and wild, untamed eyebrows, thick and sooty in appearance. Mr. Kraneger had a kind face, but Henry's dad said he was a "hard-selling businessman." Mr. Kraneger's voice was deep and quiet, almost mellow. Henry's mother said, "He was intelligent and educated." Mr. Kraneger had huge hands, but Henry's dad said they were not the hands of a laborer. Henry noticed Mr. Kraneger's hands were never raw or red, blistered or callused like his dad's. Henry heard his mom say, "Mr. Kraneger had a rare special charisma that rubbed off on others."

"Good morning, lad; are you ready to load up?" he asked.

"Yes, sir, I have everything ready to go."

Mrs. Rotyn waved hello to her neighbor from the kitchen.

Mr. Kraneger asked, "Have you had breakfast yet, Henry?" he wondered if Henry remembered they were stopping for breakfast.

Henry nodded no; "I remembered you said we were stopping at the Flying Saucer on our way."

Mr. Kraneger patted him on the shoulder. "Bobby is in the shower. We will be over to pick you up in just a few minutes. Is your father up yet?"

"Yes, sir, he's in his chair in the living room; please come in."

Mr. Kraneger walked into the dimly lit foyer. The tongue and groove floor creaked under his weight, but he was familiar with the old house; his uncle built it back in the thirties. Mr. Kraneger walked through the family room into the dimmer living room. The old dark oak columns separated the rooms.

Henry Kraneger was one of the town's founders; he raised Benjamin Kraneger when he was only weeks old. Unfortunately, Ben's parents died in the Spanish Influenza scourge in 1921.

Eileen Kraneger was a lady. Henry's mom said she was high class. All Henry knew was that she always dressed up, all the time. Her perfume was French; its fragrance left an invisible trail wherever she walked.

The Kraneger's lived in a massive stone house. The eighty-year-old gothic architecture stood within a seven-foot-high stone fence around the property's perimeter. Columns of stone bric-a-brac twelve feet high stood majestically on each side of the circular driveway and the two separate pedestrian gates. Three separate outbuildings, including a four-car garage, were located on the estate. In addition, there was a Gazebo with a stone foundation and pillars capped by whitewashed hand-carved woodwork. The four-room guesthouse was for Consuela, the maid, and her husband, Fernando, the Gardener.

Family memorabilia filled the sizeable unfinished attic with two different watchtowers at each end of the house. The estate covered half of a city block. Some people called it a mansion, but the Kraneger's did not; to them, it was just a house.

Bobby was their only son and was Henry's best friend. They were in the same grade.

Bobby had two sisters. Brandy was eighteen; she was the oldest. Bobby's other sister Barbara was his fraternal twin, but they were not alike in looks or personality. Barbara did not like her name and preferred to be called Barby.

Henry liked Barby, and all the kids thought they had a thing for each other. However, Barby had never shown any affection for him.

Seven days on the Au Sable was going to be incredibly special. Henry looked forward to catching fish, having fun in the water, and being in the wilderness with the girls.

Michigan: The Winter Water Woman Wonderland. Henry got a kick out of using that saying. He learned it from his uncle, who lived in California.

Henry wondered what adventures lay ahead.

CHAPTER 3

Summer Vacation 1964

*H*enry gathered all his things together for the outing. While he took his tackle box out to the front yard, he wished he had better fishing gear. Unfortunately, he did not have the most fantastic stuff, unlike Bobby, who had the most expensive fishing equipment you could buy. Henry's fishing gear was from the local bait store, garage sales, or family hand-me-downs. Bobby's fishing gear was from those expensive sporting goods stores in Battle Creek. However, Henry was uncomfortable with Bobby's equipment because Mr. Kraneger was particular about using it. He preached from first, catching the fish second. Henry's dad thought it was more important to see your dinner. So did Henry.

Brandy was good with the gear, which was a sore point with Bobby. Brandy constantly persecuted the poor guy.

Barby was not interested at all in fishing. She was very feminine, all girls; she never acquired the tomboy syndrome like so many of her peers.

The weatherman on the radio was reporting a thunderstorm moving toward them. Henry did not need a weatherman to tell him a storm was coming. The leaves on the trees were turning under, a sure sign of a humdinger.

Mrs. Kraneger drove the station wagon with the girls; the guys were in the pickup/camper, pulling a tent trailer with all the equipment one would need for seven days in the wilderness.

They took M60 over to the experimental four lanes. But, Mr. Kraneger said, "The entire nation will have roadways like this all across the country someday."

They stopped at the Flying Saucer Inn. It was the largest wooden structure in the county, Mr. Kraneger explained.

Henry ordered French toast, scrambled eggs, and hot chocolate. After everyone else called, Mr. Kraneger told Henry he would buy, but Henry worked topping onions most of June, and he had lots of money. It made him feel good to buy his breakfast. Mr. Kraneger understood when Henry explained his reasons for paying his way. He told Henry in front of everybody that a man who insists on paying his way in this world deserves respect.

The restaurant was on the second floor. They could see the storm clouds moving in from the southwest through a panoramic window view. The view over the treetops was Henry's favorite. Henry loved eating there.

Henry sat next to his friend. Bobby was short and overweight. He was a schemer; he was always playing practical jokes. However, he was not a mean character; he had that reputation because he was very loud. Bobby spoke as though everyone needed to hear his version of things—first, last, and only.

Bobby was very pale and had very dark hair. The dark hair and light complexion made for a rather gruesome-looking fellow. Popular opinion was only kind to Bobby if people tried to understand him. His physical appearance, as well as his personality, kept his peers at bay. Henry liked Bobby simply fine. Mr. Kraneger informed Henry he appreciated the kindness he showed his son.

Brandy got up and went to the bathroom. While she was gone, Bobby smeared her seat with some honey. Brandy sat in it when she returned and, at first, did not notice it. Henry saw him do it and bit his lip, snickering, trying not to laugh. Bobby did not even break into a grin. When Brandy realized she had sat in something sticky, she got mad at Henry because he was snickering.

"You little creep. You think this is funny, don't you, Pudge," she scolded. She did not care if raising her voice was improper in public. "You little shit."

"Brandy!" Mrs. Kraneger snapped sternly.

Henry did not say anything; he was intimidated, and everyone looked at him.

Bobby wasn't about to let her get away with that, so he yelled at her, "Leave him alone, stretch! He didn't do anything to you."

Bobby called her stretch because she was so tall.

Brandy hated it when he called her stretch because she thought it gave him a weird kind of tired joy.

Bobby looked directly at Brandy and silently pronounced "trollop" without saying the word audibly.

Mr. Kraneger stepped in, "Knock it off, Bobby." he smiled at his older daughter, "What happened, dear?" He tried to calm Brandy down, but she had a stubborn attitude.

Bobby leaned over to Henry and said, "Dad will do anything for Brandy; she's special," Henry figured it was because she was the oldest.

Mrs. Kraneger, who always seemed to resolve things formally, told Brandy to go to the car, get another pair of shorts, and change into the restroom. She said it was probably there when she sat down; after all, how much should one expect from an establishment soliciting to the public?

Barby often found herself arbitrating peace between her two siblings almost every day. So, when Brandy left, Barby went with her.

Henry watched them leave; Brandy walked away, taking dainty little steps. She wore tight-fitting, noticeably short, cut-off blue jeans. Brandy pulled at the white frayed cotton fabric on the edges as she looked back at him and shook her fist. Brandy was angry. She told Barby, "I don't have to put up with Bobby's bullshit." After she got outside, Brandy dropped the little cutesy walk and stretched out in full stride. Her long legs carried her quickly across the parking lot. Barby walked faster, sometimes breaking into a run, trying to keep up with her older sister.

When Brandy stopped at the car, her mood changed. She looked thoughtfully at her younger sister. "This is our last summer together, sweetie." she brushed Barby's hair off of her face. "You're going to break more hearts than your older sister."

Barby smiled. "Brandy, you know Henry didn't put the honey on your seat; Bobby did it."

"I figured he either did or put Hank up to it."

"You made Henry feel bad, Brandy; I saw it in his face."

"Look, sweetie, Hank can handle himself simply fine; he's not the innocent angel type. Give him a few years; he will be all hands like most boys. But, if you know what I mean, his motivation in life will be getting into your pants."

Brandy went into the bathroom to change. She looked at herself in the mirror and admired her long, graceful neck. Her long, shiny black hair enhanced her slender figure. She did not have any of Barby's freckles, but she had her father's long, thin face. She thought her mouth was too large but liked her long, delicate nose. Her dark emerald eyes sparkled under her long eyelashes.

Unlike Barby, Brandy's fair complexion amplified her looks. As a result, many people said she was as beautiful as a Hollywood star.

While studying, Brandy wondered what life would be like away from her family. Boston was a long way from home. She put on a good front, and her family thought she was an independent 60's woman. Brandy was beginning to miss them already. Brandy wanted to talk with her father but did not want the conversation to become a shouting match. Her Mother never understood the women's liberation movement. Brandy took one more look, smiled, checked her teeth, and walked away.

She had a great sense of humor, but Bobby was pushing it. Brandy was intelligent, and she had her father's businesslike personality. Her Mother taunted her and complained that a happy smile would take her a mile. Brandy felt a fake smile would become pretense.

When the girls returned, Henry realized Barby must have told Brandy what had happened. Yet, when Brandy looked his way, anger and hate were missing.

Brandy looked at Bobby and smiled. "Well, Pudge, I hope you eat a lot because Dad said we are not stopping again."

Brandy knew he was sensitive about his weight, but she stuck it to him. She did it to aggravate him, and it worked. Then Brandy retaliated against the real culprit. She reached in front of Bobby to get some syrup and knocked on his glass of milk in his lap. It was an artful maneuver; she made it look like an accident.

Henry knew better and glanced at Brandy. She winked at him and smiled. Her expression of cunning retribution lasted less than a second. Then, her feminine charm conquered the moment. "Oh dear, how clumsy of me. Waitress, we need some help, please?"

The parents never did figure out the battle going on under their noses. It was just a silent secret skirmish between two thugs. Henry was impressed with Bobby's tranquility: unmanageable bedlam was his usual reaction.

Mrs. Kraneger said she was worried about the storm, but Mr. Kraneger argued that waiting meant giving up a good campsite. She thought they should return home and wait for the storm to blow over. Mr. Kraneger insisted on continuing, so she followed his wishes as usual.

They headed west to US 27 North. Once they got to Grayling, they would head east to Mio, then northeast on some county roads north of the thumb area of Michigan.

The storm did not seem to be catching them, thought Henry. The sky was black, but they were staying ahead of it.

Mr. Kraneger told the boys this was how storms tracked across the state, southwest to northeast.

The short caravan pulled into the Park around five. Mr. Kraneger had already decided to wait until the storm blew over to set up the storage tent. He had requested a double campsite when he made the reservation. As stated in the brochure, the camp was above the other campgrounds.

Two large sugar maples stood along with the entry of the two campsites. A row of dense blue cedars in the rear created a dark green wall. Tall, thick bushes that resembled wild blueberries divided the edges of the campsite from the adjoining sites. That is where Mr. Kraneger and the boys set up the tent camper.

The pickup camper was full of all the latest amenities necessary to take the wild out of the wilderness. The storage tent was essential because the pickup camper was full of amenities, so it was highly prized.

Mr. and Mrs. Kraneger walked around the camp, talking to the other campers. He kept his eye on the incoming storm.

Mr. Kraneger considered himself a businessman with a family rather than a family man with a business. Therefore, he permitted his wife to run the household. This rule included the children. He fancied them more than loved them, but he did enjoy their company now that they were older. He had a skillful wife who was more than qualified to address their needs. He had a business to develop when they were younger, which required too much time and energy. However, he wrestled with his lack of parenting and accepted responsibility for ignoring his children. He provided well for them and, until recently, had been quite content with the arrangement.

The emotion-packed discussion with Tom Rotyn left him shaken. The man's dying wish asked Ben to help Henry. Tom was a Marine who served our country and cared for his son. Tom's example shames Ben Kraneger into realizing that Bobby needs a father's influence.

Mr. Kraneger's wife tormented him by neglecting his son. Yet, while not capitulating completely, he pursued the issue rather than ignore it and suffer the consequences.

He gazed at the billowing, dark, fast-moving clouds, thinking about how often his wife seemed to pick divisive issues. She had some remarkable intuition; he resented it viscously because he was always on the losing end. He did not have a good feeling about this storm; he had an uneasy sinking feeling in his gut that, once again, his wife had picked another winner.

Mr. Kraneger was immensely proud of his family; the children did well academically. Brandy would soon be attending an Ivy League school. She was too independent, though, and he wondered why she could not be more submissive like her mother. Mr. Kraneger dismissed those thoughts, realizing Brandy was like her father. She would be a formidable businesswoman; she had good instincts and was smart as a whip. Her spunk made him feel better, somehow.

He liked the Rotyn lad. He thought his long hair was a bit rebellious but showed the same tenacity as Brandy. Those two would be a match if she were not his senior by about four years.

Henry was intrigued by storms and noticed Mr. Kraneger kept looking at the sky. At first, the wind blew in a wavering soft gust, and it seemed to stop at times completely. Finally, at about seven pm, Mr. Kraneger directed the teenagers into the tent camper.

Barby and Brandy were playing a heated game of euchre against Bobby and Henry.

"Come on, stretch. Deal the cards."

"Hank, please help Pudge understand how near death's door he leans."

"Bobby, Brandy will kill you if you don't calm down."

"You two better not cheat; Brandy and I play fair, so you guys do the same."

"Did you hear Barby? That means no farting, hacking, winking, or anything that may cover up a cheater."

Brandy gave everyone five cards and turned one up, the Jack of Diamonds.

"Right bower," Bobby whined, sitting on her left. Henry was on her right. Her sister sat across from her.

Bobby passed; Barby said, "Pick it up."

Brandy picked up Jack and discarded it.

Bobby led with the left bower. Brandy looked at her sister, "You know what he is doing?"

"Stretch, oh no, oh hell no," Bobby's face turned thirteen shades of red. "Jungle Rules, Henry." he got up on his knees, pointing to his older sister. "She started it, not me; I always get blamed, but you heard her, Henry."

Barby looked at her sister with a slightly perturbed facial expression. She laid down the nine diamonds hesitantly. Brandy smiled at her, and Barby smiled back, but it was awaiting, you-smile-first kind of smile.

Henry laid the nine of clubs. Brandy got this evil look in her eye, looking at her brother, and said, "No help from Hank." She laid the right bower down and scooped up the cards, smiling at Bobby.

Brandy laid the ten clubs. Barby stared at her sister and got this sudden deathly look on her face. Bobby laid the queen of clubs. Barby applied to be the king of clubs. Henry rocked back and forth in his chair, raised his right arm as high as possible, and slammed the ace of clubs down. Bobby bellowed, and the two boys slapped a high-five across the table.

Brandy looked suspiciously at her sister; she cocked her head sideways as if to say, please.

Henry led with the king of Spades. Brandy laid out the ten spades. Brandy looked at her sister and hoped. Bobby laid down the ace of spades. Barby trumped everything with Jack of Clubs.

"Barby, what a doll!" Brandy, her older sister, screamed.

Barby stiffened suddenly. She pursed her lips tightly, and her large brown eyes became brutal and hateful. She hated it when people associated her with that overly famous doll that had adopted her name. Brandy knew better, she of all people. She preached women's lib; how could she be so vain?

Brandy realized what she had done. She silently lipped to her sister, "I'm so sorry."

Barby laid down the ace of diamonds, looked at Henry, smiled, and then looked at her brother with a dainty, evil smile. "It's your deal, Pudge."

Brandy looked at her sister bug-eyed and full of pride. "I love you, Barby."

Bobby pretended to puke while he was dealing. Then, he turned up the ace of hearts.

Barby looked at her brother as he looked at his cards. Then, she turned her attention to her sister. They looked at each other and sent feminine intuitions to each other at the speed of light. "Pick it up."

Bobby looked at his sister with an I-can't-believe-you said-that look. He looked as if someone had taken his birthday away. Then he got mad, puffing up like a toad. "Barby, how, why? I'm not too fond of it when you do that. How do you know?"

"Well, duh, I think it's called twins," she flashed a beaming smile at her sister.

"I can't do it. How come only you can do it?" Bobby lost his joy.

"She told you stupid. Besides, you got too much testosterone," Brandy looked at her younger sister, "he is only thirteen, and already he has this much!"

Barby giggled so hard she almost wet her pants.

Henry chuckled until he saw Bobby's reaction.

Brandy held out her arms, symbolizing an excessive amount.

Barby laughed harder, but Henry sat quietly, displaying no emotion though he secretly thought it great fun.

Bobby told Henry, "Give us two points," he laid down five hearts, including one bower.

He smiled sourly at his twin and said, "Your deal."

Mr. Kraneger kept walking past the door, still looking at the sky. Then, finally, the sky turned black off to the southwest at about eight pm. The storm front looked like a black rolled-up carpet lying in the sky, horizontally unrolling toward them.

Bobby stormed out of the tent camper, expressing remorse or outrage. Mr. Kraneger smiled. Let them blow off some steam, he thought. He rather enjoyed the way his daughters teamed up against his son. He thought the experience would help him become a more mature man. At any rate, it was good fun for now. He smiled and looked at his wife. She threw her hands in the air. Mr. Kraneger understood the signal; he walked over near his son. Bobby bent over in obvious emotional pain.

"Surely you didn't let those trollops get the best of you again?" Bobby looked up at his father. He did not want to smile, but his father had just called his sisters trollops. Bobby thought it was enormously humorous. He tried to hold it in, but his whole body involuntarily started shaking, and his frown turned upside down as his father started laughing out loud. They both laughed so hard that they fell to their knees. Brandy and Barby came out to see why all the laughing. When the father and son looked at the girls, they looked at each other, then back at them, and laughed even harder. Ironically, the girls started laughing, and then the men laughed even harder, though they did not think it was possible. Finally, they rolled down on the ground, bellowing uncontrollably.

Brandy got this weird look in her eye and grabbed her sister by the shoulders. "Barbara, quit laughing; stop it now." Her sister quieted, looked at her father and brother, and then at Brandy.

"Why?"

"They are laughing at us. I don't know what about, but believe me, these men are laughing at you and me."

The girls walked away and left the two Hyenas rolling in the grass.

Mr. Kraneger got up and then helped his son to his feet. They embraced and slapped each other on the back.

Henry was in the restroom and missed all the fun. Bobby shared with him what his father had done, but Henry did not understand the humor. Finally, Bobby glumly told him; you had to be there.

The camp was almost entire; many people stared at the approaching storm. Hardly anyone had set up a tent.

Mrs. Kraneger listened to a weather bulletin on a transistor radio. Then, finally, she called her husband. Mr. Kraneger ran to the door, "A tornado was sighted just south of the campsite. We need to get off the hill. Come on, everybody, there is a hollow just a hundred feet east."

Mr. Kraneger got the tarp and flashlights out of the camper. He headed for the hollow, and everyone followed. It only took a few moments to reach the edge. The ground dropped off sharply, and a large hickory tree stood at the top edge. They climbed down the path and hung onto the roots of the tree.

Below, the hollow twisted and turned as it fell off toward the river.

They located a sandy section that offered good protection. The bank above them hung over the dry creek bed.

Mr. Kraneger and the boys laid out the tarp, putting its bottom half about six feet down the embankment. Then they pulled the rest of the tarp up over them, pushing it down to their feet, folding it under, holding it down.

Bobby and Mr. Kraneger sat on the upper slope, the women sat in the middle, and Henry sat at the lower end of the hill. They all sat with their backs to the bank.

Henry sat beside Barby, and she whispered to him, "Scrunch up closer." He put his arm around her. Brandy was sitting on the other side of Barby. When Henry put his arm around Barby, his hand accidentally touched Brandy's breast. Brandy bent forward and gave him a mean look.

The wind started again; this time, it was steady, pushy, unrelenting, and growing more robust; they all pulled the tarp in tighter. Henry could smell Mrs. Kraneger's perfume.

Mother Nature's storm exploded, and rain pounded against the tarp. The wind became violent and sounded like a train. The edges of the tarp caught the wind. Bobby lost his grip on the end of the tarp, and it whipped away. The howling wind and frightening downpour stole their dignity. Brandy jumped up and cursed. She tripped over Barby and fell for Henry. Brandy tackled the tarp and pulled it back in place on Bobby's end. She yelled, "Get a better grip, Pudge. You're not a weakling."

Bobby started to yell something; Henry could not understand what he was saying. Mr. Kraneger yelled something, and then the ground under them began to move; they slid. Henry felt the changing shapes under him. Barby clung to Henry, but she started to panic. Henry held her tight.

Everyone was in a flash flood, moving downhill toward the river. Henry tried to grab a tree root to hang on to, but his grip was not firm enough. They hit a bump and then fell faster. The floundering mass piled against a thicket of small trees.

Henry's face smashed against Brandy's naked belly. When Henry tried to get free, he reached up to push her off him and accidentally grabbed her left breast. Henry let go as soon as he realized what he had done.

She whined, "What is it with you? Do you have some perverted fascination for my tits?" Brandy stuck her face in his and said, "Hank, you look like a girl with that long hair."

Henry did not say a word. Brandy called him Hank—she was the only one—everyone else called him Henry. Brandy could be mean, but Henry was infatuated with her and did not suffer any indignation.

The rain let up as they gathered to decide what to do. The women were complaining about the mud. Mrs. Kraneger was furious; she spent three hours at the hair salon on Friday; the mud and rain left her devastated in only a few moments. Mr. Kraneger tried to soothe her, but she caught him when he rolled his eyes and winked at Henry silently as if to add humor to the decimation. Then, finally, she threw her hands in the air and stormed off for the bathroom. Brandy and Barby waddled close behind.

Brandy was positively livid. The dirt and mud soiled her in the most private areas. How could her father put them in such a compromising situation? She could feel the filth rub against her legs as she scrambled up the muddied hillside. Her Mother should have stood her ground and insisted on waiting for the storm to blow over. Instead, she meant to take up this issue of constantly bowing to her husband. Brandy never interfered in her parents' marriage, but she was eighteen and would soon be in college. Her Mother was not independent enough, and Brandy thought to enlighten her on the subject. However, she knew the timing was not right, and her mother would need her support if her mother confronted Brandy's father. Brandy did not want to open a can of worms only to take flight herself in college. So, she decided to postpone the attempt for feminine independence.

Brandy took her mother's arm and helped her up the slippery hill. Unfortunately, her mother lacked the athletic prowess Brandy found so natural. On the other hand, Brandy respected her mom because she could pour out the charm, elegance, and gentility she learned from her generation. However, Brandy was a sixties woman who would never let a man dominate her like her father dominated her mother.

Barby climbed halfway up the hill and slid to the bottom. Brandy yelled for someone to help Barby, but Brandy responded first. The men were busy doing nothing as usual. Brandy practically carried Barby up the hill, where her mother stood in total disgust. Brandy did not see that look on her mother's face very often; she pondered over what to say but quickly decided against adversity.

Barby was her mother all over again. She did have some athletic ability but seemed shy about it. Brandy had many long talks with her sibling, adeptly instructing her never to allow a man to dominate her like her father does her mother.

Bobby surveyed the area. He had heard the rushing water but was unaware of how close they were to the river. A muddy menagerie of weeds, sticks, and leaves formed a wall against a maple sapling row. The structure looked like a wave frozen in time. Two steps beyond, the land quit on a limestone cliff. Fifteen feet below, the water swirled as it pushed against a bend in the river.

Lightning cracked, and the rain started again, but the wind stopped. The men picked up their things and returned to their campsite.

Black, muddy blotches stained their skin and clung to their clothes. Henry took a hot shower with his clothes on and then shed them after removing all the mud and dirt he could see.

Brandy and Barby showered together. Her hair was dark brown like Brandy's. Barby's eyes were brown, and her skin was brown. Yet, she never lost her summer tan. Mrs. Kraneger was forty percent Chippewa. However, she never admitted this to anyone.

While Brandy admired her sister, she suffered a bout of melancholy. She would be gone soon; she would miss this doll-like friend. "Honey, sweetie, you will write to me, won't you?"

Barby liked it when her older sister showed affection for her. "I have already started a letter, Brandy. I will write. You're the one that won't write, I bet."

Mr. and Mrs. Kraneger slept in the camper. The children slept in the tent camper. The girls were on one side, and Bobby and Henry slept on the other. It rained most of the night.

They awoke in the morning cold and tired. The dampness of the night made everything smell musty and moldy. Bobby and Henry tied a rope between the trees and hung up the sleeping bags to air out.

The parents were arguing again about how they should have listened to the weatherman. Mr. Kraneger argued again that they could have lost their campsite if they had waited.

The Park finished filling with tents and campers overnight. Bobby and Henry set up the storage tent and helped unpack the truck camper while Mr. Kraneger leveled it. The women set out a breakfast of cold cereal, grapefruit halves, and coffee. After eating, Mr. Kraneger insisted on arranging their camp and practicing their fishing form. Henry wanted to go fishing and did not care about his form.

The swiftness of the river accentuated a problem with waders; if they filled up with water, it was almost impossible to swim. If that should happen, getting them off could mean life or death. So, Mr. Kraneger made everyone practice getting out of their waders.

They scouted in the afternoon and evening, preparing strategies for the best-looking fishing spots. Then, just before dinner, the boys took some time to gather wood for the campfire.

Mrs. Kraneger cooked hot dogs and beans. They also had county-line cheese and potato salad for dinner.

Barby played her guitar; the neighbors came and sat around the fire. Everyone sang songs until bedtime.

The following day, Mr. Kraneger woke everyone at dawn. They gathered their gear and set out for the fishing spots. Henry selected a small island where large boulders were just upstream. A quiet pool free of the current lay behind the boulders. He thought this was just the spot a large Brown would hang out for some unsuspecting meal to cruise past. Bobby and Brandy were on the downstream end of the Island; Henry could not make out what they were saying, but it was apparent they were arguing.

Henry brought his dad's fly rod, but he only liked using it for small panfish. He had his grandpa's Shakespeare open-face reel with a four-foot rod. Henry put a lively night crawler on his hook. He climbed up on the rock but could not see into the water because the turbulence stirred it, hiding whatever lay just along the edge of the current. Henry lowered his line into the water, and the wind pulled it to its advantage. He played out about fifteen feet of cable and set his reel at its lightest resistance. Henry looked around; Mrs. Kraneger was upstream about six feet from the bank. He thought she was using a minnow with a standard river rig (six-ounce weight at the end of the line with the bail-up line).

When his reel started whirring, the sudden jerk almost pulled his pole out of his grasp. He pulled his bar straight up in the air while recapturing his sense of balance. The fiber-steel rod bent ninety degrees and shook violently in his grip. The jittering action sent sparks of wonderment up his spine and butterflies into his abdomen. He yelled, "FISH ON!"

Henry tried to place his right thumb on his spindle to slow it down, but the whirring reel burned him. He tried to set his drag to a higher setting but lost his balance and fell on his butt, almost falling off the rock. He leaned back and put his legs up, grasping the end of his rod; he let go with his left hand and set the drag to its highest setting. Unfortunately, the pole bent sharply, and the reel spun out of control.

Henry jumped up and ran down the rock onto the Island; he ran into the shallows downstream. He recalled his dad telling him how he had done this once. The maneuver slowed the speed of his reel, and the drag finally grabbed. Henry stopped, and his pole bent in two again. He kept moving downstream to prevent the breath from losing its hold. He kept yelling, "FISH ON! FISH ON!"

Bobby and Brandy pulled in their lines and were closing in on Henry's location. Bobby had the large net in his hands.

Brandy yelled, "Don't give it any slack; keep your line tight."

"Girls," Henry thought.

Henry stopped just before the end of the Island; he stayed outside because he did not want his fish to remain in the primary current.

Henry's reel kept slipping now and then. He waded away from the Island, trying to keep the fish out of the primary current. Finally, his theory started to work, and the fish yielded, allowing Henry to put some line back on his reel.

Mr. Kraneger was on the scene now. He spoke with a conservative voice, "Steady boy, keep your pole high, no quick movements, steady."

Other anglers were gathering on both sides of him. Henry put the butt of his pole against his belly. He pulled his rod higher and started reeling in as he let the rod fall forward. While he repeated the procedure, the crowd kept getting bigger.

Old fishers talked to one another about what kind of fish they had hooked into size, weight, and length. Henry did not care; he did not want to lose it.

Mr. Kraneger grabbed the net from Bobby's grasp, but Bobby did not like giving it up. Finally, Mr. Kraneger realized he had made a mistake and returned the net to Bobby.

Brandy was yelling, telling people to keep back and not to touch Hank's line. Then, an intoxicated man tried to grab Henry's line, saying to pull it in. Brandy yelled at him, "If you touch Hank's line, it'll snap like a twig."

Bobby finally positioned himself close to the large Brown. He lowered his net behind the fish and plucked it from the water.

The Brown weighed in at fourteen pounds four ounces, and it was twenty-eight inches long.

The following two days went without incident. They swam in the afternoons, fished in the mornings, and fought the mosquitoes in the evenings.

The Brown was in the freezer. Mr. Kraneger said he would have his taxidermist mount it. He told Henry it would be his treat.

The swift current of the Au Sable was powerful and exciting. It silently wove through the uninhabited wilderness, and there was not a straight stretch longer than a football field.

Henry had difficulty keeping his feet on the bottom of the water above his knees. He tried using his feet to stop him, but he would slide from one rock to another in the swift current if the bottom were rocky.

The campers sat around the campfire at night, talking and singing songs. Mrs. Kraneger, Brandy, and Barby had the voices of angels. Henry had difficulty keeping his eyes dry when they sang songs like Bambi.

Sometimes at night, they took flashlights to the riverbank; they could see crawdads fluttering against the current, holding their own—big ones too. They were much too fast to catch without a net. So, the old-timers took a pitchfork and jammed it into the bottom. They fastened a wire basket with bacon to the pitchfork and trapped many, but they would not share even one.

Those prized baits would bring in giant Browns and rainbows; the trout hit them instantly. Henry wanted a large crawdad but only had night crawlers and leeches.

Every night after supper, a prize went to the angler for the largest catch of the day. The private campground held the contest every night. Henry Brown brought second place that first day; he won no prize, though only first-place fish won awards.

A dense fog moved into the campground on the third morning, and visibility deteriorated to less than twenty feet. Someone tied pieces of ropes to saplings to mark the way back and forth to the river. The fish would not hit anything. It was cold, about fifty degrees or less. Mrs. Kraneger was getting sick with a sore throat and a headache.

The fog cleared overnight, and it got warmer, and Mrs. Kraneger felt better. Everyone left the campsite and went out for breakfast. Mr. Kraneger always said breakfast was the best meal to buy because it was the cheapest. Henry had one Paul Bunyan pancake hanging off the plate and could hardly eat it all.

Brandy sat next to him on one side; Barby was on the other side. Every time Henry's eyes met Brandy's, he could not help but get this big smile. She called him a pervert, but he did not understand why.

A caravan of trucks carrying canoes took them twelve miles upstream.

Bobby and Henry were in one canoe, Mr. and Mrs. Kraneger were together, and Brandy and Barby shared a canoe.

Every canoe had to have a life preserver for each person. Then, after a short demonstration and simple reminders, each crew could float downstream back to camp.

Brandy and Barby did not get far when Barby dropped her paddle. She reached out to get it just as Brandy told her not to, and they went over. Bobby let Brandy have it. The girls had to float in the water until they found a sand bar shallow enough to allow them to get back in their canoes.

"Hey, stretch. You're supposed to ride in the canoe!" Bobby yelled.

Mature trees dotted the meadow-like landscape along the river. The dense brush and thistles did not start until the dark wall of evergreens dominated the forest in the background fifty or sixty feet from the river—deer feeding on the lower leafage that created the manicured trunks with branches well out of human reach. The deep snow in the winter lifted the deer high enough to feed off the pine needles. There were clusters of birch trees with their white bark partially shedding. The slim, elevated tamaracks reached eighty feet into the sky, swaying in the heavens along the banks and wetlands. Further from the river, thick stands of poplar trees lined the forest's edge just before the dense wall of evergreens. Limestone outcroppings came and went as the river slithered through the uninhabited wilderness.

The teenagers lightly splashed each other with the paddles and enjoyed the thrill of the new experience. Everyone laughed and giggled as they reveled in their new environment. It was hot by noon, and the cool water was refreshing in the hot afternoon sun.

Because of logjams and brush piles, the Kalamazoo and St. Joseph rivers needed to clear every quarter mile. No logjams or brush were blocking the Au Sable River. The river was 138 miles long, and it fell 650 feet. The quickness of the current, combined with the canoe's speed, created the illusion of racing downstream. Several families were navigating the river together. Groups of canoes lagged or sped ahead, disappearing downstream. The river was, at times, one hundred yards wide.

Mrs. Kraneger did not like getting wet, so the kids stopped splashing when her canoe was closed.

Brandy taught Barby how to use her paddle. She explained that short, quick strokes kept the canoe on a straighter course. The two sisters struggled to find a rhythm at first but began to show some promise. On the other hand, Bobby and Henry automatically seemed to find a natural synchronized rhythm. First, Bobby poked fun at his sister's lack of coordination. Then, he and Henry began showing off and easily navigated the swift water.

Brandy was in the back of the girls' canoe and spoke calmly to her sister. "Don't look back at me; just listen. We will act like bird watchers, but when the opportunity presents itself, we will ram Hank and Pudge and pretend we made a mistake."

Staring straight ahead with a gleam in her eye, Barby said, "Aye-aye, Captain."

Bobby and Henry were downstream ahead of everyone by several canoe lengths. They were showing off paddling in circles.

Both Bobby and Henry noticed the speed Brandy and Barby had attained. The boys stopped paddling and were watching the bottom. The girls were coming right at them. Bobby and Henry were sideways in the current when Henry saw them coming. He yelled, "Bobby, the girls."

Bobby turned and yelled, "Paddle right, but Henry was already paddling to the left. When Brandy and Barby rammed into their side, the impact did not flip them, but the boys' reaction did. They both leaned away from the jolt, and the canoe flipped over.

Mr. and Mrs. Kraneger began clapping.

Brandy yelled, "Oh no, are you guys all right? You floated in front of us. We are such poor navigators we could not avoid hitting you. Gosh, we are so sorry." Then, the girls began whooping it up.

Bobby and Henry looked at each other in total disgust. Then, finally, Bobby yelled, "I told you to turn right because the current was too strong to go left."

Henry calmly shouted back at him, "I knew we shouldn't have slowed in the middle of the river; you dope."

"Let's get them," Bobby cried. "Get in. Hurry up, get in, get in!"

The girls had a significant lead on them and paddled fast, and they were still whooping it up.

Bobby and Henry jumped in their canoe and paddled like madmen. Their pace was furious, totally out of control. They almost caught the girls when they came to a sharp bend to the left in the river. The girls were on the right side of the river, just past the turn. The boys took the curve wide, thinking they would be on the girls quicker. Unfortunately, the brunt of the river bounced off a rocky outcropping, creating a white-water backwash, and the boys were on course to ram into its bank. Unfortunately, they did not recognize the danger until it was too late. Their canoe sped along with the primary current, and they did not have enough time to maneuver. Bobby managed to turn the front of the canoe slightly and yelled to Henry for help. He and Henry were paddling hard to get out of the current, but it was no use as the canoe hit the rocky embankment with a thud.

The river eroded the rock, creating an underwater vault. The front end of the canoe scraped against the curved rock and slipped underwater. Bobby leaped to the left into the river feet first as it slid under the hidden inset. His thrust pushed the canoe even deeper into the sub-surface current. The rear end of the canoe suddenly rose and twisted violently to the right, catapulting Henry into the side of the rock wall. Henry tried to get his hands before him to absorb the shock, but the force was too dynamic. His chest struck a portion of rock protruding out of the limestone wall. The thump knocked the wind out of him and caused temporary paralysis. Henry's limp body slid into the white-water face down. The current sucked him into the vault and flushed him into the swift stream. Henry could not move, and he could not breathe. He saw frothing white bubbles between the green and blue pebbles, gray rocks, and boulders on the bottom as he floated past them.

Brandy and Barby saw the canoe twist and toss Henry against the wall. Barby screamed, "Henry!"

Brandy leaped into the shallow water, yelling at Bobby to help Hank. Unfortunately, Bobby injured himself jumping out of the canoe and was not responding.

Brandy pushed herself as she fought against the current in the hip-deep water. She was still a hundred and fifty feet downstream from Henry. He was floating toward her but on the opposite side of the river. She figured she had three minutes left to get to him. Unfortunately, Brandy lost her left tennis shoe and was sure she had already cut her foot badly on a sharp rock. Two minutes later, Brandy was at the brunt of the river's current. She thrust her hands in a shoveling motion, assisting her legs as she went against the wild, unrelenting force. Brandy was scared. She was thrashing wildly, "Hank! Hank!" Her eyes were full of water, and she could not see very well, but she ignored everything: her eyes, the pain in her left foot, the side aches, and the pain in her heart. Three minutes later, she was frantic to intercept him.

Henry's limp body floated closer to the primary current. Brandy tackled him and twisted him over on his back. She grabbed his neck, pulling him back toward the shoreline into the lesser wind. Brandy could not see what was behind her. She backed into a flat, muddy barrier at the end of the limestone outcropping.

Brandy stumbled over the small boulders, pulling him with all her might backward, lunging up onto the muddy embankment. She kept kicking her heels into the muck, struggling out of the water into the thick sludge. Brandy's foot began to throb, her back arched, and her shoulders were tired. She transferred all her remaining energy to her arms and yanked Henry out of the mud onto herself in one final challenge.

Barby was crying, "Hurry, Brandy, hurry." Finally, she yelled, "Daddy, Daddy!"

Bobby made it to shore as his parents pulled up. His mom jumped out of the canoe and helped him escape the water. Mr. Kraneger paddled hard for the opposite shore, where Brandy pulled Henry onto the muddy bog.

Henry was still stunned when he felt someone grabbing his chin and turning him over on his back. Fingernails dug deep into his throat, and he began coughing and choking but could not catch his breath. Henry gagged and floated headfirst over the water on his back. He felt the mud sliding under him but was still struggling to breathe. The person pulling him collapsed. Henry felt himself lying on top of someone. He tried to fill his lungs between the spasms.

Brandy cried quietly. Henry had never seen Brandy cry before. She tried to sit up but could not break free of the muck. Finally, she reached out and stroked his face with her muddy palm.

Henry turned over and buried his face into her bosom. He tried to push it off, but the mud was too deep when he put his hands down. His face fell back into her bare belly. Brandy reached down with both arms and pulled him by his shirt until his head rested snugly between her breasts.

Sniveling and breathing heavily, Brandy asked, "Hank, are you alright?"

Henry managed to take a few short breaths. Brandy laid back and rested. Henry did not move, but he regained some composure. Brandy's legs had embedded themselves into the black bog, and the muddy mire began to stink. Barby wadded into the knee-deep mud, coming to where Brandy and Henry were stuck. She sobbed uncontrollably. Barby spread her arms out, fell over them both, and hugged and cried. "Henry, I thought you were dead."

Brandy whined, "I did too!"

Mr. Kraneger arrived and helped extract them from the mud. Brandy whined about the smell. The stirred-up, grimy, sticky muck reeked of mold, fetid plant life, and putrid rotting soil.

Bobby twisted his knee, jumping from the canoe; he was on the opposing shoreline waving at Henry. Henry waved back.

Brandy, Henry, and Barby swam in the shallow water. They twisted and turned and rinsed most of the mud off their bodies. Brandy bent over Henry and rubbed the ground off the back of his neck and hair.

She recalled babysitting for him. But, she wondered, when did he suddenly grow up? The transition from a boy to a young man seemed to happen overnight, like a mushroom. When did he become taller than her? His maturity puzzled her and stirred her to imagine him as a man. She loved his hair. She remembered washing it for him on those nights his parents had entrusted her to watch him.

She ducked his head repeatedly, removing the mud from his entangled nest. Then, he finally stopped her and said, "Brandy, I do need to breathe," she dunked him again.

While Henry helped wash her hair and imitated her routine, Brandy's tee shirt opened, and Henry saw both breasts. They hung in the open as the stretched and broken fabric that was her bra fell loose. Brandy caught him all goggle-eyed, and then she dunked backward, coming out of the water with her hair trailing in perfect symmetry. "You like them, don't you?" she inquired with a smile.

He looked her in the eye with a sheepish grin. He helped her up; she was almost as tall as Henry. Brandy embraced him.

Brandy kissed him and whispered, "Hank, I love your hair; please don't ever cut it."

Brandy stumbled when she tried to put weight on her injured foot. Henry caught her, and when he saw the painful expression on her face, he knew something was wrong. Barby noticed her bloody foot when she fell. She grabbed her leg while Henry held Brandy. It was a deep, clean cut before the heel in the center of the foot. Barby removed her scarf and tied a temporary restraint that closed the wound. Henry picked up Brandy and sat her in the canoe.

Brandy had no idea Henry was so strong.

Henry thanked her for pulling him to shore; he secretly and silently supposed she saved his life.

The others climbed into their canoes and floated gently toward the campsite.

On the way, they saw various wildlife: deer, otter, mink, muskrat, beaver, fish, and many ducks.

After returning to the campsite, Bobby and Henry carried Brandy to the car. Henry could not help but notice Brandy's breast nipples as they showed through her tee shirt. He liked looking at them; she caught him staring and gave him a cat-like look.

Mr. and Mrs. Kraneger took Brandy into town to get stitches and returned to a blazing campfire hours later. Brandy hobbled over and found a stump next to Henry. Barby began entertaining them with some Hank Williams tunes. She was about to play Henry's favorite: "I'm so lonesome I could cry."

Henry loved the water, camping in the woods, and fishing. He loved Barby, and he loved Brandy in a confused kind of way.

This far north in Michigan, the stars in the night sky lit up like jewels. One night, they saw the Northern Lights.

It was past midnight when Mr. Kraneger went to the bathroom. He overlooked Mother Nature's artistic gift in the heavens until he was returning to the camper. He woke everyone in his camp, but many other campers also woke their children to allow them to see the rare phenomenon. Narrow beams of crisscrossing light filled the night sky. They were like giant beams of pickup sticks strewn in the heavens. Some were fuzzy, and some were very distinct looking.

Barby and Henry lay on the grass on their backs. They formed a straight-line head-to-head with their feet going in opposite directions. They discussed their future, school, friendship, and the incredible northern lights sky.

Barby asked, "Are we going steady, the boyfriend-girlfriend thing?"

He said, "Barby, everyone knows that we dig each other. Do you want to go steady with me?"

She said, "Yes, I want to go steady with you very much."

Henry turned over, looked into her eyes, and said, "Pretty girl."

She blushed and, out of the blue, chimed, "Silly boy."

Henry pulled a wild wheat stem and bit it lightly, tasting the bitterness. "Barby, we're going into the ninth grade. Can you believe it?"

"I know, Henry. Isn't it exciting?" She smiled at him and thought he was trying to act too cool with the weed in his mouth. She liked Henry because he was quiet, not loud like Brandy and Bobby; those two argued continuously.

The campers spent several more days fishing, canoeing, swimming, and picnicking.

While fishing the day before they had to leave, Bobby slipped on some rocks, and his waders filled up with water. "Hey, you guys, I need some help."

The current pulled him down, and he gagged and flopped like a fish into the swift part of the stream. His arms thrashed violently. He tried to stand up, but the current was too strong.

Brandy heard him yelling and saw him in trouble. But unfortunately, she was upstream in her waders too far to help. "Hank, we need to help Bobby!" she screamed.

Henry was closer, but he had his back to Bobby, and he was still in his waders and could not move extremely fast.

Barby was the closest one, but she was helping her father roll up the tarp.

"Barby, can you help Bobby? He's coming toward you," Henry yelled.

"Where is he? I don't even see him," she muttered.

Bobby was sucked underwater for a moment. Barby saw him and took off like a bullet.

Bobby needs help. Bobby, I am coming. Daddy, come on!" she screamed.

Barby leaped from shore and scraped the bottom, but she ignored the pain and came up from the bottom and swam hard.

Fortunately, two fishermen downstream were able to capture him. Bobby was so scared he relieved himself in his wanders; the smell was awful, even mouthy. Brandy knew enough to avoid any teasing.

Bobby was not injured. His bruised ego from the embarrassment of it all was injury enough.

On the trip home the next day, Bobby remarked how they had dodged several bullets.

Barby scraped her right knee over a rock, but the glancing blow did not break her skin.

Barby was sitting between her dad and mom. Brandy sat between Henry and Bobby in the back seat. Bobby leaned against the door; sound asleep.

Brandy leaned against Henry's shoulder. Her eyes were closed, but she whispered into his ear. "You are becoming a very handsome young man. Barby told me she loves you. I think she is suffering from puppy love syndrome. We had a lot of fun, didn't we, Hank?" she admitted.

Henry nodded and rested his head on hers for a moment.

"You don't smell like onions anymore. That is hard work, Hank," she said.

Henry smiled and slumped his shoulders.

"I'm going to take a nap, Henry. Do you mind if I snuggle a bit?" He smiled and nodded yes.

She snuggled closer and pulled his right arm against her bosom.

Henry was perplexed. Brandy was something special, but Henry felt an extraordinary relationship with Barby. He tried to put into words how he felt. Finally, he leaned back into the seat, closed his eyes, and dreamt about Brandy.

CHAPTER 4

Fatherless

Henry was thrilled to see his mom and dad. Sparky ran up to Henry, meowing and rubbing against his legs, weaving first against one, then the other. Henry ignored his cat's attempted affection as he greeted his parents. Then, finally, when he reached down to pick up his cat, it ran off and hid. Henry knew Sparky disapproved of Henry's absence and lack of feline etiquette. Henry knew where his hiding spots were and would locate him later.

"Henry, I hope you are hungry. I am making a nice dinner. Why don't you go into the living room and spend time with your father?"

"Let me know if you need some help, mom."

Henry sat on the couch across from his father. "Dad, how were you while I was gone?"

"Awe shucks, Henry; one day is about the same as the next. Did you have a good time with the Kraneger's?"

"I had a lot of fun, Dad. Thanks for letting me go. What book are you reading?"

"Nevada by Zane Grey."

"Zane Grey wrote a lot of books. I've read about six of them." Henry said.

"Listen, Son, and I want to explain a few things. Most importantly, you have Chippewa blood flowing in your veins. You stand proud because of your heritage. Chief Aslin came by for a visit while you were gone. He wants you to be active in the Chippewa nation. Pow Wow does not have very many young natives. Henry, you are 40% Chippewa and qualify for many Native American benefits. You are an American son. Always wear that fact in your heart. I never got involved with my heritage. I regret this immensely. Be proud, son, and don't take a back seat to anyone."

Henry's mom made chicken and dumplings—his favorite meal. Finally, his dad felt good enough to join Henry and his mom at the table. Henry would recall his father sharing his favorite meal for many years. The precious time with everyone at the table enjoying each other's company would be Henry's last memory of a family meal. Unfortunately, Henry's dad suffered a major stroke a week later and died.

He could still see his mother's face on Thursday morning. She projected a calm, caring, worried look on Henry. He knew what had happened, and she did not have to say anything. She was sitting on the side of his bed and about to speak. Henry reached up and touched her cheek with his finger. He whispered, "It's dad, huh?"

The ambulance was outside but could not remove the corpse until the coroner arrived.

"Henry, do you want to see your father before they take him away?"

He looked at his mother; he could tell she had been crying. Her eyes were still red and puffy. She was brave for Henry, and he could tell she was in a fragile state of mind. "Yes, Mother, I will go see him now," he kissed her cheek and hugged her.

"Do you want to be alone, or do you want me to go with your honey?" she asked.

Henry patted his bed with his hand. "Get some rest, Mom, while I go say goodbye. You look exhausted."

Henry walked into his parents' bedroom, the only room where he felt uncomfortable. His father looked like a small man lying on his bed in his pajamas. His father's head was against his pillows, hands folded in his lap. His mother combed his hair. His eyes looked sunken and grayish, sadly staring at the ceiling. He was inquiring, almost like he was about to ask a question. His skin was a blotchy mix of red and gray over pale blue.

Henry recalled one of the last conversations with his father when he came home from camping with the Kraneger's. "Henry, I will be gone soon. I want you to know how much joy you have brought to your mother and me. You and I have spoken many times about what I expect of you. Enjoy your youth, son. It will not last much longer. See Chief Aslin, too. Get involved with your heritage. Remember, son, you are America! Soon, you will be supporting a family of your own. I want you to be happy. I want you to be a kind man. I expect you to be civil, moral, fair, and virtuous. Help your mother; she is a strong woman, but my passing will be intricate. Remember to be ethical. Never ask another man to do something you would not do yourself. Love yourself, but always be humble in front of others. Avoid making the same mistake twice, be bold, and stand up for a good cause. Henry, you are my only son. I have fought enough to fulfill our family's obligation to our country for ten generations.

One more thing, son, your hair; wear it proud, wear it long, and wash it often!"

Henry remembered the smile on his face: it was joyful and caring, but mostly it was free of pain.

Many of the points his father recited were familiar to Henry. But, except for a couple, his father had never told him to be a kind man, and he did not think his dad ever approved of his long hair. So why did he express those things to him now? Could his father indicate somehow that he had not been a kind man? Henry searched his memory and could not devise a single act of unkindness perpetrated by his father.

What did he mean? Henry walked over and put his right hand over his father's hands. "Dad, I will try hard to be a kind man. I will work hard at being virtuous. I will never cut my hair and take care of Mom. I love you, Dad."

Henry tried to cry, but nothing would come; he felt overt sadness and an uncomfortable fear. The VFW hosted the Funeral, and an entire military Honor Guard stood alongside the coffin.

Henry's father died Thursday night, and on Sunday morning, Henry watched as his coffin lay over the hole that would intern his dad. Henry never cried. He felt no emotion at all. Instead, as he sat at the gravesite waiting for the ceremony to begin, he thought about the events of the last few days.

During the ceremony, Henry's mother broke down several times. Henry tried to comfort her. He felt nothing. Speakers who served with his father told stories of his father's heroism and exceptional service to his country. His mother accepted the folded flag from the honor guard. Too many strange men shook Henry's hand and patted him. Henry knew none of them would help him and his mother. Several military officers made indignant remarks about why a man like Tom Rotyn would allow his son to have long hair. He watched and listened as the ceremony dragged on and on. Henry wanted it to be over.

Henry helped his mother to the black military Sedan and sat silently back to Jackson. He could not figure out why they had to drive back to Jackson. They were in Barneyville. Why couldn't they have worked things out differently?

Mrs. Rotyn noticed Henry had not cried all day. She worried about him but decided not to say anything and let her son grieve his father's way.

Henry rode home from Jackson later that evening with Mr. Kraneger and Bobby. Mrs. Kraneger rode with Henry's mother in another vehicle.

"Your father was a good man, Henry. I am going to miss him very much. How are you doing, son?"

Henry looked out his window; mainly, the large flat farms in this part of Michigan were grain producers. Fields of soybeans, corn, and oats came and went as the car sped along M60.

"Your mother is a good woman, Henry, who worries about you. I am here for you if you want to talk, son. If not today, then maybe tomorrow or the next day."

Henry felt like talking less today, tomorrow, or next. He felt nothing.

The following week, he passed quickly. Henry visited his father's grave at the riverside every morning before school. He still felt nothing, and he could not cry, and it bothered him that his heart could be so cold.

Brandy left for college in Boston to be a freshman at Dartmouth University.

Bobby, Barby, and Henry went to Barneyville High School's first football game of the season. They rode the bus together because the game was in Athens. Henry and Barby sat in the back of the bus because the chaperones were in the front. Although the night was still hot, it was only the first week of September.

Barby was worried about Henry. She asked, "Are you still thinking about your dad a lot?"

Henry sat forward in the seat. "In the morning, when I first got up, I still looked for him in the living room, sitting in his chair. Dad was always up before sunrise, reading the paper.

"This morning, for example, I knew he wasn't there, but I still looked for him. The living room seems eerie now. Dad was almost always in his chair. Sometimes it feels as if he isn't gone."

Henry felt a surging sorrow erupt deep in his chest. He sat silently, attempting to quell the raging emotion.

Barby studied his face. She kissed his cheek.

Henry was all teary-eyed. He did not want her to see the tears, so he put his arm around her neck, pulling her head into his shoulder. She smelled wonderful.

She sensed his emotional pain. She put a hand on his shoulder. "Henry, listen to me."

He buried his face in his hands, ashamed of his tearful lack of composure.

She leaned against him and softly whispered. "Henry, you're going to be simply fine. I am going to be your friend for life. You are going to be my first love and my last love. I swear to God above and all the angels." Barby was intent on caring for Henry.

Henry was overwhelmed with grief and could not say a word. He tried to fight off the tears. Finally, Barby pulled at him, and he turned sideways, holding his head down. She pulled him against her shoulder, and Henry could feel the tears coming. Barby was wearing a windbreaker over a velour sweater. Henry buried his head into her softness and cried silently.

Barby put her arms around his neck. She felt his hot tears soak through her sweater, and a kindred love for Henry swelled in her heart.

Henry cried for a long time. "I should have stayed home," he whispered.

She pulled him tight against her and held him as he grieved and grappled for a life without his dad.

Barby and Henry had been close friends for a long time. In the third grade, they sat next to each other in class. In the fourth grade, they passed notes back and forth. Henry's mom taught them, and they started ice skating together in the fifth grade. They did their homework together in the fifth, sixth, seventh, and eighth grades; they walked to every class together and kissed for the first time.

On the ride home, they sat close to each other; it was great therapy for him. In a quiet time during the trip, he looked into Barby's delightful brown eyes and said, "Pretty girl."

When Henry arrived home, his mother was waiting for him. She was overly concerned about her son's mental condition. However, as soon as his eyes met hers, his constitution broke again. All he could manage to say was, "Mom?"

He ran into his mother's arms. He cried loudly until his chest hurt.

Jessica Rotyn caressed her only child tenderly. She cried as she held her most precious possession. I know it hurts Henry; I know it hurts."

CHAPTER 5

The Headship Seat

*H*enry walked into the living room every morning and stared at his father's chair. His father was always there, reading a book. The chair was like a family heirloom in his mind. One morning, he walked to the chair and sat down. He had sat in it before, but it was not very often. Warm memories flooded his mind. He felt better for the first time in a long time.

Henry was in his science class on a Friday afternoon in late November 1963. His Mother knocked on the open door and stepped into the room. "I'm sorry to interrupt your class, Mr. Robinson. But unfortunately, I have some awful news. President Kennedy was killed today in Dallas, Texas. Vice President Johnson is being sworn in as President right away." Tears dripped down her cheeks, and Henry ran up and held her. All the other children walked up quickly and draped themselves around Mrs. Rotyn. The boys wiped their eyes and stared at each other with strong jaws.

Barby knocked on Henry's door. "Henry, I want to be with you."

Henry held out his arms, and she fell into his grasp. She cried hard for a few minutes. Henry closed the door and looked at his mom. She walked up and put her arms around both.

Barby was taking the assassination traumatically. "We all loved President Kennedy. Why did this happen? I don't understand." Barby blurted.

Henry tried to be strong for her. Barby and Henry came into the living room and sat on the couch. Barby cried hysterically. Henry looked at his father's chair. "I know what Dad would have said, America will remember this day forever. However, we live in a strong nation. Stand tall among your peers."

Bobby quietly walked into the living room. Walter Cronkite explained the process of the Vice President taking the oath to become the new President.

Other students kept coming into the living room because they had no TVs.

Henry's Mother served milk and cookies.

The three friends walked to school together every day after their morning runs. Bobby, Barby, and Henry waited for each other in the afternoon and walked home together. Henry met Barby at her locker between classes. The simple comfort of seeing each other brought them esoteric Security. The passing of time and their repetitive fraternization aided them in dealing with daily stress. Henry was becoming an adult. Barby liked his maturation.

After school, Henry came over and did his homework with Barby. The Kraneger's were Henry's extended family. As a result, many people in the community thought he was a Kraneger.

The Rotyns spent the evening at the Kraneger's every Sunday night because they had a color TV. Walt Disney's {Wonderful World of Color}, followed by Bonanza. The girls prepared BLT sandwiches and a Coca-Cola. Mr. Kraneger made homemade ice cream. One of the mothers usually made a cake, or sometimes they would have a fresh apple, peach, cherry cobbler, or dumplings. Bobby and Henry usually overate.

Many of their peers spent Sunday afternoons at Rotyn's because Henry's Mom helped all the kids with their homework. That always made Henry feel good: he loved his mother very much. Henry told his mom he loved her often, even in public. Henry never let any peer fear stop him.

One evening, Henry sat with his mother in his father's old chair in the living room. "Mom, I'm going to sit in the Headship seat. I am the man of the house now."

His mom smiled. "You haven't been a teenager for that long, young man. However, I will allow your headship to begin, but I am still the boss." He sat and looked at her. He did not seek her approval. He was the man of the house, and she could feel comfortable in his presence. He should be careful with the man of the house thing.

Mrs. Rotyn did not smile or frown. She did, however, silently acknowledge the changing of the guard. She had often wondered how long it would take for Henry to step up and become the man of the house. Her love for her son changed that night. It now included respect, honor, and virtue.

When Henry first spoke with his mother from the headship seat, he did so with a virtuous courtesy befitting the occasion.

"It's tranquil without a dad in the house. I don't remember him making much noise, so I don't understand how it can be so quiet."

"I know what you mean; some nights, as I sit here, it seems odd to hear noises I didn't hear before your father died."

Henry smiled at his mother, and she returned his smile with a perplexed expression. Mrs. Rotyn languished in a sudden rush of emotion. "Why do I hear them now?"

Henry recognized her delicate sensitivity. "Mom, you know it must have been audible. I heard the wind blowing the old cedar limbs against the shutters last night. It never bothered me before, but now it sends chills up my back."

She studied her son's face. He was already much taller than her, and now she saw the man beginning to emerge from the boy. His tender attempt to seem manly touched her deeply.

"Mom, I lay awake at night sometimes, and I can't hear you snore as Dad did. It frightens me, and I came to your room last night to see if you were safe."

Mrs. Rotyn smiled at her son. "I didn't know you worried about such things. But, honey, my bedroom is my private room. Just like your bedroom is your private place. I would prefer you to knock on my door. Then, you can wake me up any hour of the day or night." she smiled.

She made him smile. She made him feel safe even though he was now the man in the family.

"I was talking with Bobby and some of the guys; we want to spend the day Saturday on the Millpond. Do you have anything planned for the weekend?"

Mrs. Rotyn did not like the Millpond at this time of the year. "No, but you must be wary of thin ice, agreed?"

Henry gave his mother a whining stare, then removed it quickly before she noticed and replied, "Yes, Mother."

"Monday night, I want to start spending quality time together; one night a week will do us both good. You give me some ideas, and I will share mine with you. Then, we can have some fun together and complete a few projects. What do you think?"

"Sure, Mom. Can we discuss this tomorrow, though? I think I'm going to go to bed. I'm tired and have a math exam to review with Bobby in the morning." Henry kissed his mother on the cheek. "I love you, Mom!"

She smiled as Henry went to his room. Jessica Elizabeth Rotyn sat in her lonely living room reading a magazine. It was late; she knew she, too, should be retiring soon. Nevertheless, she enjoyed the pleasant conversation with her son.

She missed her husband. He had been gone almost a year. She was only thirty-four years old and wondered if she would ever meet anyone as excellent as Tom Rotyn. Of course, the focus of her life now needed to be Henry. Her simple needs could wait, and her son required all her attention. She worried about the future, Tom had taken care of everything, and now she had to make decisions. Henry's Mother did not want to worry Henry. They had money from Tom's life insurance and her mother's work at the school. Social Security she received for Henry, the meager savings Tom accumulated, and the pay from her job were undoubtedly ample enough to cover their financial responsibilities. She even saved a little from her wages for a rainy day. She wondered what would happen if Henry moved away. Of course, college would be a problem. Little Barneyville had nothing to offer in the way of a college education. She came to realize that this was what bothered her. She would not have the money to send him to a good college. She needed to speak frankly with Henry and help him see the need to keep his grades up. They may be the only chance he would have to further his education.

CHAPTER 6

Skinny Dipping

$\mathcal{B}$obby and Henry loved to swim. They also loved to be mischievous. It was New Year's Day, and they were ice fishing on the Millpond with their friends from school.

Tom and Terry Lickliter were identical twins, but only their looks harmonized. Both had short-medium builds. Tom was reserved, kind, moderate, friendly, and a straight-A student. Terry was his opposite. He was outgoing, pushy, competitive, proud, and moody. He struggled to keep a B average and used terrible language.

Gary West was as tall as Henry. He was wiry, brilliant, quiet, and reserved but could be surprisingly daring. He ran as fast as Henry. Henry secretly felt if he ever had a brother, he would be like Gary because the two were so alike. Except for the way they wore their hair.

They were not catching anything and were beginning to get bored. The boys were sitting in a circle around a hole in the ice. It was a sunny, cold day, but it felt warmer because there was no wind. Finally, Terry pulled his line out of the water. "Hey guys, let us go swimming. The water is clear, and it is a warm day. I bet it is almost thirty degrees."

Bobby grimaced and whined, "I'm not swimming. You will freeze your balls off in that water. You have a screw loose, Terry."

Henry pulled his line out of the water. "We would be the first kids in town to swim if we did it on New Year's Day. I'm willing. How about you, Gary?"

"Damn, Henry, maybe we ought to think about this one. I'm not wearing my swimming trunks. It is a long walk back to town. I know we'd freeze our ass off, but what the hell, let us do it." Gary pulled his line out and looked at Tom.

Tom looked at his brother. "Where do you dig up all this, Terry? If Mom and Dad find out, we're grounded."

Terry pushed his brother's shoulder and said, "Wary weasels. I am going swimming. If any of you guys have any balls, you will join me.

"Come on, you guys. We're at the southeast end of the Millpond. The walk back to town will be more than a mile." Tom argued.

"Tom, we're around the bend away from the highway. Nobody can see us." Henry smiled.

"Now listen, if we do this, we need to stay close to shore and away from a current," Tom complained.

"Too bad we couldn't take some photos. girls in school would dig this shit." Terry laughed.

The boys couldn't see hidden ice huts and houses on the shoreline.

Terry, Gary, and Bobby took turns using an ax to make their hole in the ice.

"Damn, the sun will be down in an hour. This fricking ice is too thick, you damn idiots. We're too close to the shore. I bet we won't have more than a foot of water. I'm not swinging this ax anymore. This work is useless, shitheads." Terry whined.

Henry and Tom gathered wood along the shoreline. They brought the wood twenty feet from the hole and started a small bonfire.

Bobby talked to himself as he worked. He knew the others were not paying much attention to his words, but he did not let that stop him from talking. "We're all going to have numb nuts for doing this."

Everyone ignored him as they continued pulling the broken pieces of ice out of the water.

Tom yelled from the shore, "Hey, one of you guys, come to help me."

Gary looked at Henry first, then went to his aid. Tom was trying to break off a tamarack shoot to use as a depth gauge. "I got the tool, Tom. I could cut down a tree with this hunting knife." Gary grinned.

They brought the tamarack shoot over and measured the depth of the water. It was about four feet deep.

"The depth could be deceiving when you look into the icy water." Tom related.

Bobby whined, "It's too cold to take our clothes off."

"You're a pussy, Bobby." Terry jeered.

"You go first if you think you have the balls, Terry." Bobby snapped.

Terry knew Bobby never did anything first.

"Bobby, we will have a friendly bonfire until you can feel it from the shore.

Terry went over to the fire and started removing his clothes.

Gary removed his clothes while Terry and Bobby argued and slipped into the water. He hung onto the fish stringer when he ducked under the ice out of sight. Tom had hold of the other end of the stringer. He cried out, "Hey, where is he? Where's Gary?" He held up both ends of the stringer for all to see. "This shithead is going to get us in trouble," Bobby complained. Henry started to remove his clothes when Gary came out of the water and slid across the snow-covered ice like a lizard.

Gary stood up. "What the hell happened to your pecker?" Terry yelled.

"Look how tiny his junk looks, you guys." Henry laughed.

Tom yelled, "Oh no, I won't do that to myself." Tom looked at Gary's tiny penis and asked, "Does it hurt?"

Gary flipped him the fickle finger of fate. "Holy shit, that's cold," Gary grumbled. He ran across the ice in tiny strides. When he reached the fire, he stood on his coat and put his clothes on. "The water is warmer than the air, you guys. You have to dunk your head underwater to qualify!"

He stammered.

Henry knew this was dangerous because the river was still moving. The current could suck one under the ice and sweep them downstream. "Hey, you guys, we need to keep hold of the rope. Don't let go of it." he turned toward Gary and asked, "Was there much of a current Gary?"

"No, there wasn't much current. However, some of these guys do not swim that well. I think the stringer was a good idea. It was dumb letting go of it, I guess," Gary said.

Bobby was the second boy in the water, and the others were all amazed because Bobby rarely did things first or second. When Bobby came up out of the water, his teeth were chattering. His balls and penis were very tiny.

"Damn, it is colder up here than in the water," Bobby cried. He jumped back in and splashed Tom and Terry. They got mad and would not let him out of the hole. Gary and Henry had to intervene because Bobby was turning blue.

Henry removed the rest of his clothes.

Terry yelled, "Damn stud muffin, the girls will love you, Henry! But, hey, you guys, Henry's hung like a horse!"

Henry was very embarrassed. He quickly slipped into the icy water. The freezing water took his breath away when Henry ducked under the surface. His head began to pound violently, shaking violently while his body tried adapting to the icy water. Henry's headache eased off after a few moments. He opened his eyes and saw sharp, crystal-like ice facing him. It was not smooth at all, like on the surface. Large pockets of trapped air looked like invisible balloons flattened and fluttering below the ice. He pushed off the bottom and slid onto the ice. The first thing he checked was his penis; it was the size of a pencil eraser. His balls shriveled into a wrinkled sack the size of a small peach pit.

The boys laughed as they pointed to each other; the tiny shrunken organs were so out of place. They held a contest to see whose penis and balls shrank most. To his chagrin, Bobby won the prestigious prize. "My baby brother has a bigger pecker than you, Bobby." Terry teased.

The icy drenching shocked every fiber in their bodies, and Gary was right; the water was much warmer than the air.

The rope was frozen stiff, and each time it went into the icy water, it became harder to manage. Also, if any part of the rope touched bodies, it left welts.

The boys stood around the fire warming up, continually teasing each other. Finally, they decided to make this an annual event, but they agreed to bring towels and blankets next year.

Bobby, Henry, Gary, Tom, and Terry formed the Rowdy Rogues gang. Someday, they envisioned themselves doing something monumental. So they all bought black leather coats and sent away heavy denim emblems in a magazine. When they got the patches, they went to an upholsterer, and he sewed them on the back of their jackets. The symbol was a joker standing on one side of the scales of justice. The round emblem's background was orange with a blue border. The Coat of Arms was gold, and the Joker was black and red. Rowdy Rogue was in Silver at the bottom of the emblem. The boys wore coats whenever the temperature dropped.

CHAPTER 7

The Log Cabin Bungalow

The thick cover of cat-o'-nine-tails partially hid the view of the island cabin from the highway during every season except winter. Since it was not incredibly attractive, many people may have let that impression distract them from experiencing the remarkable sanctuary. The small log cabin bungalow was accessible only by boat, except during winter. The small island it sat on could only accommodate one building.

When Henry looked at the Bungalow in seasons other than winter, he saw its hidden esoteric quality during the summer. He knew that by Christmas, the fascinating and enchanting aspects of the Bungalow came magically alive.

The local fire department built a one-room log cabin on the island in the center of Millpond. The Bungalow only had one entrance, a thick, heavy beam door. The door was not very tall, and when entering or exiting, most people had to duck under the heavily beamed doorway header. There were no windows, but it had an open fireplace.

In the deep winter, the fireplace's light lit up the one-room cabin with a yellow glow. The sunken round brick fireplace sat in the middle of the Bungalow. It sat on the firm rock bed at the peak of the tiny island. Two feet high around the double-brick wall surrounding the fireplace.

A narrow cement floor at the bottom followed the curvature of the building. Five pews circled the cabin, with each one at a higher level. The pews were thick slabs of wood dowelled together—six inches of sawdust covered the walking surfaces. The sawdust insulated the floor from the frost, which seeped up through the ground.

A large, inverted funnel had a double wall hung from the ceiling covering the entire fireplace, acting as a chimney. Its width and breadth provided a safe, warm ledge for everyone to lay mittens or gloves and head coverings on to warm and dry.

Every Saturday morning, youngsters from all over town worked to clean off the snow from the ice around the cabin. Then, everyone skated in a large circle with the log cabin in the center.

Henry's mother was one of the adults who watched over the behavior of all the teenagers. She was an exceptionally excellent skater. She taught Henry and Brandy, and Brandy taught Barby.

Boyfriends, girlfriends, and other people of all ages came to share in the fun. In addition, Henry's mom and dad taught many children in town to skate.

Over the holiday, Brandy was home from college. Henry's mom taught her how to skate as a little girl. She was by far the most talented skater, but she did not have the fluid grace of Mrs. Rotyn. Brandy, in turn, also taught youngsters the art of cutting ice on a blade. Both talented ice skaters were immensely popular with all the town's children.

The Rowdy Rogue's hockey team took on all challengers on Saturday mornings. They had a small rink configured near the cabin. Piles of snow scraped off the ice, creating a high bank on both sides of the rink. Bobby whittled pucks out of pickle barrel ribs. The boys made hockey sticks out of dried hickory slabs.

The park department posted a schedule that reserved weekend afternoons for families. Friday and Saturday nights were for teenagers. Entering the cabin provided a quick way to warm up, make friends, and tell stories. Entire families would come and take part in the winter wonderland.

Bobby, Barby, and Henry spent many winter Saturday afternoons at the Bungalow. One of the moms packed a picnic lunch, usually ring bologna, banana, French bread, county line cheese, hot chocolate, and snowball cakes. In addition, the Village of Barneyville provided hot cider on Saturdays and hot chocolate on Sundays.

On one frigid and sunny Saturday morning, the wind blew out of the west. As a result, wisps of snow blew across Millpond. Skaters could only skate for about ten minutes before needing relief from the cold; the temperature never got above ten degrees all day.

A combination of hickory and applewood burned in the fireplace, providing a warm glow capable of thawing the ice from the skates and the cold from the bones.

Barby and Henry sat in a dim, secluded spot in the right corner. The cold bursts of chilly air from the opening door did not reach that far. So, they shed coats and sweaters and were quite comfortable. Henry sat with his back in the corner, against the skins; Barby sat leaning against him on his right side. One of the problems in a small town is that everyone knows everyone. So, they had to be careful, or their parents would find out they were alone in the Bungalow. Mrs. Kraneger constantly harped to Barby about not being alone with a boy. Of course, Bobby was always there, but he gave Barby and Henry a lot of privacy.

These were the innocent years. The two teenagers sat and talked while warming themselves.

"Henry, I hate you."

Henry looked at Barby bewildered. "What did I do now?"

Barby reached out and pulled his hair over his head, covering his face. "Your hair looks nicer than mine. I refuse to associate with a boy who has hair like that. It's bad enough that it's longer, but it looks nicer too!"

He looked at her; she rolled her eyes back and forth. "So, wash it once in a while."

She slapped him across his shoulder with her open palm. "Ouch," she cried, "Now you are trying to hurt me." Her face broke into a repressed grin.

"Barby, you hit me; I didn't hit you."

She pouted and stuck out her bottom lip. "Do you think I'm pretty?"

Henry put his hands over his face and hid his response. "I think Brandy is pretty," he snickered in a low voice—almost a whisper.

Barby's brown eyes became enormous and round; she pursed her lips tightly and tried to look mad.

Henry whispered, "Your nose is smiling."

She snickered and then choked on her snicker. "How can a nose smile? A nose can't smile." she giggled.

He reached out and handed her his hanky. "You have snot hanging out of your nose; it's not smiling now."

She took his hanky and blew her nose several times, then wadded it and daintily handed it back to him. "How can a nose smile, Henry?" she turned her face as if to allow him to view the side of her nose, "See, it doesn't smile."

Henry stared into her eyes as she brought her nose close to his. "Barby, a few minutes ago, your face was glowing. You have beautiful brown eyes, soft, wet lips, and lovely eyebrows. However, your nose was happy; it was smiling."

Her face beamed brightly. Her response in a shrill high voice was both charming and petite, "Oh Henry, if you say so, dear."

Henry leaned back against the coats. "Barby, you know I think you're beautiful. My hair is not nicer than yours, and you're the only girl I know with a nose that can smile!"

They got dressed and went outside to skate. The two teenagers skated together and were eloquent partners because they relied on each other for support, which worked. They smoothly glided around the bungalow arm in arm. Each time they completed the large circle, they would change positions. She would skate backward, or he would. Henry and Barby understood it was the only time they could embrace each other freely. They could woo each other on the ice, and no one ever noticed.

She loved his strength on the ice, and he loved her agility and rhythm.

Barby did not have the athleticism of Brandy, but she was a better dancer both on the ice and off.

Henry's face was remarkably close to Barby's. "I want to kiss your round, wet, ruby lips," he begged.

"My goodness, Henry, where are you learning to flirt with a girl?"

"I'll never tell, honey. You seem to enjoy colloquial amorality." Henry bragged.

"Yes, love, I do yearn to hear you express your love for me without judgment," Barby confessed.

"I cannot express how I feel about you with words alone. A young lady's kiss would convey much more, my dear." Henry smiled.

Their routine allowed them to skate cheek to cheek. Each winter, they became a little bolder with the touching and snuggling.

Barby's cheeks were rose-petal red in the cold air. The tip of her nose also glowed like a rose, but so did Henry's.

Barby was light as a feather, and Henry could spin with her in his grip, hold her high in the air, and catch her easily when she fell into his arms. They practiced a dance routine like Olympic skaters. Of course, they could only do some complicated maneuvers, but no one in Barneyville saw anything like their routine.

Henry's mom worked with them for years, and finally, patience and hard work began to pay dividends; the talented pair looked elegant and brilliant together.

Onlookers admired their dedication, even congratulating them on how wonderfully they performed together. The two skaters would smile politely and continue their winter courtship on ice. The only time they even discussed their paranormal romance was when they were skating. No one could hear or interfere, and they liked that simply fine. However, Barby had to remind Henry of his wandering hands continually.

"Henry, I love skating with you. It's the only time we can touch and hug. I can tease you, silly boy."

"Barby, I want to tell you secrets while we skate. I can smell your perfume and stare into your eyes. I can tease you, silly girl."

"When anyone questions our intentions while sitting so close, the answer was always the same. We are discussing our routine."

It became too cold to skate by five pm, and everyone stayed inside. Barby brought her guitar, and so did Gary. There must have been twenty teens and several parents in the Bungalow. The young musicians sang songs by the Mamas and the Papas, Peter Paul and Mary, and many other groups.

Henry's favorite song was "Breaking up is Hard to Do," Gary and Barby played and sang it together as a duet. Everyone joined in on the chorus.

Henry was intrigued by the design of the female body. He loved looking at Barby's delicate neck. Most boys his age bragged about knowing about girls, but Henry was silently learning.

Henry loved skating with girls in high school. His strength and prowess on the ice made them less likely to be intimidated. The juniors and seniors were the girls he was especially fond of because they usually gave him money for teaching them to skate. Henry learned that they showed green empathy when they realized he was fatherless.

There were other benefits, too. Brandy taught him how to kiss in the Bungalow. She let Henry ask her about girl things. Brandy was his babysitter when he was younger. She told him about those girls as quiet, calm, and peaceful boys. She also said that girls wanted boys who were not afraid to share their feelings.

Henry missed Brandy when she went away to college. She was his friend, and he felt close to her.

Barby always had piano lessons on Saturday mornings. Brandy and Henry often met at the Bungalow and skated together until she left for college.

CHAPTER 8

Mouse Hunt

$\mathscr{B}$obby, Gary, Tom, Terry, and Henry went rabbit hunting on a cold Sunday afternoon in February. Unfortunately, the day was fading fast, and the Rowdy Rogues did not have one rabbit for their efforts.

While cutting across a wheat field on the way home, mice kept jumping out from under the crust of snow covering the wheat stubble. The boys walked on the raised rows of stubble because the ground under it was still solidly frozen. The land between the rows where patches of snow had thawed was ankle-deep in mud.

At first, the boys ignored the mice. However, this was too much to ask of Bobby. He tried stomping on them, but the mice were too fast for him.

Gary asked Henry, "Do you want to try the south side of the river next weekend?"

"We could, but I promised Barby I'd go to Valentine's dance with her. It starts at about five. It is a long way around the railroad bridge. Would we have enough time? I cannot go in the morning because I must go with my mom to Battle Creek. How about going to the blueberry farm on the other side of the millpond?"

"Hey, I forgot about that place; we should've gone over there today, Henry."

Terry yelled, "Bobby, shoot the creatures. You are not ever going to kill one. Your fat ass."

Bobby got lucky and stepped on a mouse that turned the wrong way. "I got one. Holy mackerel! There isn't anything left."

"Yeah, right. You probably stepped on a sick one, you dumb ass." Terry said.

"Watch where you point your gun, Bobby," Tom said.

Bobby stepped on another one and yelped. When he turned to face the others walking behind him, he slipped and fell, and his shotgun discharged.

Henry looked at all the others. "Anyone hit?"

Terry was dancing around, holding his knee. "Bobby, what the hell? You are a fat, dumb bastard."

Gary and Tom grabbed Terry. Gary took his gun, and Tom steadied his brother. "How bad is it?" Tom asked.

"I'm not hit. I bumped my knee with the barrel of my gun." Terry cried.

"Bobby, leave the damn mice alone," Henry yelled.

"Bobby, you could've shot someone. Knock off the stupidity!" Tom yelled.

Gary gave Terry his gun and went over and shoved Bobby. He slipped and caught himself. "Grow up, Bobby, use your brain occasionally." Gary urged.

"You fellers better get a grip," Terry said.

"Alright, you guys. Stop yelling at each other." Henry said. "Unload your guns."

Everyone unloaded their guns.

"Point them up," Henry said. "Take your safety off and pull the trigger. Then put your safety back on."

The hunters did what Henry ordered. "Now, you can stomp mice," Henry said.

They walked in silence for several minutes. Finally, a couple of mice jumped out, and none of the boys did anything. Another one leaped up in the air and landed on Gary's boot. He kicked at it, but it got away. Another one darted in front of Henry, and he calmly adjusted his stride to step on it but missed.

Tom tried to stomp the same mouse but quickly gave up.

Terry jumped in, "Kill the little bastards; I hate mice."

"It takes a pretty low-down rat to stomp an innocent little mouse," Tom said.

"Hey now, that was pretty witty, Tommy," Terry said.

Gary stepped on one and walked on as if it were nothing.

Bobby stabbed it with his pocketknife.

Terry stomped one into the mud.

Bobby dug it out and stuck it in his pocketknife with the other.

"Bobby, leave the damn mice alone." Henry scolded his friend.

Gary said, "Farmers hate mice; they get into their grain bins, eat the wheat, and take a dump in it. Mice eat their weight every other day. Lots of mice equal lots of mouse droppings. When farmers sell their wheat, the mouse droppings make it lose value."

That was a good enough argument for the angry rabbit hunters. The mouse massacre began.

"Alright, Rogues, each one of you can straddle two rows. When a mouse leaps out, kill the dirty little monster. If a mouse crosses rows, he is fair game to the Rogue walking that row." Gary yelled.

Sometimes, ten boots were trying to stomp on one little field mouse.

"The little bastards are fast; you're way too slow, Bobby." Terry teased.

The boys cursed and spat upon the mice who escaped. One of them was so fast Gary called him Mighty Mouse.

Terry bellowed, "Here I come to save the day. That means that Mighty Mouse is on his way."

After that, each crushing blow was by deriding comments. "You sure as hell are not related to Mighty Mouse."

"Listen up, you guys. Try stomping your foot ahead of where the mouse is at your numb skulls." Tom said.

"What the hell, Tommy? Where are your mice, shithead?" Terry screamed.

"Hey, numb nuts. What do you call this." Tom taunted. He held up his jack-knife with three mice dangling.

"Way to go, Tommy." Henry badgered.

When you flatten a mouse, its brains and guts spill out and create a grotesque specimen. Sometimes, little physical evidence that was identifiable as a mouse survived. It often required several stabs to find enough to stick to a knife blade.

When Henry walked on top of the stubble, the icy crust occasionally collapsed into the soft earth underneath. Sometimes, the ice collapsed in mid-stride. The jolt was only a couple of inches long but always made him stumble.

Terry caught several of the tiny critters alive with his hands. Then, he threw several of them at the other boys until Henry recalled what his father told him about standing up for a good cause.

"Terry, kill the little bastards, but don't be cruel." Henry usually spoke softly, but this time, there was some irritation in his voice.

Terry stopped throwing the mice but did not like being corrected by Henry.

By the time the light-hearted lunatics reached the end of the field, everyone had at least six or seven mice or parts of mice dangling from their pocketknives. Terry had eleven; Henry had thirteen, and Gary had seventeen mice impaled on his pocketknife. He walked away a buck and a quarter richer.

The boys dropped the mice off at older man Turleksen's dairy barn. He had about six cats. Typically, cats want to kill what they eat, but they eat their little heads off for the mice. However, most of these mice did not have a leader the cats could identify, which confused their feline senses. So, the barn cats growled at one another and ran off with a sampler. They did not go too far; they returned to the pile, sniffing and taking tiny nips, shaking their cat lips vigorously, trying to kill what was already dead. The boys walked away laughing, leaving the cats in a quandary.

The Turleksen's farm was one of the biggest in the area. Mr. Turleksen permitted the boys to hunt on his property if they stayed away from his milk cows. As a result, most of the boys worked for the Turleksen during the hay season. Henry helped with the last cut but was usually in the onion fields during the earlier cuts. After dropping off the mice, they lit about two miles down the railroad tracks for the town.

"Hey, you guys, we ought to wear our coats tomorrow," Tom said.

Henry remembered the last time they all wore their Rowdy Rogue coats. "The principal would throw a fit again," he said.

"Dad said he'd kick Splinter's ass if he tried to send me home again," Gary laughed.

"I'm wearing mine by God," Terry said.

"I'll wear mine too," said Bobby.

Henry looked at Gary and Tom. "Guess we all wear them then," he said.

"We all stick together. But, hell, hell, the gangs are all here," said Tom.

Henry walked down the tracks with his friends. It felt good to travel with the gang, with companions and guns.

CHAPTER 9

Spring Vacation

Bobby, Henry, Gary, Tom, and Terry had wanted to go camping over spring vacation for several years. Every spring, the Rowdy Rogues planned a weeklong camping trip, but the parents always put a stop to their dreams. However, this year, nothing was stopping them.

Gary called to Henry from the sidewalk. "Where's Bobby at, man? He was supposed to be here fifteen minutes ago."

Henry waved at him through his screen door. He phoned Bobby.

"Hello, Kraneger's," Barby answered.

"Barby, has your brother left yet?" Henry asked.

"I don't know, Henry. He was in the kitchen the last time I saw him. Is he late again?" Barby asked.

"Yeah, he is a jerk sometimes," Henry said quietly.

"Henry, why are you guys doing this? Look at the weather. The snow is coming down in buckets. You are going to catch pneumonia. I know this is going to be a disaster. Why don't you stay here and spend some time with me?"

"Barby, come on. We can skate on weekends. Please tell your brother to get his butt over here." Henry muttered.

"Are you even going to miss me, Henry?" Barby snickered.

"Barby!"

"Oh, Henry!"

Barby hung up. She yelled for Bobby.

Henry walked outside with his sleeping bag and a sack of canned goods. Bobby was coming around the corner, yelling about something.

Henry waved at Terry, stepping out of the back of the van. "Henry, is your gun in here yet?" Terry asked.

"Yeah, I gave it to Tom. It's in there somewhere." Henry said.

Gary was helping Bobby with his things. Bobby carried all his stuff in one trip and kept dropping things.

Terry yelled, "Just about left your ass, fatso."

Gary's dad gave Terry a dirty look.

"Oh, sorry, sir," Terry said.

Tom had the list of supplies and started reviewing it with his dad. Finally, the boys loaded the rest of their things in the van.

Gary's dad dropped them off at the railroad tracks, and the pile of supplies was more than they had imagined. They had four tents, fishing equipment, guns, and sleeping bags. In addition, they had two lanterns, a milk can for water, and various cooking utensils.

The campsite was about a half-mile into the woods.

"How the hell are we going to carry all this shit?" Terry asked.

"Do we need all of this stuff?" Henry asked.

"We need a sled," Tom said.

"We can't leave anything here; if we do, some asshole will rip us off," Terry said.

"We can't carry all this in one trip," Bobby complained.

"Form a relay," Henry advised.

"Bobby, can you stay here and guard the camping and hunting equipment," Henry asked kindly.

"I'll start pulling everything with the sled as far as the first fence line," Henry advised.

"Gary, can you pull our stuff over the fence." Henry smiled and padded Gary's back.

"Tom and Terry, load our toboggan and pull as much as possible to the river?"

"We got about six hours to get three tents up, and a fire started. We need to hunt for rabbits, too." Henry grimaced.

"Why do we have to move everything in a few hours?" Terry asked.

"When we talked about this trip into the wilderness, we didn't know we would have eighteen inches of snow and fourteen degrees." Henry moaned.

"Henry has a good idea, Terry. Quit being a prick." Tom said.

Terry got in his brother's face. "Don't piss me off, Apollo!"

Henry got in Terry's face. "What's wrong with you? Why are you such a prick?"

Terry backed down. "To hell with the lot of you." He picked up his backpack, a tent, and gun and started for the river.

Gary walked beside Tom and Henry. "What's up with the Apollo thing?"

"I got mad at Terry the other day and called him Artemis. You know, Artemis is the goddess of hunting in Greek literature. Artemis was always a hothead. So, when I get mad at Terry, it is my way of responding to his bullshit. It angers him, so now he thinks calling me Apollo is some retort." Tom laughed.

"He does act like a bitch at times," Henry added.

"He acts like Bobby most of the time, but I don't think he'd agree," Gary said.

"Maybe it's a bad twin thing," Henry said.

"Yeah, hey, that's rather good. Barby and then Bobby; Terry and then Tom. Good analogy, Henry." Gary said.

Tom opened his coat pocket and pulled out a small bottle of whisky. Meet Mister James Beam.

Terry slowed down and let the others catch up. Then, he sat down in the tent and lit a cigarette. "Hey, give me a shot, Tom?" Terry asked.

"This is for tonight, asshole," Tom said.

Terry threw his hands in the air, picked up his load, and walked beside Henry. A rabbit jumped through the fencerow, ran across the railroad tracks one hundred feet ahead of the boys, and then disappeared.

"Shit, there goes dinner." Terry grimaced.

"I could've bagged it." Tom moaned.

"You'll get your chance. I'd like to see you hit a rabbit on the run that far away." Gary said.

"Henry got one like that. I saw him do it." Terry said.

Henry looked back at Bobby. He waved, but Bobby did not see him. He felt sorry for Bobby. Everyone always picked on him. Henry felt the same way about Terry. There could be something about being a twin and being considered troubled.

Henry made eye contact with Terry. "Think we can stick it out for seven days?"

"If we had some sweet young things to keep us warm at night, we could," Terry said.

"You wouldn't know what to do with a sweet young thing if you had one," Gary said.

Terry pointed to his brother.

Tom looked away.

Terry pointed to him and said, "He knows. Ask him."

"What? Hey Tom, what's he talking about." Gary asked.

"Tommy got caught with his pecker poking our cousin," Terry said, trying to keep from laughing.

"What's up with this? Tommy, you're not a virgin?" Henry asked.

"She's seventeen! She snuck into my room last weekend, and we did it. It is no big deal. She is not our real cousin, anyhow. Her mom and our mom are half-sisters." Tom insisted.

"So, you got laid by a half-cousin. That's cool." Gary said. He and Henry did a high five.

"Let me tell you, boys, she is a real looker, too," Terry said.

"How so," asked Gary.

"What do you mean?" Tom asked.

"Who does she look like?" Henry urged.

"She's not as foxy as Brandy, but she has a nice ass," Terry said.

"Brandy is nice, very, very nice," Gary said.

"She's out of your league, Rogue," Henry exclaimed.

"How's about Barby?" Terry asked.

Henry turned to him and asked, "What about Barby?"

Terry saw that Henry was mad. "Nothing, just wondering."

"Wonder in private. We don't talk about Barby!" Henry said.

Terry held his hands in the air and took out another cigarette. "Be cool, man; I didn't mean to walk on sacred ground."

They reached the river, and Henry, Terry, and Gary returned to get the rest of the gear.

A large bonfire lit up the forest later that night. All the boys set up tents and ate dinner—rabbit stew that Gary shot and four fish that Bobby caught.

"You should've brought your guitar, Gary," Bobby said.

Terry kicked at the snow. "Yeah, as long as you didn't have to carry it, fatso."

Bobby got up and picked up a large stick. "You call me that again during your lifetime, and I'll kick the ever-living shit out of your hillbilly ass."

Terry had a big grin on his face. He looked around at the others and tried to maintain it, but his grin turned into a frown when he realized the others would not back him up. "Be cool, man. Hell, Bobby, I have been calling you fat since we were kids. I do not mean anything by it. Hell, I like you, man. You are my friend, Bobby, who was supposed to be a gang member. You mean we can't tease each other anymore."

Everyone was quiet.

Henry picked up his log and moved closer to Terry. He put his hand on Terry's shoulder. "You're right, Terry. We are all friends, but we need to quit disrespecting each other. It's all right to tease, but don't do it like you hate the other person."

Tom took out his bottle. "Hey guys, let's drink for the Rowdy Rogues."

"Guys, listen up, damn it. We never wear our Rogue coats to school. But, when we return to school, we should wear our coats, Rowdy Rogues! Bobby yelled.

'We can do it, Bobby, but we'll be kicked out of school." Terry said.

"Bobby, leave this for another day, pal." Henry smiled and patted Bobby on his back.

Gary got some paper cups, and Tom filled each with the same amount of whisky.

"Sip her easy, boys, because she'll have some kick," Tom said.

Terry built a fire in the morning before anyone else was up. Then, he set up the tripod for the coffee and began heating melted snow for the water. The twins brought a milk can with good water but only used it sometimes. Then, he set up the frying pan and started cooking bacon. The air was calm but stung your cheeks. The snow had a thin crust of ice on it, but the sky was clear.

Henry came out of the tent first and ran for the woods. He returned afterward and walked up to where Terry was sitting near the fire. "How about we go rabbit hunting together this morning," Henry said.

Terry should have looked up. "Sure, we can get four or five good ones."

Henry moved his seat closer to the fire. "How long have you been up?" he asked.

"Half an hour," Terry said.

"Nice fire. That bacon sure smells good. Coffee ready yet?" he asked.

"Nope, water not hot enough yet," Terry said.

Gary came out of the tent and ran for the woods.

"Where the hell is he going in such a hurry?" Terry asked. He smiled at Henry.

"Look at that sky. I hope it does not warm up too much. Then, I'll make the coffee." Henry said.

Gary came over and held his hands out over the fire. "Nice fire, Terry."

Henry and Terry had four rabbits. Bobby caught six nice bluegills, and the boys went to bed with full bellies.

On Monday, the temperature got up to forty-five degrees. That night, the boys were in the sleeping tent.

"My uncle told me about this trick. Watch this, Rogue's." Gary said. He breathed deeply, kneeled, wrapped his arms around his knees, and held his breath. Then, he fell unconscious almost instantly.

Terry poked him until he woke up.

"That's pure bull shit," Terry said.

"Try it. Gary said.

Terry breathed deeply six times, then kneeled and held his breath. Finally, he went out like a light.

Tom tickled him, but he did not move.

Terry woke up after a few moments. "Wow, holy mackerel. Did I do it?" he asked.

Henry tried it, too. He fell over as soon as he grabbed his knees.

Bobby would not do it.

Gary did it again.

Tom did it again.

Terry did it again.

Henry did it again.

Bobby still would not do it.

The rain started after dark and warmed the air to fifty-five degrees. The snow melted, and the ground thawed, but the melted snow could not drain through the thirty-two-inch frontline. The floor turned into a muddy bog. Fog settled in over the woods.

"Bobby, you better wake up," Henry whispered.

"What's up, Rogue?" Bobby asked.

"It has been raining hard. Thank goodness the tents are on a hill." Henry said.

"Why did you wake me up, Henry?" Bobby wondered.

"The milk can tip over, and the lid wasn't tight. So, we lost most of our water. The sleds won't do us any good. It's our turn to get water. The snow is gone, Bobby. There is not enough clean snow to melt anymore. The Bishop's Farm is the closest. It's about a mile away." Henry said.

Bobby got dressed. Henry dumped the remaining water into the coffee pot. He grabbed one side of the milk can, and Bobby grabbed the other. The mud was a foot deep in places. It kept pulling their boots off. They made it about two hundred yards before they gave up.

Bobby looked at his friend. "We've got three more days. After that, what will we do without water?" he asked.

Henry looked at the river. "The water on top of the ice is mostly snowmelt or rain. So, I'll bet it's clean enough to drink," he said.

"I don't know, Henry; we can't start a fire. But, if we could boil the water, I'm sure it'd be good enough to drink." Bobby said.

"We have the little camp burner. So, we could boil water in our coffee pot. But, of course, the water wouldn't taste perfect." Henry replied.

"Guess what, the LP Gas is almost empty. We don't have any spare cans." Bobby said.

"What are we going to do, quit?" Henry asked.

"No, I guess not," Bobby said.

They filled the milk can up to three-quarters full of nice-looking river water. Then they made river water Kool-Aid from the rest of the water in the milk can.

Everyone loved the Kool-Aid; it was a big hit, and confidence was high in achieving their goal. All five Rowdy Rogues were still at the campsite.

Late Thursday night, Tom got sick. He threw up all over the tent. He went home.

Terry abandoned that tent and moved in with the others. On Friday afternoon, Gary got the runs, and he went home. He said it was a constant leakage.

Bobby threw up all over the other sleeping tent early Saturday morning. Bobby told Terry Lickliter what he and Henry had done with the water. Terry punched Henry in the nose. Terry did not give him a warning or anything; he just walked up and slugged Henry in the nose.

Henry went home with a nosebleed. Terry never did get sick, but Henry learned later he did not drink any of the Kool-Aid.

Henry got sick that night. He had a high fever. His mom said it was 102 most of the night. By noon the following day, his fever had elevated to 103, and Henry's mom took him to the hospital. Henry was dehydrated because he could not keep anything in his stomach.

Henry did not remember much of that week; his mom said he almost died, and his temperature reached 105 several times.

After five days, his fever broke to less than 100, and he became aware of where he was. Henry's doctor told him that some minor bugs caused all the problems. He said to him that he could have killed everyone, including himself.

Bobby, Gary, and Tom contracted dysentery and spent time in the hospital. Tom's fever was the worst. Later in his life, he would learn he became sterile because of the madness. Henry's last name suffered abuse for many years.

The parents had to go into the mud and vomit-soaked tents to clean up the equipment. They all said the smell was unbearable. Every parent questioned Henry's intelligence.

Henry wondered for a long time how he could have been so stupid. But school was about over, so the teasing did not last long. River water Kool-Aid had a nice enough ring.

Bobby was sick for a long time but never said anything wrong to Henry. He seemed to lose stamina—just was sickly for months.

The Rowdy Rogue gang lost its appeal to its members after river water Kool-Aid. The boys wore their coats occasionally, but the club was always different.

CHAPTER 10

Thunder Jumpers

Topping onions was an excellent job for a fifteen-year-old, Henry told himself as he worked feverishly. He was happy to be back in the onion fields. Nobody wanted to be around him, and that was fine with Henry. The river water Kool-Aid was still an issue, and Henry was thankful for the solitude. Sure, he smelled like onions for days on end. Friends and loved ones referred to him as the kid who smelled like onions. Having a rotten last name kept things stirred up.

Henry started working in the onion fields shortly after sunrise. The hot sun cooked his shoulders, and he knew the sheets in his bed would feel like sandpaper. Henry was getting very tired by early afternoon, but he had had a perfect day and wanted to finish with a flurry of activity. His back ached to work between the two rows, pulling two handfuls of onions from the row on his right and then quickly performing the same maneuver on his left. As he moved down the long row, his knees plowed deep into the cool, dark muck. The drier gray muck on top was hot and would burn his knees if he did not use the plowing action. One of the migrants showed him how to protect himself this way. Below the surface, the muck was fantastic and had some moisture in it. Each time he moved, the coolness of the damp earth soothed his aching knees.

To be a good onion topper, you had to be fast on your knees and have a strong back. Henry pulled five or six onions, held them over the crate, and cut off the tops with scissors. The onions fell into the box, and Henry tossed the tops. He always worked two rows at a time. Henry worked the rows fast until he got tired, then turned around and worked backward. Occasionally, Henry would nick one of his knuckles while cutting off the onion tops. If Henry accidentally cut his left forefinger knuckle, he would switch hands and use his other until he cut it too. Henry quit at lunchtime, and the migrants took a two-hour siesta.

During the morning, Henry could fill twenty crates of onions an hour. So at fifteen cents a box, that was three dollars an hour, fifteen dollars a day, seventy-five dollars a week. So he would spend forty or fifty dollars during the summer and save the rest.

For three years, in early summer, he worked three weeks in mid-June to early July. The five-week job provided enough money to carry him through the summer. He put $100.00 in his savings account. He gave his mother $100.00 and saved the rest for special occasions.

After each onion topping season, Henry went swimming, took long hot showers, and scrubbed his body vigorously, but it always took two weeks before the onion smells subsided.

Later in the summer, Bobby, Barby, and Henry went on day trips on their bicycles. Barneyville was a flat town, except near Millpond. There were a lot of hills along the Millpond. The three teens often met up with other friends cruising throughout the neighborhoods. The tall sugar maples, poplar, white and red oak trees created a cool canopy along the sidewalks and streets.

In a small town like Barneyville, friendships flourished. The cyclists often stopped and talked to older folks who sat on their porches; of course, the Kool-Aid and cookies were part of the experience. In August, driver's education classes started, but bicycles were great.

Bobby and Henry loved to fish along the Millpond. The fishing could have been more fruitful, but the idea was what was necessary. Sometimes, other agendas would surface during their languid hours on the bank of the Millpond. The conversations almost always turned to girls, cars, or baseball. Bobby was an automobile and baseball nut, but Henry did not share his passion. Henry was interested in girls. He often spoke to Bobby about his affection for Barby. The conversations were almost always one way. Bobby wanted to sell pickup trucks. Henry wanted to be a teacher. On the rare occasions that Barby accompanied them, she made it known she wanted to be a chemist and have a large family.

Henry's uncle Fred came to visit from California. First, Henry told him about all the exciting things he was doing. Then, his father's brother told him about something he did as a kid in Barneyville. His uncle Fred said that the Millpond had a large pipe near the state highway bridge as a level control drain.

Henry knew about the drainpipe. It was a large vertical pipe next to the highway. His uncle explained that he, his friends, and Henry's father used to jump in it and come out on the other side of the bridge.

Henry knew the water came out below on the other side because a large pool of bubbles and foam was always present. Even in the coldest of winters, the ice never froze in that spot. So, he always stayed clear of it because the ice was never safe.

Henry did not know that the pipe made a long, sweeping turn under the highway. Then, the tube opened on the other side of the road in fifteen feet of water. His uncle said that only the most courageous boys would dare jump into that dark, scary pipe when he was growing up.

Henry asked his uncle why kids quit doing it. His uncle said repetitive summer droughts reduced the volume of water so low that the fun dried up over the years.

The eight-foot-wide water level drainpipe was about ten feet below the highway bridge. The river on the opposite side of the bridge was thirty feet lower. So, the tube came out fifteen feet below the water level. Henry dove to the bottom many times over the years. He knew how far the pipe was from the bridge. Kids used to jump off the bridge until a drunk driver ran over a little girl. The total drop, they reasoned, was forty-five feet, thirty-five feet underwater. No one Henry knew could hold their breath long enough to dive to thirty-five feet.

Henry contacted the Rowdy Rogues, and they agreed to meet at the dam the following day. Henry was woken up during the night by lightning and thunder. He went around the house and closed all the windows. The sun shined when he woke up, but tree limbs scattered around the yard. Pools of rainwater covered the landscape.

He jumped on his bike, and Bobby came around the corner. They met the twins and Gary at Mill Pond. The water was high, and the roar from the level control pipe was deafening. They silently surveyed the situation.

"Niagara Falls would be safer than this," Terry stated loudly.

"You know a guy just survived going over Niagara Falls in a barrel a few years ago," Gary yelled.

"How are you going to float over the lip of the pipe? You'd have to do it during a drenching rain," Tom hollered.

"How do you know there is no waterlogged timber plugging up the opening? Water can flow through all kinds of garbage, but I don't think I'd trust a sinking five-dollar bill." Terry lamented.

"Hey guys, I got an idea. We need to measure several things. First, take a rubber ball the size of a softball, tie a twenty-pound fishing line to it, and let it free fall. Time how long it takes from the millpond level control to the river's surface. We need to perform this test ten times.

That gave Bobby an idea. "There are old pickle barrels behind the old pickle factory.

"Hey guys, let us move away from the thunder. If we find a pickle barrel that is still usable,

First and foremost, we need to measure how long it would take for a barrel to travel under the highway and surface." Henry said.

The boys rode their bikes over to the old pickle factory. They found a solid barrel and tied it on a large Radio Flyer wagon. It could have been a better fit, but it worked. Gary pulled it behind his bike to his house. Gary climbed into the barrel. It was a tight fit, but he could get in and out without help.

"Let's take it over to the millpond and drop this piece of shit into the bowels of hell," Terry said.

They got the pickle barrel to Millpond.

"Holy Moses, we can't swim out to that thing. It would suck us over the side like a leaf. Shit, man, how the hell can we do this?" Terry yelled.

"Hey, look at this Rogue. There is a steel beam down here going out to the drainpipe. It sure looks like a support beam, maybe. It is about six inches below the water. The beam is wide, too," Gary said.

The boys rolled the barrel down the hill and floated it to the level control pipe. Unfortunately, the water pulled it over the lip, and the barrel disappeared.

"Shit, did you see that, Rogue's?" Bobby said.

"What the hell, Bobby?" Tom yelled.

"Where's the barrel, Bobby?" Henry asked.

"That thing sucked her away from me," Bobby whined.

"Holy mackerel, run across the highway, fools. We need to get the barrel back," Gary yelled.

Terry and Henry ran like hell. They got across the highway, and the barrel was floating downstream. They scrambled down the narrow, winding fishing trail and leaped into the river, chasing the barrel. Finally, they caught up to it and began pushing it back toward the spot on the shore where the fishing trail stopped. Henry and Terry wrestled the barrel back up the hill and rolled it across the highway.

"Doesn't look like it's damaged you guys," Bobby said.

"Tommy, you have a watch. Does the secondhand work?" Terry asked.

"Yeah, it works fine. What do you need for Terry?

"We need to measure how long it takes for the barrel to pop up below," Gary said.

"Tommy and Bobby, you guys go down along the fishing trail. Terry goes over to the other side of the highway; make sure Tommy and Bobby see you. Gary goes up on this side of the highway, and we must see each other. So, I will wave at you, Gary, when the barrel drops. You wave at Terry, and Terry, you wave at Tom. Tom, you watch your secondhand; Bobby, you watch for the barrel. That is how we can figure out how long it takes for the barrel to travel," Henry said.

They dropped the pickle barrel through the black hole a dozen times. It took eighteen seconds each time to pop up on the other side.

Gary volunteered to get in the barrel to see how it felt. So, they waited thirty seconds, opened the barrel, and Gary was breathing hard.

It did not rain for two weeks. Then, finally, after a three-day soaker, the big day arrived. Gary could hold his breath for more than two minutes.

The water plunging into the black hole made a lot of noise. The noise was deafening up close. It sounded like thunder. The boys had to yell at the top of their lungs to hear each other while standing near it. The land dropped about thirty feet on the opposite side of the highway. Bubbles and foam bubbled up and drifted downstream in the middle of the basin.

They planned to push the barrel into the throat of the drain. Instead, six inches below the waterline, they found a flat concrete curb along the side of the staging area.

They stationed two guys on the other side of the bridge, one guy on each bank close to the pool of bubbles. Gary took some deep breaths. Bobby and Henry quickly closed the lid and pushed the barrel over the side.

The barrel bobbed up in twenty-eight seconds. Tom and Terry jumped in and pushed the barrel to shore. The barrel was heavier with Gary in it, so it took longer to move it. Finally, Gary popped it open, and fifty-four seconds had elapsed.

"Hey, you guys. Could you have tossed me around a little harder?" Gary complained. "This shit scared me, you guys."

Tom looked at his brother. They did not move; they did not look at Gary.

Henry and Bobby came down the hill quickly. They slowed their approach when they saw Gary. He was naked, and he was rinsing his shorts in the river.

Bobby looked at Henry.

"I shit my pants," Gary complained.

"Gary, I'm sorry, Rogue," Henry said.

"Hey man, Gary. Damn it all. I'm sorry." Bobby said.

"It's your turn, Henry. You will love this, Rogue. Tie a fricking rope around this thing and pull it to shore. It takes too long, and these honyocks spin you around like a drunken fool," Gary whined.

"Watch what I do, Gary. Lickliter twins, you watch for me," Henry looked at Bobby, and Bobby gave him a thumbs up. Then, Henry shouted, "I'm going to get wet."

Henry tried to remember what his uncle said, "You have to wait for a good rain." Well, it rained hard the night before. The water was gushing into the drain. Henry knew his uncle would not lie to him. He remembered his uncle said that the current would push you hard, but the bubbles would lift you to the surface like an elevator. He remembered, too, that his uncle told him to count to twenty-five; counting would calm the natural inclination to panic.

The pipe was twelve feet in diameter, and Henry stood above the drain on the bridging a foot below the throat. The thunderous roar of water tumbling into the drainpipe vacillated. The water nearly closed the throat of the pipe, forming a black hole like the pupil of an enormous eyeball. The roar increased when the eye opened but muffled the thunderous roar eerily when it closed. The deck vibrated in unison with the sound. Henry's legs shuddered as fear crept into his heart. He watched as the black eye opened, reformed, filled in again, then reformed again. He was trying to find the nerve to take the plunge.

Henry looked up at Bobby. His friend formed a perplexing expression. Henry understood; if he did not jump, their friendship could continue indubitably replete. Henry's ex-marine father shared many stories about courage, bravery, and valor. Henry sorted the late-night conversations reminiscently. His dad told him that courage was the nerve to face danger. Bravery was the capacity to act with courage. Valor was bravery and courage in action. Why wait for courage or bravery when what he needed was valor? Henry needed to clearly see the task at hand and then act on it. That was true valor: action associated with bravery and courage. Henry grabbed his nose and leaped in feet first.

As his body fell, he realized he was not jumping into the water because the water was falling with him at the same speed. Globules of water clung to each other like clusters of grapes. As Henry fell further into the darkness, more water seemed to join the fun. Suddenly, he began twirling. Henry suffered severe vertigo. The water was moving with him, and the sensation became almost intolerable. He closed his eyes and counted. Everything around him was going in four directions, spinning and falling. Henry did not feel the turn. The dominant sensation of going down continued unabated. He was free-falling, and the speed of the rushing water kept pushing him downward.

He blew hard on his nose, clearing his ears. However, he became dizzy, and each time he equalized, it made him dizzier. His count was now at fifteen, and there was no sign of rising to the surface.

Suddenly, the spinning stopped, and millions of bubbles began to attach themselves to Henry, pushing at him. They seemed to grab at his belly, neck, arms, legs, and face. A fearful dread was building in his gut, but he fought off the urge to panic. Instead, the overpowering thrust continued pushing him into some incredulous bottomless pit.

He opened his eyes and saw bubbles everywhere. The bubbles were fluffy, bubbly, and fizzy. He could not swim; nothing reacted to his thrusts with his arms or legs. Henry experienced narcosis, mayhem, and confusion. He tried to grab the water and push upward or what he thought was up, but nothing he did seemed to work. He concentrated on his count—twenty-six, then twenty-seven.

Unexpectedly, abruptly, it was over. Henry was on the surface, floating downstream. How did he get to the surface?

It took Henry several seconds to regain his composure. He watched the white billowing clouds spin in the sky and decided he had never seen such a thing. It was so neat, so calm, so groovy.

Tom swam up next to Henry. "How was it, man?"

"Bodacious Tommy. I cannot wait to do it again. Why is the sky spinning?"

Gary jumped into the thundering waters seconds after Henry. He bobbed up, screaming, "Yahoo!"

Bobby followed Gary, and he popped to the surface, uttering unintelligible sounds.

Tom and Terry jumped next, followed by the others. Someone always waited along the bank. Terry, with his less-than-moral expletives, dubbed the experience; "being screwed senseless."

The Rowdy Rogues talked excitedly about their brush with unknown sensations, impressions, responses, and reactions. They unanimously agreed to be screwed senseless was the most fantastic feeling a guy could ever experience.

Henry and Bobby sat along the bank, talking and waiting for Tom, Terry, and Gary to come down through the pipe again. "I never touched the side of the pipe or anything, did you, Bobby?"

"I don't think so, but it was so quick, and the water moved so fast; I guess I didn't."

"Did you have any problems clearing your ears, Henry?"

"Yeah, but I waited too long to start; my ears ache a little."

"I started blowing against my nose right away and didn't have any trouble at all," Bobby tapped the side of his head with the heel of his palm, urging the water to drain from his ears.

Tom popped up just then. "Yahoo," he yelled. Gary popped up just ahead of him with a wide grin. He flipped Bobby and Henry the bird. They both gave him a double dose on his proper back. Terry broke the surface, gagging; he had blood running out his mouth and nose. Henry and Bobby both leaped in and scrambled to his aid. Terry had a slight cold, and when he tried to clear his ears, they would not equalize. He had to blow hard; as a result, the mucus membrane in his nose ruptured. Tom said, "It isn't a big deal; it happens to both of us occasionally when we swim." Terry did not jump anymore that day.

Terry timed the jumps; the descent to Davy Jones' locker took less than twenty-five seconds. Unfortunately, the current carried the boys twenty-five to seventy-five feet downstream before they could escape it.

Gary noticed that staying in the swirling current just outside the primary current would bring you right back into the pool of bubbles. However, shortly before getting to that point, they realized they could swim out of the swirl just fifteen feet from shore.

Climbing up the embankment wore on them; after about five jumps, the boys were exhausted.

Ever since that first day, whenever a hard rain fell, all the stouthearted swimmers in town would beat feet for the Millpond drainpipe. Of course, kids from other towns would come and join in the fun; however, not all would participate.

Even the best athletes shared Henry's experience of struggling to get the nerve to jump in the drain for the first time. Many of them failed in their first attempt. Most just wanted to see firsthand how such a thing was possible.

The parents who always ruined everything did not like the fun. They said it was too dangerous. Several of the parents tried to get thunder jumping banned. They kept whining. Someone was sure to get hurt. For a long time, the city police came and watched. Sometimes, a firefighter would show up; they knew the kids would be there if it rained.

News agencies like radio stations and some newspapers published articles, some for, some against thunder jumping. One journalist wrote, "Courageous young men like the Barneyville Thunder Jumpers displayed the strength, vigor, and nerve needed by those who intend to be leaders of their community." The Rowdy Rogues liked the name "Thunder Jumpers," which stuck from that day on.

Thunder jumping defined the Rowdy Rogues more than anything else in the small town. Rumors, often blown out of proportion, continued to hound the young men. But, except for Terry's big mouth, the gang never caused any problems.

CHAPTER 11

Henry's Abnormality

In late July, the Kranegers and Henry spent their summer vacation at Yankee Springs State Park. The Park was in the state's interior and was known for good fishing, swimming, and water skiing. Several lakes were linked, allowing boaters to play on the water for miles. In addition, there was a large sandy beach and great picnicking sites. Yankee Springs was Michigan's second-largest State Park.

The days were hot and dry; the nights were warm and damp. Huge campfires lit the dark, woodsy nights. Barby played her guitar every night around the campfire. Neighbors often moved in and around the Kraneger's fire and listened as Barby and Brandy sang familiar songs.

Mr. Kraneger purchased a new nineteen-foot Chris Craft ski boat with a hull made of fiberglass. It could seat six passengers and be stored comfortably. The windshield folded in the middle and allowed access to the two seats in the front. An Evinrude eighty-five horsepower outboard engine powered the boat. Everyone except Mrs. Kraneger learned how to ski. The ship could pull three skiers at the same time. Brandy and Henry were the most talented. Bobby and Barby liked to ski together because they liked riding the waves slowly.

Mr. Kraneger, Brandy, and Henry learned to slalom. Brandy and Henry often skied together. The swift turns and high-water spraying antics were comical, graceful, and entertaining. They both pushed each other to perform the craziest stunts. Their favorite was to whip out wide, one skier on one side of the boat and the other on the other. They would twist their skis against the water on their mark, cutting a deep swath and causing a sharp, hard turn toward the boat. Just as they came upon the boat's wake, they would jump it, and upon landing, they turned violently to the outside again, spraying the opposing skier with a thick blanket of water. The coxswain needed to open the throttle at that point as the boat could almost reach a standstill. The skiers created a real problem for themselves at this point. The swing outside often pushed the skiers faster than the boat. If the skiers had to wait too long for the ship to catch up, they could sink too far to overcome the sudden jerk when the slack came out of the rope.

Mrs. Kraneger did not like to swim, but she enjoyed boating; she did not like getting wet.

Barby and Bobby were skiing on the lake on a hot early August afternoon. The lake was empty except for a few pontoons. Mrs. Kraneger was at the helm. Mr. Kraneger faced the two skiers, spotting them in case one went down.

Henry and Brandy sat in the front, leaning out over the bow. They had been out on the water showing off earlier. She thought her slalom style was better than his, and he would never admit to that, even if she were right. They had worn each other out with their outlandish antics.

"It's tranquil and peaceful up here, Hank. I love to sit and watch the boat slide over the water."

Henry was trying to get the nerve to ask Brandy about sex. He thought she would be the perfect person to explain it to him. She would not make fun of him but would understand his need to know. So late the next night, he stayed up with Brandy and finally got the nerve to speak with her privately.

"Do you have a boyfriend in college, Brandy?" Henry asked.

She looked at him, startled by what he asked. "Freshmen don't normally have time for boyfriends, but I have been on several dates."

Henry felt quite bold because she did not seem annoyed yet. "Anyone you care to talk about?" he asked.

Brandy's facial expression sank, and she looked dumbfounded. "Hank, you sound like my FatherFather! It is none of your business!"

Something told him to back off; maybe it was her crass statement, but his abnormality was raging. "Come on, Brandy, tell me about college life. I hear it's wild and crazy."

Brandy looked around the campsite. Her Mother opened a window in the camper. She waited to see if her Mother could hear, and after deciding she could not overhear their conversation, she smiled slyly at him. "Look, dimples. I have dated a couple of guys, sleazy, pimple-faced, all-hands kind of guys. Why do you want to know? Look at you all guggle-eyed. You like me, don't you? Hell, you are infatuated with me. Look at the way you are drooling. But, Hank, listen to me; I am too old for you. I am not your girlfriend, and I will not tell you anything about my private affairs! I used to be your babysitter, you little boy!"

Henry saw the rage in her eyes, but he would not back off now. "Do you have free sex? I hear free sex is the popular trend now."

Brandy could not believe her ears. Her mouth fell open, and she turned away from his gaping stare. "How old are you, you little pervert?"

Henry saw that she was surprised and intrigued by his curiosity. "Hey, I want to know about sex, and I thought you would tell me; it's not like we will ever do it together. Okay, secretly, I'm crazy about you, but I get confused; sometimes I feel like you're my older sister, and I feel abnormal, well, you know."

Brandy thought, I do not know, and was about to let him have it.

"Brandy, you're the most beautiful girl I know. I do not have an older brother or sister, but do not worry; I am a realist. I know you're much too old for me, but I have these dreams." Henry realized too late that he had said too much. His guilt made him sink back into his seat, and his face became repressed with fervid sorrow.

Brandy sat and looked at him without saying a word. Her face turned from a red rage to a peevish grin. "Hank, you are a pervert; you cannot have dreams about me, dream about Barby, no, no, don't do that either. Are you reading pornography?" She tried to be serious, but she was about to laugh, and she had to force herself into a languid disposition as the emotion subsided.

"No, I have virtues, Brandy, you know I do," he said.

Brandy wondered if he understood his ideology. "If you want to know about sex, ask your mother."

Henry could not believe she said that. "Brandy, I can't ask my mother about sex; that would be absurd."

She turned her head, thinking what audacity. "Ask my father then." She knew her father secretly loved Henry as if he were his son. But she always needed to understand why.

"Wow, that would work well; I'm going steady with Barby. I think he knows something about our liking each other; when I ask him to tell me about sex, what do you suppose he is going to think?"

Brandy thought about what her father would think about Henry's true nature. The hidden esoteric Henry, who seemed infatuated with her and went steady with her fifteen-year-old sister?

"Well, have you forgotten, I am Barby's older sister!" Brandy saw the innocent look on Hank's face and realized he meant nothing improper towards her little sister. "Hank, someday, maybe, but not here with my parents."

Henry was losing his edge, and he knew it. "They cannot hear us, and they are not watching us. Besides, I'm not asking for a demonstration."

Brandy suddenly got tired of the animated, naïve schoolboy. "Hank, alright, I'm sure in school you have seen the movies in Home Economics?" She did not want to pursue this any further.

"Sure, but they don't tell you about feelings; I know about the mechanics, but I don't know about the feelings."

She could not believe she was going down this road with him. "Why do you need to know about feelings?" She looked again to see if her Mother had heard any of the idiocy.

"Brandy, it's a guy thing; when I'm with my friends, sometimes we talk about sex. I don't want to sound like an idiot. I don't need to do it; I want to know how it feels."

How old are you? Brandy asked herself the question again. "Hank, believe me, you do not need to know how it feels!" Brandy touched his face and brushed his hair to the side. "Look, sweetie, give it some time. I know your hormones are raging right now, but you need to cool it with the sex stuff, okay." He looked like a little boy that had just lost his favorite toy.

"Sure, I understand." Henry felt betrayed; he hoped Brandy would explain everything to him. However, he was sulking as he supposed it was only suitable for the abnormality to continue; after all, he was not quite sixteen years old.

Henry's Mother waited for him Sunday night until the vacationers arrived home. He told her all about skiing and their fun on the water.

Brandy warned Barby about Henry's raging hormones. The older sister warned her not to be alone with Henry because he may act imprudently.

Brandy left for college in Boston: a sophomore at Dartmouth.

CHAPTER 12

Sophomore Year

Henry, Bobby, and Barby were in their sophomore year in high school. Bobby, Henry, and Gary started the first string on the varsity football team.

Bobby slept in late almost daily; his tardiness at school almost disqualified him from the football team. His mom took him to the doctor, but he said nothing was wrong with him. Bobby had grown four more inches by the time football season was over. Bobby's body needed the extra rest because he was growing so fast.

Henry walked to school every day with Barby.

"Henry, my grandfather owned an old sailboat. The boat is in South Haven. I think the Kalamazoo River flows into Lake Michigan at South Haven. My grandfather had fifty acres of farmland on the river. I don't know how far from Lake Michigan. The sailboat is in a barn on the farm close to the river. A farmer grows crops on the farm every year and posts profits for Dad. Brandy doesn't want the boat. Bobby doesn't want it either. I'm thinking about going up to look at it. Nobody knew Grandpa owned a sailboat until he died. My grandfather died before I was born. Would you go with me, Henry?" Barby asked.

"You know I will, Barby. Have you ever been on a sailboat?" Henry pulled her closer as they walked.

"No, I have never sailed anything, Henry."

"Would you be responsible for the sailboat?" Henry asked.

"Not right away, but sailing it during the summer might be fun. Maybe for years, Henry."

"I don't have my driver's license yet. You have yours, don't you, Henry?"

"Yeah, but where will we get a car, Barby?"

"My father has hundreds of cars, Henry. I'll ask him tonight when everything is just right."

"Your dad will give you anything, Barby."

"I know, honey, but I don't want to take advantage of him, dear." She flashed her eyes.

Saturday morning, Barby knocked on Henry's door.

"Hello, young lady. Henry is in his room getting dressed, I think." Jessica pondered.

"I can knock on his door, Mrs. Rotyn. Do you mind?" Barby wondered.

"Nope, just be careful, dear. Henry has a habit of running around the house in his underwear." Jessica advised.

Barby walked down the hallway to his door. She was about to knock on his door when Henry opened it with one hand and had the other holding a towel overhead. He was otherwise naked, and she couldn't take her eyes off his dangling thingy."

"Mom, can you check if my clothes in the dryer are ready," Henry yelled.

"Hello, Henry. Could you cover it up just a little, please?" Barby asked.

"Barby, please tell me you had your eyes closed," Henry inquired.

"Your mother told me I should be careful. I was going to knock on your door, silly. I got an eyeful. I mean, I saw you. It made me smile, dear. I don't think I ever saw anything like this, honey. Wow, I don't know what to say, silly boy. No, you most certainly are not a boy," Barby blushed.

"How are you, silly girl," Henry asked while he lowered his towel around his torso and pushed his hair back.

"I do not think I'm a silly girl anymore," Barby smiled beautifully.

"Be quiet, honey; please don't let my mother know what happened," he whispered.

"This will no doubt become an extraordinary secret for us to marvel at many years from now," she looked down.

"Why uh, uh hum, are you staring at me, Barby?" he rambled.

"If I step into your room and close your door. Would a second performance be appropriate?" She pushed him into his room and pulled the door shut.

"What are you doing, Barby?"

"She pushed the lock and smiled. I'm waiting for you, dear," Barby said.

"You want me to drop my towel," he asked.

"Maybe, but what isn't important? The encore is the most important; however, the performance was indescribable."

"Barby, do you need to see it again?" He was puzzled.

"Henry, tell me the truth. Did you know I was in your house?"

Henry cringed. "I did hear people talking in the kitchen. I didn't know it was you. I wasn't waiting for you to come to my door." Henry promised.

"I don't care; the show must go on. It's imperative, dear, you placed the serving on my plate, Henry, and I wish to consume it now," she smiled.

"No, seriously, Barby, I won't expose myself."

"She pushed him onto the bed and pulled the towel away. He was swelling in front of her. Wow, this thing is huge, Henry. Will it ever stop getting bigger? But don't tell me, dear; I'm all done. Here, honey, take your towel. We leave in ten minutes. I'll get your clothes, too."

They drove the car for twenty minutes before anyone said a word.

"Henry, I brought a swimsuit; your mom shoved yours in with mine."

"I'm sorry I abused your idea about life. We are much more than a few glimpses of our bodies. You are beautiful in so many ways. I think we know we love each other. I love everything about you. Some things will mature faster, and some will have to wait until they are mature and capable of dealing with our objectives, whatever they might become. I am sorry; please forgive me, darling?" Barby confessed.

"I love you, Barby. I love you from the bottom of my heart. But I am embarrassed by exposing myself to you. Neither of us is ready to take on an adult life. Oh, I looked up the route to South Haven. Two hours there and two hours back home. I brought some money, too." Henry explained.

"South Haven is twelve miles. Do you have directions to the farm?" Henry asked.

"Henry, I left the map; Dad drew it for me on my desk in my room. Shoot, I'm sorry, honey," she mumbled the last few words.

"Henry looked at her with a smile. But, Barby, don't worry, this is a small town. There is only one river, right?"

"I'm mad at myself. But, Henry, we could call the house and ask someone to enter my room."

"Look honey, is the farm on the north side of the river or south side, Barby?"

"Henry, I don't know, honey. Grandpa lived there for fifty years. Someone will know where the farm is at, silly boy."

"Barby, you decided not to call me a silly boy."

"Henry, I changed my mind. You will always be my silly boy until we make love."

"Barby, you cannot tease me like this, honey."

"Henry, keep it in your pants, silly boy."

"Barby, you are impossible. What am I going to do with you?"

"Turn right here, Henry. There is a bridge down the hill. I just saw it, but the trees are blocking our view, honey."

"Look, Barby; it is a covered bridge. Covered bridges are so rare."

"Turn left on this road, Henry. There isn't a road sign, but this must be River Road. I remember the name of the road, honey."

"I didn't see downtown, Barby. Do you think we are close to the lake?"

"I don't know, Henry. The forest is to think to see anything. This road isn't much more than a cow path."

"Wow, Barby, this road is weaving back and forth and getting smaller."

"Look, Henry, a farm. Is that a ditch running up to that old barn? The road stops, honey. Many driveways exist between the farmhouse, the barn, and the corn bin. There's an old silo and three sheds. Go to the mailbox; it looks like a name is on it."

"let's go wipe it off. It coated with dirt, Barby."

"Kraneger, this is it, Henry. But, Gee whiz, look how long that barn is, honey. Look, Henry, does the ditch go into the barn?"

"I don't know, Barby. There are two barn doors on rollers. Let's open them and get a glimpse. There might be a sailboat in there, honey."

"The river isn't very far from the barn, Henry. Look, there are ropes on both sides of the ditch. They pull the doors open. How do you get on the other side?"

"Let's pull this side open, Barby, then I can walk around and open the other side.

They pulled the door, and it slid open with minimal effort.

"Henry, this takes my breath away. The woodwork is magnificent, honey. Open the other door and let the sunlight brighten the boat."

The boat was sitting in a wooden cradle. The cradle was on two twelve-inch beams. Two eight-inch straps could lift the boat with a large wheel that could manually raise it and lower it to the water.

"How does this work, Henry? There was a lot of engineering designed into the lift."

"I know, Barby; how long has this been stored in this barn?"

"There is a wooden ladder over there, Henry. Can we use it to get up on the boat?"

"Let me look at it, Barby. Yeah, this looks like it's in great condition."

Henry dragged it over, and they both lifted the ladder into a safe position.

"Wow, this is sturdy, Barby. Let me go up and check everything. Then, if it's safe, I'll have you come up too."

Barby climbed up behind him. "This boat is covered in dust, Henry. How can we clean this without being covered by dust?"

"Let me open the barn doors on the other end. Why don't you come down, for now? Maybe we can find an air compressor? Come on, little lady, why don't you go first," he climbed onto the ladder and saw her breast bounce loosely in her bra. She looked up and caught him staring. I hope you are enjoying yourself. What the hell, Henry? What has gotten into you?"

"I don't know, Barby. I swear I didn't plan anything. I can't help myself. But, wow, we should get used to seeing each other, you know, naked, maybe?"

"No, sir, you will not get used to seeing me naked. Henry, do you want me?"

"Not right now, Barby, but you want me to. I think you do."

"Of course, I want you, but we are not old enough, silly boy."

"I'm not trying to force myself on you, Barby. I look at you more than I used to."

"You can look all you want. Just don't let me catch you. Do you understand, Henry?"

"Barby, I didn't mean to look at your boobs. So, let's drop all this nonsense, please?"

"Stop looking at my tits. That can't be that hard, Henry."

"Henry, is this an air compressor?"

"It's an old one, but it is an air compressor. So let me open those doors, Barby."

Henry opened both doors. "Wow, feel that breeze, Barby. Stay at this end, and maybe you won't get dirty."

"Henry tested the compressor. Then he dragged the airline and began blowing the dust off the boat. He was amazed by the beauty of the sailboat. The dust cloud settled quickly.

"Henry, the hull is a beautiful blue. Can I come up now," Barby yelled.

"Come on up, little lady. I'll hold the ladder."

"Step back, mister, and don't stare at my boobs, Henry."

She climbed the ladder in a hurry and stepped onto the sailboat. "Henry, this sailboat looks like it's new. Let's go down below."

Henry slid the hatch and let Barby go down first.

"Henry, it's beautiful down here, and there isn't any dust. Come on down, honey."

They spent an hour opening all the doors and storage spaces. Finally, they found the owner's manuals and took them to read on the way home.

"Hello up there; anybody in the boat?"

"Who is that, Barby? Does anyone know we will be here today?"

"Maybe the farmer knows, Henry."

Barby climbed up onto the deck. "'Hi, you must be the farmer and caretaker for our property. I'm Barby Kraneger. My boyfriend is here with me."

"I'm Richard Johnson. Your dad called my daughter yesterday and said you'd be here today. Have you ever sailed a boat like this before?"

Henry climbed up the deck with Barby. "Hello there, Richard. I'm Henry. We thought maybe we'd see you, folks, today. How far is it to Lake Michigan?"

"From the water, maybe four miles. Are you folks thinking about sailing to the lake by the river? My girl motored a sailboat to the lake three or four years ago. There has to be good rain because there are no navigation markers on the river."

A girl pulled up on a small motorbike. "Hello, you guys. I'm Ellen, who are they, Daddy."

"I'm Barby Kraneger, and this is my boyfriend, Henry."

"You all still in school, Barby?"

"Yeah, we're both in high school in Barneyville," Barby answered.

"I'm a senior in South Haven. I've sailed this old boat a few times over the years. This lift is an engineering marvel. We'd need good rain to navigate the river. However, the depth gets much better half an hour down the river. Just let me know. I'd love to oblige you as best I can."

"I need her when we pick corn. The lake isn't very nice in late October, anyhow."

"We didn't know this boat was in the family. Henry and I would appreciate some help. Three or more would work well, better yet for an overnight."

"We were getting ready to close up things, drive downtown, and see the piers. But then, we want to buy lunch. Do you know where we can find a good restaurant?" Henry asked.

"Dad has to take a load of corn to the mill. Do you need me, Daddy?"

"No, you go with these fine people. Appreciate your hospitality."

"Is the lake still warm enough to swim?" Henry asked.

"The water is great, but the nights have cooled off. Body surfing sounds like fun," Ellen added.

They had lunch and body-surfed in the lake for two hours. Ellen was taller than Barby and was very pretty. Then, they all went to Ellen's for dinner. Mr. Johnson was still gone because he was taking his truck to Illinois for repairs.

Barby took a shower after dinner and took a nap on the couch.

Ellen washed Barby and Henry's clothes while he took a shower. Barby and Henry sat around in a towel until his clothes were dry.

Henry woke Barby, thanked Ellen, and drove off in a hurry.

CHAPTER 13

Henry's Innocence

*M*any families were on the ice at the Millpond the night before Christmas Eve. Henry was skating with Barby. They were both thinking about their ice-dancing program. The township set up lighting from a utility pole on the small island. The lights lit up the skating rink from just before Christmas until after the New Year until eleven.

Henry and Barby started skating together around the rink for their warmup. They were flying almost full speed as they approached the log cabin, completing one circle. Barby was on Henry's right side. She turned on her left skate just as Henry dug his left toe into the ice, spewing chips high into the air. Henry held onto Barby's hands as she flung herself into the air ahead of him, and Henry slipped under her, grabbing her waist, and pushing upward until she was above him with his arms fully extended.

Barby was supposed to let go of his arms and spread hers out, pretending to fly like a bird, but she clung to him unsteadily. Henry touched his left toe again, and they began to spin gently. The two silhouettes turned faster and faster, and then he lowered her ahead of him, and she touched the ice, going backward. Many people had come out on the ice to watch because the two skaters were the talk of the town. The onlookers gave them a resounding round of applause.

Henry held Barby close as she continued skating backward, picking up speed. "We did it, Henry!"

Henry smiled, but he was breathing hard. "You're beautiful tonight, Barby."

Her smile was enthusiastically gleaming. "Let's go around twice, Henry, but you look tired. Are you tired?" He smiled and pulled her tighter. "Henry, everyone is looking!" She did not fight him, though, and sunk deeply into his embrace.

He looked down into her eyes. "I want to kiss you right here before our parents and everyone!"

Barby pursed her lips and dipped her eyes in a sensual expression. "Silly boy, be patient."

The second turn was coming up next. "Remember to hang on tightly, Barby!" She nodded daintily in the affirmative. Barby swung out to his left, and now they were going together. They pushed until the speed increased beyond the ability to stay within the parameters of the cleared ice. Henry and Barby planted their left toes into the ice and sprayed the crowd. They both began spinning; he spun behind, and she ahead. They raised their trailing right legs into a double Camel. The thrust of the flying twist propelled them to turn faster and faster.

Individually, they spun into the top position with their hands pointing towards the bright full moon in the icy air above them. He bowed, and she curtsied, and they skated off together. Another round of energetic applause filled the night air as they joined the crowd arm in arm.

Her smile was angelic. Henry stopped breathing to view her glowing face. "Pretty Girl." Her feminine charm won him over totally.

She was fascinated with him but interpreted her feelings as true love. She adored him as she studied the outline of his face; she imagined a lifetime of revering this most honorable young man.

"Barby, you look like an angel tonight."

She took her eyes off him for an instant. Then she returned to meet his gaze. "Silly boy."

Henry's mother took the ice next. First, she performed figure eight in the camel position, an exceedingly tricky program. Then, she performed a few single jumps, which surprised Henry because his mother had not tried any leaps in many years.

Brandy took the ice and put on a demonstration of true athletic prowess. She performed several doubles and one triple-axle.

Then Henry and Brandy tried to make a helicopter twirl together, but he fell, and she landed on him unhurt except for her dignity.

Then came the ice dancing, and this was Barby and Henry's time to shine.

They danced across the ice to "Love Me Tender," Barby had to push continually and slap Henry as he was all over her.

"It's part of the routine." He argued. They skated fully embraced, her left hand resting on his neck, his right hand wrapped around her back, holding her close. Henry's left hand and Barby's right hand joined in the typical fashion. After the first stanza, everyone joined in the fun.

"Henry, don't you think we are just a little close!"

He smiled, ignoring her prudishness, and pulled her tighter into his chest. She enjoyed the way he held her and snuggled into his strong embrace. But she was worried about how it looked.

Next, they danced to Cherish by the Association. Brandy cut in, and Barby was furious.

"Hi, good, looking Hank." Henry looked for Barby, but she was skating off to the Bungalow.

"Hello, stretch."

Brandy gave him a severe, petulant stare. "You were dancing too close with Barby; you two must cool it. Why not skate with me, Hank?" She put her head on his shoulder.

They danced well together. Brandy skated backward, clinging to him, swaying gently back and forth to the rhythm of the music. Brandy began sucking on his neck, and she smelled wonderful. Henry suffered a mesmerizing spell. He pulled her tighter, and she cuddled into his grasp, encouraging his romantic intentions.

He broke their silence. "Brandy, what are you doing? You're driving me nuts."

Brandy stopped and looked into his eyes. She kissed him on the lips lightly. "Bye." She skated away.

Henry drifted alone across the ice. Then he remembered his date and left to find Barby. He found her in the Bungalow, sitting in their spot by herself. She had her knees up and buried her face between them. Henry stumbled past other skaters warming themselves. He sat next to Barby. He put his right arm around her and whispered. "It's me." He slid closer to her, but she remained in her repressed position. Henry gently pulled her over, and she swayed without hesitation or restraint into his arms. The Bungalow was full of people of all ages. Several adults frowned disapprovingly, but Henry ignored them all. Barby buried her head into his shoulder. She snuggled into his arms, and the nervous, empty feeling in her tummy simmered down.

Henry felt the stares acutely. However, he did not discourage Barby's embrace. When Barby began crying profusely, Henry was glad the place was noisy because no one noticed her involuntary convulsions and sobbing. Her mother, aunts, and teachers told Barby she was too young to know what love was, but she knew in her heart that she loved Henry. Barby would always love Henry. Then she saw the hickey.

She looked into his eyes with her wet face, red eyes, and full-blown pout. "Why Henry?" Then she started crying again and flung herself away from him.

Henry overlooked Mrs. Kraneger. She had stepped inside earlier and watched their every move.

Mrs. Kraneger kept watching her daughter. She looked like a lovesick cow. Whatever possessed her to leave these two youngsters unsupervised? Everything she saw she interpreted as promiscuous mischief. Their shameful, ardent exhibition during their dance routine was not artful or athletic; it was indecent.

She came over and demanded, "Barbara, get up and go home this instant." Mrs. Kraneger was so furious with Henry. She supposed he did something to provoke tears and hoped it was not immoral.

Brandy walked in, stumbled through the crowd, and kneeled close to Henry. "Why is Barby crying, Hank?"

Mrs. Kraneger stared at him and badgered him. "Speak up, young man; what was happening here." Then she saw the hickey.

Henry's mom walked in just then and approached the crowded corner. "Henry, what's going on?"

Henry looked at Brandy, then his mother, and avoided Mrs. Kraneger. Barby tucked her face into his arms. She was still crying. Henry did nothing wrong, but Barby's mom made him look like a deviant pervert.

Mrs. Kraneger began shaking her fist at him. "What did you do to my daughter?"

Henry could not take any more of her accusations. He leaped up and pushed his way out towards the doorway of the Bungalow. The woman shouted at him to stop and explain himself. Several of the men grabbed at him, but he shoved past them. His eyes were watery, and he could not see well. The door opened, and Henry lunged for it. He was desperate to free himself from the den of harping women.

He forgot to duck his head. As a result, he broke his nose when his face slammed into the icy beam, and blood began oozing from the fracture.

Henry was alone when he woke in the emergency room, and everything was white. His face burned like fire, and he could not breathe very well. He suffered confusion along with acute nasal pain. An emerging awareness brought a headache that made him feel nauseous.

Henry reached up to feel his nose, finding it numb and sore along the edges. He could sense something in his nose but was reluctant to handle it because it was too painful to touch.

Mrs. Rotyn visited the lady's room. She returned to the cubicle where her son lay battered and unconscious. When she saw he was awake, she called for the nurse. The Doctor came in with her.

Henry noticed his mother and realized she had been crying.

The Doctor began asking questions he could not understand. Henry wanted to avoid being bothered by all the questions. He wanted his mother to come closer, but these annoying people were in the way.

It was then that Henry realized he could not hear them. So, he studied the Doctor's face but could not listen to what he was saying.

Jessica Rotyn saw the terror in her son's eyes; she went to his side. The Doctor was talking to his mother, and she was crying again. Henry was flailing his arms, trying to touch her, but he could not.

She took a pen and a piece of paper, wrote a note, and showed it to Henry. It read, "It's only temporary." She bent over, kissed his forehead, and laid her head on his chest, hugging him. Henry was overcome with emotion and started to cry. He did not want to, but he could not control it. Everyone left the room but his mother. She embraced her son and sobbed with him.

Henry slept through the night. As a result, he suffered a severe concussion and a broken nose. The Doctor had to pack his nose with string to stop the bleeding.

By Christmas Eve, Henry's hearing had returned partially. However, he still had a headache, and his entire face throbbed. In addition, both of his eyes were black and blue.

Mr. and Mrs. Kraneger visited Henry at the hospital.

Mr. Kraneger informed him, "We are so sorry you got hurt. I hit that low door frame myself. Your hearing will improve, Henry. Barby wants to see you but is still too young by hospital rules. We toon all spend the holidays together."

"My father taught me to be a virtuous person, Mrs. Kraneger. Barby knows that very well."

"Henry, I know that you are a fine young man. I felt terrible about how I bugged you. But, Henry, you reacted the only way any child would when pushed beyond their breaking point; you ran away. Barby told us that Brandy gave you the hickey. Silly thing to do, but Brandy apologized to Barby. Goodness me, I used to pepper young men with hickeys, including this man next to me." Mrs. Kraneger said.

The two mothers hugged and reassured each other of their mutual respect; Mr. Kraneger told Henry's mother to cover the hospital bill. Henry thanked him because he knew his mother was about to say no. He also knew his mother could not afford it.

Henry was discharged after lunch and was able to go home.

Barby visited Henry on Christmas Eve after dark. He was so happy to see her; it lifted his spirits.

"Henry, you look like a cute, oversized raccoon."

Barby and Henry were alone in his room. She kissed him on the cheek.

"Ouch, he said playfully."

She slapped him tenderly, "Silly boy. Does it hurt terribly?"

Henry's eyes became large. His nose felt like it was the size of a watermelon. Finally, he formed Donald Duck's lips and nodded in the affirmative.

"Do you want me to kiss it and make it better?" Again, he repeated the same facial features. She kissed his forehead and cheeks and then quickly touched her lips to his.

"Henry, I'm so sorry." Barby loved him so much, and all the suffering he endured now was because of that love. She struggled with her feelings for Henry. Too bad she thought poor Henry had to suffer to quell her turbulent feminine impulses.

Henry dozed off while she sat beside him. She was gone when he woke up later that evening, and he wondered when she had left.

He fell asleep when his head hit his pillow and slept comfortably.

When he woke up Christmas morning, Brandy was sleeping beside him. Brandy wore blue jeans and a Michigan sweatshirt. Her feet were bare, and Henry did not see any shoes. Her long, black, shiny hair fell softly across her breast, and Henry was infatuated with her beauty. Henry's bed was a full-sized standard mattress, and Brandy lay precariously on its edge.

Henry's face felt tight and swollen. He could see better today, and his hearing had improved. He could not hear Brandy breathe but could see her chest rise and fall. Barby was cute and pretty, but Brandy exuded a beauty about her that Barby could not match.

"Did you fart?" Henry bolted as her surprise statement caught him off guard.

"Sure, I have been rotten to the core. I might have to give you mouth-to-mouth a couple of times because you struggled to remain conscious."

She opened her sullen green eyes and smiled at him. "Sweet, Merry Christmas, Hank. You look bad."

He lay back and thought he could smell her perfume.

She reached over, grabbed his hand, and squeezed it gently. "My family was worried about you, but I wasn't. I know how strong you are inside and out. Feel bad?"

"Yeah, I feel pretty tough." He looked at her, giving him the once over.

"Can I get you a pill or something?" She gave him her patented catlike look.

He pointed to his bedside table. "Merry Christmas, Brandy."

She stared at him but did not say a word. Instead, she picked up the bottle. "Darvon, not bad, Hank!" She went to get some water for him.

Henry heard his mother's voice as she talked with Brandy.

"How is the patient, dear?"

He could not hear Brandy's reply, although he could tell she did say something.

Mrs. Rotyn came into his room. Her hair was uncombed, and she wore blue jeans and a Michigan sweatshirt. His mother had a natural beauty like Brandy, and it made him feel good that she was not an old hag like so many of his friend's mothers.

"Time to rise and shine, good morning, Henry. Merry Christmas, can you hear me, honey?"

Henry nodded quickly and tried to smile, but the pain prevented him from communicating his joy.

"We have to be at the Doctor's at eleven a.m. He will be on duty in the emergency room but told me to bring you in so he can check your dressing. Do you want me to bathe you?"

Henry looked at her with a desperate repulsion. "Mom, I don't need you to give me a bath."

Brandy came in with the water. "I can help Mrs. Kraneger."

Henry pulled his pillow over his head and forgot about his nose.

"That's alright, Brandy. I think Henry will be able to take care of himself. He doesn't remember how we both used to see him bare ass naked." The two women laughed, and Henry continued ignoring them, hiding carefully behind his pillow.

"If you need help, Jessica, just call me; I could bathe Henry." So, the woman left him alone and went into the living room.

"Thank you for coming over, Brandy. The Doctor was concerned about the dressing. Did you see all the string up his nose?"

Brandy felt a special closeness with Jessica Rotyn. She had always been there for her, especially at school. Brandy came to enjoy being in the presence of a real lady. Having Jessica in her life was like having a second mother, and Jessica was more liberal, not the conservative Brandy's mother often portrayed.

"How much string does he have in his nose?" Brandy asked.

Barby knocked at the door and came in instead of waiting for someone to answer it.

"Hello beautiful Barby, Merry Christmas; how are you feeling, dear?" Jessica smiled warmly.

"Merry Christmas, Mrs. Rotyn. I'm exhausted; how is Henry?" she asked desperately.

Jessica waved at Barby. "You can go in, honey."

Barby removed her shoes, smiled at her sister, and entered Henry's room.

"Jessica, what would you tell me about the string?"

Mrs. Rotyn wondered just then if Henry was still decent. Then she dismissed her worries; she did not hear any commotion from his room.

"The Doctor told me he packed over fifty feet up to his nose."

Brandy saw Barby's shoes and realized she had not worn any but wished she had taken the time to put something on her feet.

"Why did they use string?" Brandy asked.

"It is a common procedure to stop the bleeding. Weird, huh?"

When Barby came into Henry's room, he smiled, but it made his face burn like fire. Then, finally, she came over and kissed his cheek.

"Silly boy, what am I going to do with you? You about lost your head over me."

He reached out and held her hand. She leaned over and kissed him. He could not feel or smell her and wondered why he had missed such a fantastic opportunity.

She helped him into the bathroom and removed his pajamas and tee shirt while his bathtub was filling. She put in some bubble bath beads, then smiled at him. "I can remove your boxers if you want, Henry; I don't mind?"

He shooed her out of the bathroom, but Barby would not leave until she embraced him tenderly. Then she went into his bedroom and removed his sheets and pillowcase.

The front door sprang open, and this time, it was Bobby.

"Hey, common Pudge, you don't just walk in without knocking on the door. Where are your manners?" Brandy put her hands on her hips and sternly demanded a reply.

Bobby slept longer than he should have, again.

Sorry, Mrs. Rotyn."

Jessica was used to the intrusions, especially from Bobby.

Bobby tried to ignore his older sister, but she embarrassed him, and he desperately tried to invent some form of retribution.

"Mom is waiting for you to stretch." His statement was blunt and very intense.

Whatever for, Brandy wondered, but she drew a blank. "I guess I need to find out what my mother wants. I am always glad to help Jessica. You have been so nice to me. It's the least I could do."

Brandy gave Jessica a big hug, and then she left quietly.

Bobby smiled and grinned; he watched his sister leave. He looked at Mrs. Rotyn and smiled slyly. "Mom's not home. She left early to visit her sister in Battle Creek."

Jessica knew he was a rascal, but now she saw he was also devious and despicable.

"Bobby!"

How's Henry, Mrs. Rotyn?" He was still smiling until he saw her sour look. He did not think she would make a big deal out of it. He shrugged his shoulders and said, "What?"

"Why did you do that to Brandy?"

Bobby sucked in his bottom lip and shrugged his shoulders again. "She needs to return some phone calls anyway, Mrs. Rotyn."

She stared at him to see how long he would maintain his composure but gave up after a few moments. "Barby is with Henry, but I think you can go in. Knock first, young man!"

Mrs. Rotyn left the room, leaving him alone in the living room.

Barby was in her bedroom later that night when her mother came in and wanted to talk.

Mrs. Kraneger did not approve of her sixteen-year-old daughter spending so much time with only one boy. Henry was Bobby's friend anyhow, and it seemed to her that Barby was spending more time with Henry than Bobby. "Hello, dear. How is Henry?"

Barby knew her mother did not care about Henry. Whatever her mom wanted to talk to her about would not include a sincere concern for him. She thought her mother was incredibly old-fashioned, but her parents were always kind to Henry; Barby thought she owed them that much. "He is much better, Mother, thank you." Her voice was a matter of fact, and Barby knew her attitude was disrespectful. She needed to try harder to seem grateful, but it was hard. She did love her mother and felt terrible about the tone of voice she used. "It was nice of you and Dad to visit him in the hospital. Henry also told me how Dad paid all the medical bills, thanks, Mom. I will thank Dad, too, in the morning. Did you want to talk?" She tried to smile and hoped she was convincing.

Barby washed her hair earlier, and her mother brushed it slowly.

"Barby, you're only sixteen; how involved are you with Henry?"

Barby knew she was about to suffer some prudish, unreasonable mothering. "We're classmates, and we're going steady. Henry and I dance and skate together, end of the story."

She stared at her mother with a perturbed expression.

Mrs. Kraneger was always closest to Barby; she felt a bond between herself and her youngest daughter that did not exist with her other children. However, her little girl was growing up, and it frightened her to think they would soon no longer share their mother/daughter moments. "Barby, Henry is a very nice boy, but you know how I feel about you spending too much time together." She saw the resentment forming in her daughter's eyes.

"Mom!"

Mrs. Kraneger made up her mind about this, and she would not back down. "Henry is a wonderful boy, and I care for him deeply."

Barby hated her mother at times like this; she loved her but hated her. "You're never satisfied. Henry has always been a gentleman. He is not a bad person or immoral, but you do not like him because of his family. They do not have enough money to suit you, do they, Mom? I may never meet another man like him in a hundred years. So why isn't Henry good enough for you, Mother?"

Mrs. Kraneger was getting a headache. "I want you to date other boys for a while, dear, and Henry is not a man yet. You will see my point if you date other boys for six months. If you feel the same about Henry after six months as you do now, I will quit bugging you. I promise to keep my word. It's difficult for me to come to you with this, dear."

Barby was almost in tears. Why does it have to hurt to be young and in love? She wanted to describe to her mother how Henry made her feel. She always smiled when she was with him, how the air around him tingled with life. She would understand if she could feel how Barby understood his loyalty, virtue, and kindness. But, instead, Barby began to cry, and her sorrow overwhelmed her fragile composure. "Don't tell me how hard it is for you. Why do you treat me this way? I do not want to hear it. Stop explaining; I do not need your reasons. Don't tell me because it hurts."

Her mother let her cry. She recalled how difficult her puberty had been.

Barby looked up at her mother; her pleading eyes spoke volumes. "Mom, why does it have to hurt so much?"

Mrs. Kraneger took her daughter into her arms. She held her as Barby's raging hormones ravaged her fragile spirit.

Mrs. Kraneger changed the subject, and Barby felt a comforting glow begin to warm between them again. They spoke for over an hour about Barby's schoolwork and her choices of classes. Barby talked about college and what sort of education she wanted. Then her mother rubbed her back and tucked her into bed.

CHAPTER 14

Breaking Up Is Hard to Do

*H*enry and Barby were walking to school on a bright, sunny morning. They both turned seventeen in August.

"Look at the sky, Henry." Barby looked into Henry's eyes.

"You seem to be in a cheerful mood, Barby."

"I'm trying hard, Henry."

"Oh, oh. What happened to the bright sunny day, Barby?"

"Henry, I can look into your eyes on a bright sunny day, and your cerulean blues melt my anxieties."

"I hope our morning sky can melt any nasty anxieties. But, honey, your bright eyes have dimmed, Barby."

"Henry, we need to ease off our relationship. There I said it; oh my god, this hurts so much, Henry," she burst into tears.

"Your mom is back at her trash talk. Barby, how much ease do we need to promote in our relationship?"

"Mom is a member of the Michigan Society of Women's Rights. Unfortunately, the entry fee is so expensive; well-to-do women join."

"I knew your dad had a membership in the country club. Bobby revealed that to me. Rich people promote those things to ensure they won't mix in with us poor people.

"I've never heard you express those feelings, Henry."

"I don't look down on poor people. But I don't see myself living like that too. So, I don't feel any trepidation either way, Barby."

"Mom wants our family to have dinner with a family in Jackson. So, she is always promoting association with wealthy people, Henry."

"Mom told me Brandy is dating a man in medical school. Her emphasis was ridiculous; Brandy wrote to me and said she was dating several boys. I have never heard Brandy express anything like my mother."

"You seem to be explaining your way out of our relationship, Barby."

"No, Henry! We're close to school, and your lack of understanding will make me cry."

"Ellen Johnson has been writing to me. I haven't replied; maybe I should, Barby."

"Do you like her, Henry?"

"I'm not going to waste my time, Barby."

"What do you mean, Henry."

"Why should I waste my time with you anymore? Have you made up your mind, Barby?"

"Henry, why are you so mean?"

"Go on, Barby, and mix in with the well-to-do. I'll stick with the farmers' daughters."

"Henry, I'm not trying to hurt you."

"Go ahead and twist the knife, Barby. The injury is already fatal."

Barby burst into tears and ran into the girl's bathroom.

CHAPTER 15

Saturday Night Dances

*S*chool ended, and Henry was topping onions by the third week in June. No one wanted to be around him except Bobby. They played tennis together in the evenings.

Henry's Mother was taking a summer course; she needed a State Certificate for her job at the school.

It rained a lot in July; there were seven or eight good days of thunder jumping. Some of the girls in town tried thunder jumping. It went well until a girl from Litchfield lost her bikini top. Henry was there, and everyone was goggle-eyed glances. Finally, one of the guys gave her his tee shirt. It was wet, and everyone said you could still see her tits.

Every time girls came to join in the fun, the boys tried to get them to wear their wet tee shirts. The boys argued that it was the initiation requirement. Some of the girls fell for it, but most did not.

The boys talked the girls into a wet tee shirt contest one hot afternoon. Barby left early, but it did not matter because she would not have gone along with anything of the sort. Brandy, however, was still present. Henry informed Brandy, he wanted her to enter the contest and that she would get his vote. She did not like the idea at first but finally agreed. Henry gave her his shirt, and Brandy took off her bikini top after putting his shirt on. Brandy was a big hit; she got all the votes, all of them.

Later that evening, Henry walked home with Bobby and Brandy. They had spent the entire afternoon thunder jumping and were exhausted. Brandy was taking everyone to the drive-in theatre after dark. The Kraneger's were a remarkably close family, and Henry saw their loyalty, care, and concern for each other. Henry did not know anyone else with this family's money without it going to their heads. Brandy was a bit pretentious but never to Henry. Barby and Bobby were very down to earth; Henry liked that quality, which he emulated himself.

Henry and his mom listened during their evening meals as Walter Cronkite chronicled the changing world conditions. The Vietnam War protests and demonstrations were dismantling the illusive superior image of the American way.

On Saturday afternoons during the summer, the Flying Saucer restaurant was for teenagers until dark. Parents took turns chaperoning the dances. The dances were always very upbeat; DJs from the surrounding cities brought the big city appeal. Teens gathered at famous spots as far away as Indiana and Ohio. They consumed cherry cokes, root beer floats, and popcorn as they mimicked a lifestyle soon to be their own.

Henry went to the dance with his mother on a Saturday night in July. She was there because she was a chaperone.

Henry saw Barby when she came in with her sister. He smiled and waved, and they both waved back to him. Henry and Barby were still close friends. They still talked and joked in school, but he did not think her feelings for him were the same. She had lots of friends. Some days, she spent so much time with her friends that they hardly spent any time together. Since summer vacation started, Henry has been unable to spend one hour with her. He began to wonder if she had any feelings for him at all. He did not want to push himself on her, though, so he did not pursue her when she arrived.

Henry was talking to Tom when someone tapped his shoulder. It was Barby.

"Hell, Henry," Barby smiled.

"Tommy or Terry, whomever, Terry or Tommy. How have you been?" Barby gave him a halfhearted smile.

Tom greeted her and then excused himself. Henry was left alone with Barby.

"Hello, pretty girl. Would you like to dance?"

She smiled and winked at him. "Henry, I'd love to." She took his arm, followed him onto the dance floor, and hurried into his embrace.

"You look genuinely nice to such a short girl. Are you ever going to get any taller?" He was ornery and sensed his words came out worse than he intended.

She did not get upset at his taunt. Instead, she tried to smile and ignore his triteness. "I'm delighted, Henry. Do you know why?"

He frowned; his initial reaction was to repeat something harsh or insensitive, but he decided not to say anything. They danced without saying a word for some time. He pulled Barby closer and wanted to say something but did not trust his emotions. Finally, after taking a deep breath, he broke the silence.

"I'm still crazy about you." But unfortunately, his words were much louder than he meant, and several people gave him strange looks.

She tipped her head to the side and gave him a sad stare. "Is it too late to say I'm sorry?" Her voice was lucid but compelling. "I've thought of you every night and day. I was on the verge of breaking down and running over to see you every night this last week, but I believe in our love, Henry. I believe in you."

He pulled her close—too close, but she did not resist. They spun together across the floor, dancing to the music. His moves were sharp and quick, but she did not miss a step.

He stopped abruptly and pulled her into a captivating embrace. "Barby, I didn't give up on us." His tone was sharp and critical again. Finally, he lowered his voice and suppressed his anger. "Sometimes love does not feel like it should, sometimes it hurts, but true love is indefatigable."

She grinned from ear to ear.

"You liked that one, huh?" He grinned, displaying his dimples.

She loved his knack for unusual words, primarily if they expressed his love for her.

They separated a bit as another song began. They danced to "California Dreaming'" by the Mamas and the Papas.

She looked up into his eyes and saw the strength of his love for her. "You're my favorite mistake, Henry."

He looked at her again, wondering about the ditz syndrome. "What do you mean?" he asked.

She smiled, held her head high, and rocked to the music, looking into his eyes. "I know you're in love with me. If a girl is going to do something foolish to her boyfriend, she is smart to do it to the one who loves her. True love will survive even the worst mistakes."

He knew she was talking about not standing up to her mother. "Barby, I have never hidden my love for you. My heart is yours. It's as fragile as spring snow."

His face looked as if he were about to cry. "Henry, silly boy. How do you think I have felt about dating other guys? I went out with a creep from Litchfield. I never told you about it. He is a junior. I was not in his car for three minutes when he tried to get in my pants. My Mother thought he was a great guy because his parents had money. I walked home four miles that night. I did not have to, but it gave me time to think. Did you ever walk by me in school and not see me looking your way? That is why you are my favorite mistake, and I believe that with all my heart."

They left the dance floor and went over to sit with their mother. "Hello, Jessica. You look beautiful tonight. I see where your son gets his looks."

Henry kissed his mother; he still thought a real man should not be embarrassed to kiss his mother in public.

Barby whispered, "Henry, you have your mother's eyes." Henry looked at his mom and winked.

"Barby, you two were dancing too close. Has something changed? Is there something you want to tell me?" Jessica knew about the pain Henry experienced. She liked Barby but was unhappy about her lack of devotion to her son.

Boldly, Barby held her arms out to Henry, and he embraced her lightly. She pressed up against him. He adjusted his grasp to accept her revealing hug. No elbows or hands were pushing at his chest. The embrace was unlike any other she had allowed. She made eye contact with Henry's Mother and smiled.

Later in the evening, Barby caught Jessica alone. "Jessica, I love Henry. I have loved him for as long as I can remember. My Mother does not think I am old enough to know the difference between infatuation and love. So, I want to tell you today that I love Henry. I hope you understand."

Jessica wondered what to say. She was quiet for a moment, then spoke. "Dear, people often hurt those they love. Be careful not to make that mistake."

Barby hugged her and kissed her cheek. "I'm guilty; I admit it. But I will try my best."

It could have been the summer air, the young hearts, the sixties music, and the need to love when all around them, so many people were defining ways to hate. But maybe it was love or a sincere desire to feel loved.

Two young hearts survived the short test, reaffirming their mutual affection. Then, in the summer of 1966, their young love matured.

Barby and Henry both dated different people during the six-month test. Then, finally, they fell into a comfortable relationship again. Both were confidently aware of the other's loyalty. The teens felt an overwhelming need to be with each other constantly. Until they went away to college, Henry and Barby seldom missed a Saturday night dance.

CHAPTER 16

Brandy's Surprise

*H*enry and his extended family went on vacation in late July. This year, they traveled up north to Traverse City and stayed in a motel on Grand Traverse Bay. They ate fine dinners and danced at the most exclusive restaurants every night. In addition, Mr. Kraneger took Henry golfing with Bobby.

The women shopped in the many tiny shops along the bay. Then, on several occasions, they swam and sailed in the harbor during the daylight hours.

Late one evening, while Barby was taking a shower. Henry went for a walk with Brandy. They went by the water, crossing under an overhanging footbridge that crossed a road near the bay. Brandy asked Henry, "How big is it, Hank?"

"How big is what?" he replied.

She walked up to him and pulled him into her bosom. He put his arms around her instinctively. She put her palms on his cheeks, drew his lips down to hers, and kissed him.

Her sudden affection caught Henry off guard, but he returned her kiss.

She slipped her hand into his pants and stroked him tenderly. She pushed her tongue into his mouth and twittered with his tongue. His legs became weak, and he was suddenly dizzy.

"Hank, what the hell." She pulled her hand up and wiped it on his shorts. Then, she smiled and walked away in a hurry.

Later that night, Henry was in bed wondering why Brandy grabbed his privates. Her actions did not match her personality. He felt satisfied at first, but he also felt violated. He often heard that expression applied to females who men mistreated. He struggled with the idea that Brandy committed a crime, but she did humiliate him. He liked her curious nature. At least, that is what he told himself. Something was going to happen. Her discovery might lead to an experience that made him feel giddy and wonderous. He wanted to be alone with her. He could not do that because Barby was in his heart. However, Brandy opened a secret door. Henry needed to keep a cool head and go with the flow. He fell asleep.

When Henry saw Brandy the next day, she acted as if nothing had happened; Henry was confused. Her only comment was, "Hi, Hank."

Henry tried to talk to Brandy, but she glanced at him with her patented Cheshire smile. Why would she do that to him? He desperately needed to speak with her, but they were never alone.

Henry loved this family. He loved Barby, but he struggled with his commitment to her. Was his love for her imaginary? He was not sure how he felt about Brandy. His abnormality attacked his elusive innocence. His virtue was weak.

The trip back to Barneyville was filled with joy and laughter as the family shared their exciting experiences. Henry tried hard to laugh and be part of the merriment.

Brandy sat next to her sister in the back seat of the station wagon. Henry and Bobby sat in the middle chair.

Mr. Kraneger was becoming a real family man and much happier. The large station wagon comfortably sat the six travelers, and they carried their baggage on the roof in a container made just for that purpose.

Barby, Bobby, and Henry were almost seventeen. Henry's birthday was January 16, and Bobby and Barby's were February 16.

Barby, Bobby, and Henry planned what classes they would take in the fall; the three wanted to attend college. Henry would need a scholarship. Barby and Bobby already had bank accounts with more than ample funds to pay for their education. Henry's dad had been correct; the Kraneger's did have money.

CHAPTER 17

Junior's

$\mathscr{B}$randy left for college in Boston, a junior at Dartmouth.

School started, and Bobby, Barby, Gary, and Henry were Juniors. Bobby had grown almost two inches since spring and was taller than Henry. Henry also grew some, and he was six feet tall.

Gary was the starting quarterback for the varsity. Gary was unusually talented. Bobby began to be at center, and Henry was the running back, kicker, and punter. He also played defensive end. He had the coach's eye on offense as much as on Defense. Barneyville High School's only loss was Litchfield on Barneyville's field last year.

Barby, like her sister Brandy, was a cheerleader. Brandy was immensely popular in high school: she was queen at homecoming and gorgeous. Barby followed in her big sister's footsteps.

Henry and Barby went hayride on a Saturday night in late October. Kids around the county attended the annual event at old man Turleksen's farm. The ride started about a half-hour before dusk. The two-hour-long trip wound along the St. Joseph River, passing under massive trees lined the edge of the lane encircling the six-hundred-acre farm.

Henry and Barby conversed quietly, covering themselves with straw. Henry stacked up some bales in the back of the wagon. He and Barby sat between two rows and had some privacy.

"Henry, do you think I am prettier than any other girl in school?" Henry sat against the last row of straw bales, and Barby lay with her head in his lap. He covered her face with the straw, and she kept pushing it away.

"NO!" Barby cried. Henry pushed a giant pile over her face.

"Henry, don't do that; stop it." She grabbed a handful of his hair and pulled his face down to hers.

"I'm going to kiss you; I mean, really kiss you!"

"Barby, you are pulling the hair out of my head!"

She let go of his hair and sat beside him, leaned over, and kissed him.

Henry returned her kiss as tenderly as he could manage. Her lips were warm and wet, and she did not squirm or return from his embrace. Instead, he wrapped his arms around her and pulled her into his chest. He felt her breasts pressing against him, and there was much more to them than he suspected. He noticed the fresh scent of lilacs as his nose touched her hair.

The caravan of farm wagons passed into the hilly section close to the river. People in the lead wagon fifty yards ahead of them yelled and screamed.

"Henry, what's wrong up there?"

He looked but could not see anything wrong except that everyone on the wagon was walking on the ground and looking into the trees.

"Snakes, they see Blue Racers in the trees!"

She looked at him in disbelief. "Right, snakes can climb trees. Nice try, silly boy!"

He grinned at her and decided to leave things as they were. "Barby, whatever you do, do not look into the snake-infested trees."

She pinched his neck.

"Ouch; stop it, you trollop." He kissed her quickly on the lips before she could reply.

"Henry, what did you call me?" She slugged him in the belly as hard as she could.

The solid right uppercut caught him off guard and took away his wind. He had no idea she was that strong.

Suddenly, Barby let out a blood-curdling scream. Several other girls probed the trees and yelled snakes. Henry looked but could not identify anything at first, but then he saw the branches moving above them.

"Barby, look, Blue Racers go into the trees after sleeping birds." Henry saw three snakes; they were each about five feet long.

Barby buried her face in his chest. "Henry, get me out of here." she wailed.

"Barby, they're harmless. Look how beautifully they slither from tree to tree."

He slid his finger down the front of her blouse. Barby sat up quickly, kissed him, and choked him at the same time.

Henry laughed while he kissed her. She stopped trying to choke him and pounded her palms against his shoulders while they kissed.

Henry held her tenderly, and she did not push him away. They fell over in the deep straw, tasting each other for the first time. She allowed him to press against her totally without apprehension.

When they finally parted, she stared into his eyes. "Don't touch my breast!" she said fiercely.

When she remembered the snakes, she smiled, dove back into his chest, buried her head, and grabbed him frantically. "Tell me when we are clear, Henry."

The caravan pulled away from the river as the lane crossed the back of the farm. It was dark now, and they could not identify the people who sat a few feet away. A full moon blinked behind thick dark clouds, and it was too dark to see anything.

Little dark birds followed them across the span. The elusive winged varmints kept dive-bombing the wagons. Henry and Barby watched them hover above them, darting in circles, and then suddenly down they would come within inches of their heads.

The moon showed between the clouds breaking, and a woman screamed in the wagon behind them. There was a loud commotion, and the frightening announcement came: "Bats!"

The dive-bombing birds were bats. Barby dove back into Henry's chest. "Henry, I can't stand bats; get them away!"

Henry lay beside her in the straw; he disliked bats. Some young men stood up, swinging their coats and sweaters, trying to drive the winged menaces away. Barby and Henry stayed on the floor of the wagon.

"Henry, you should be protecting me. Why aren't you driving them away?"

He ignored her and stayed on the floor.

"Come over here, Henry." He slid over next to her, fluffed up the straw, and spread it over them. "Kiss me, Henry."

They kissed each other, hiding under more than two feet of straw. She was cold and snuggled closer to him. The fledgling lips pressed together and created their unique impression of what it must be like to love someone intimately. Finally, she put her index finger on his chin and pushed him away. When they parted, her beautiful brown eyes affixed to his.

"Where's Bobby at Henry?" She looked around for her brother but could not recognize which silhouette in the darkness was her brother.

"Henry said, "I don't think Bobby is coming up for air." Barby kissed Henry again.

"Who is he with Henry?"

"Bobby is with a freshman. Her name is Sherry. That's all I know about her." He stroked her cheek with his fingers. "You are the most beautiful girl in school," he said.

The trip ended, and the four teenagers rode back into town with Mrs. Kraneger. They talked about the snakes and the bats, the darkness, and the smells of farm life.

CHAPTER 18

Mr. Kraneger's Offer

*N*ew Year's Day was one of the coldest days so far that winter. The ice on the Millpond was still too thin, though. December was unusually mild, and there was no ice on the Millpond until late. So, the five foolhardy teenagers broke the thin ice along the bank. It was a dark day with heavy snow falling about an inch an hour. The Rowdy Rogues slipped along the muddy embankment. The water was too cold to rinse the mud, so it froze their skin and clothing. The teens looked like a bunch of hogs wallowing in the mire. It was not a fun time. Breaking clean ice and jumping into clean, freezing water was okay, but the frozen mud was a bummer.

On a late February afternoon, Barby and Henry were at the log cabin on the Millpond. Henry waited patiently for the opportunity to be alone with Barby. Instead, she leaned against him to get warm. The fire blazed, and a yellow haze lit the dim cabin. A mother and two children left the log cabin bungalow. "I didn't think she would ever leave." Barby twisted around and kissed him. Her cheeks were cold, and her lips were wet. "You are a perfect kisser, Mr. Rotyn. Who has been teaching you?" She kissed him again, this time pressing her bosom into him slightly.

Henry pulled her timidly into his chest; she allowed him to feel the fullness of her breast.

Again, she asked, "Who is teaching you to kiss like this? Henry, you're incredible." Her face was flushed, as was his. She studied his face, and his dimples delighted her. His smile was gentle, and his kisses sublime. Barby loved his kind face. She was almost jealous of his long, luxurious hair. But his light blue eyes captivated her; those pools of radiating cerulean blue subdued her intrinsic female defenses.

The two lovebirds sat and talked until dark. Then, when other families began overrunning the cabin, they left to skate together.

Later, they clung to each other as they trudged through the snow on the way home. Halfway between streetlights, darkness covered their path. They began sharing long, sensual kisses in the dark shadows.

Barby invited Henry in for some hot chocolate. Mr. Kraneger was watching the Tonight Show. Mrs. Kraneger was on the telephone talking with her sister. Bobby was sitting with his father, making fun of someone on the program.

Barby went into the kitchen to prepare the drinks. Mr. Kraneger shut off the television.

"Hello, young man; how is your mother, Henry?"

Henry sat next to Bobby on the oversized leather couch.

"She's fine, sir. Thank you."

Bobby interrupted, "We're going to the Indiana game tomorrow. Dad bought some great seats; wish you would go."

Henry liked college basketball, but he had to keep his part-time job. "Thanks, Bobby, but I need to work."

"What colleges are you applying to, Henry?"

"I am planning to attend San Diego State. My uncle lives there, and he offered me a job. But he told me I had to have residency for one year. Then I'd be able to attend college for free except for my books."

The room became quiet as they listened to Henry's conversation.

Mr. Kraneger continued. "Barby has her heart set on the University of California, Berkeley. Unfortunately, it is too far to go to college, but she has her sister's independent spirit.

Barby entered the room with a pot of hot chocolate. She smiled at Henry and asked him how many Marshmallows he wanted. She gave her father a dirty look. Henry held up two fingers.

Mr. Kraneger smiled at his daughter, giving her his choice. Then he looked curiously at Henry.

Barby bent over while serving him and gave Henry a free glance down her blouse, but she stomped on his foot when she realized he was staring.

She whispered to him, "Peek, don't probe." He winced in pain. His feet were still cold, and he took his boots off at the front door.

"Bobby says you want to be a teacher and a football coach; is that right?" Mr. Kraneger asked.

Henry looked at his friend. Bobby tipped his head and shrugged his shoulders. "I want to teach, sir. I also think I can bring some fresh ideas to the game."

Mr. Kraneger nodded and smiled at Henry. "I'm in a position to help you attend the college of your choice, young man. You choose the university, and I will take care of the rest. It would make me incredibly happy."

"Mr. Kraneger, this is incredible. I'd have to ask my mother first. Henry hesitated."

"Henry, your father, worked part-time for my business for many years. He put half of his wage on his mortgage. Your father invested the other half in our business. We kept his investment on the books with interest for your college education."

"He never told me he worked for you, Mr. Kraneger," Henry added.

"Those funds helped my business grow. Money was tight during those years. Your father invested that money wisely. Your father's concern for you was very foresighted."

Henry looked at Barby. She smiled and raised her eyebrows, twisting her face slightly to the side. She was behind this.

"Thank you very much, Mr. Kraneger. My father never mentioned this. I know you are very sincere, but my father taught me that a man should provide for himself. I mean no disrespect, sir."

Barby got up out of her chair and sat next to Henry. She elbowed him and pinched his butt.

"I understand, son. However, this offer was born before you. It will remain open indefinitely with no strings attached." Mr. Kraneger saw a lot of Tom Rotyn in his son. Henry had his father's tenacious pride.

Later that evening, Mr. Kraneger talked privately with Henry. He explained the agreement he had with Henry's father. Mr. Kraneger reasoned that his responsibility to look after his friend's boy was inclusive in that he should do what he reasonably could assist Henry. When Henry understood the complete picture, he accepted Mr. Kraneger's offer instead of discussing the matter with his mother. If she agreed, Henry agreed to investigate his options thoroughly.

When Henry spoke with his mother about Mr. Kraneger's offer, she was upset that Henry had not consulted with her first. She knew her husband worked part-time, and they were old fishing buddies, but she would never have guessed Tom Rotyn was putting that much money into Mr. Kraneger's business. So, she told Henry to wait until she could speak with Mrs. Kraneger.

While Henry was at work the next day, Mrs. Rotyn visited Mrs. Kraneger. Jessica and Eileen had known each other for many years, though Jessica constantly intimidated Eileen with her terrific figure. But then, of course, Eileen, with her fashion-conscious wardrobe and high society etiquette, was always a little too prim for Jessica. Nevertheless, the two women were tolerant of each other but not close friends.

"Hello, Jessica. My, but the years have been kind to you. How do you keep your schoolgirl figure? I am so envious?"

Jessica was impressed; Eileen seemed very sincere. The usual I-will-compliment-you-while-keeping-you-subservient connotation was not evident. "Hello, Eileen. Thank you for taking time out of your busy schedule. As I mentioned on the telephone, I wanted to discuss your husband's proposal regarding Henry's education. Tom certainly kept this a tight secret. I knew he worked for your husband before we met. Tom put a down payment on our house with the money saved while in the Marines. He confided in me that he had never spent a dime in four years. Ben and Tom secretly agreed to care for the other's family if one of them died. Do not get me wrong, Eileen; we are not complaining. Do you remember the long fishing trips those two went on? They would disappear for days on end. You and I do not get to spend much time together anymore. I miss your company."

Eileen gave Jessica a warm hug. She was taller than Jessica, but the short woman was beautiful. Unfortunately, Eileen's hair was stiff and unmanageable without professional help.

"Ben offered to send Henry to the college of his choice. He claims Tom asked him to look after Henry. What do you know about all this, Eileen?"

Both Jessica and Eileen graduated from Barneyville High School. Eileen graduated in 1940, and Jessica in 1948.

"Jesse, I know Thomas and Benjamin had some silly pact. Benjamin previously mentioned it, but I gave it a little thought. I do not know a thing about any other agreement. As you know, Benjamin handles all the financial matters. He has generous accounts set up for the children. I, of course, have my accounts to manage the household. My expense account is moderate, but Benjamin is always thoughtful if I need anything. Beyond those accounts, I am averse to investments or other financial matters. I will ask Benjamin to meet with you and explain his intent. It would help if you had some say about these things, dear. I cannot imagine life without my husband. It must be exceedingly difficult."

"Thank you, Eileen; my only concern is Henry; he has his father's temperament and independence. Thank you again."

Early the following week, Benjamin Kraneger visited the Rotyn family home. Jessica was home alone as Henry was at the high school gym with Barby.

"My goodness, Benjamin. Come on, for goodness's sake. I just opened a cold beer. Would you like one?" She went to the refrigerator, took out a bottle, and opened it for him, not waiting for his answer.

"Come on in the living room, Ben." She had forgotten how large a man Ben Kraneger was until he stood close to her. Ben was not obese, but his two hundred thirty-five pounds were solid at six feet three inches. His arms and his hands were too large for his body. When he took the beer bottle, his enormous hand swallowed hers and the bottle.

"Henry is at school, but I am glad because this will give us a chance to talk privately."

Ben sat on one end of the couch while Jessica sat opposite. Her youthful vitality aroused him. He noticed her flawless face remained wrinkle-free, and her figure was astonishing.

"Jessica, I guess we haven't talked since the funeral. I am sorry, time can steal your life from under your nose."

Jessica wore a short pink and white pleated skirt and silk pullover blouse. She had removed her bra earlier, and the outline of her nipples showed through, making it hard for Ben to concentrate.

Jessica had never been uncomfortable around Ben before, but today, she sensed a wary uneasiness. He stared at her as though she had spilled something on her blouse. She did not want to look at herself in front of Ben. His eyes remained fixed on her; now, she was sure something was wrong. "Ben, Henry informed me about your very gracious proposition." Why did she use that word? She did not mean to say proposition; she meant to say proposal.

Ben dropped his stare while drinking his beer, and Jessica became more comfortable.

"Jessica, I am truly fortunate to be financially sound. However, I think—no, I know Tom would have done the same. Money was tight back then. His investment helped. I the funds he invested I matched. He always said his children would need it for college."

He noticed her nipples again without staring.

"Ben, your agreement with Tom was terrific. Tom and I didn't keep secrets, Ben. Of course, if needed, I could get a mortgage on the house, but Tom wanted the place to go to Henry free and clear; it was in his will.

"Jessica, you won't need to get a mortgage. The money Tom invested in my company is real. I can have my accountant show you where and how much the money is yearly."

"We are very comfortable, but I must admit there is no money for Henry's college education." Jessica did not want to show emotion because this was business, and her son's welfare was at stake. So, instead, she grabbed a tissue from the coffee table. "Oh no, I am sorry, Ben. I don't know what came over me."

Ben got up, entered the kitchen, and returned with two more beers. "Here, Jessica, have another drink. It's on the house."

She smiled at him and had a big drink.

"Thank you, Ben. Henry and I have relied on you and your family since Tom died. Thank you for all your kindness." She stood up, went over to him, and kissed him on the cheek, but when she backed away to stand erect, her foot tripped on the edge of the coffee table. She tipped back, falling, and his large hands suddenly grabbed her. He pulled her into his embrace, and she instinctively wrapped her arms around him. When she looked up into his eyes, she saw his desire.

Over the years, Jessica had wondered about Ben. While she pondered over their past, she was in a bit of a stupor when his lips found hers. Jessica responded curiously at first. She wondered what other surprises she might uncover about him. Jessica had not slept with a man for over three years. Benjamin's smoothness stirred her need for physical pleasure.

Jessica felt herself lifting. Her clothes came off quickly. She was fully aware of what was happening but had no desire to stop him.

Afterward, he fell asleep while she caressed his neck and chest. She waited a short time and then slid out of bed. She went into her bathroom and started to draw a tub full of hot water. She bathed and then soaked in the bubble bath. She exited the bathroom an hour later in her yellow terrycloth robe.

Ben was putting his clothes on. "No, Ben. Please." She helped him out of his things and pulled him into the bathroom. She put him into the tub and bathed him like a little boy. They did not talk, but she did kiss him often. Finally, she dried him off and dressed him.

"I didn't intend for this to happen, Jessica."

She smiled at him. "I know, Ben; I didn't either."

He hugged her tenderly and was about to leave. "We mustn't ever relate any of this to our families. I am sorry, Jessica. I should have been stronger."

She kissed him, captured his hands, and held them to her breasts. "Don't be sorry. You were wonderful. Thank you, Ben. You know how to make a woman feel splendid. I do not want to ruin your marriage, Ben, and I will never hound you. However, I will never kick you out of my bed."

She kissed him on the cheek. "That is all I meant to do earlier. I can't explain what happened, but I'm glad it did."

He admired her cleavage and wondered silently. We both wanted it; maybe we had secretly wanted it for years.

She felt his apprehension. "Don't chastise yourself, Benjamin. I will keep this secret until the day I die." She straightened his clothes and leaned against him.

"I haven't made love to Eileen for over six years. That is both our fault. You are a good, decent woman, Jessica. I will forever remember this special occasion."

She smiled and hugged him again. "Too many sparks, huh?" She said, smiling.

"Yes, and Tom was a fortunate man." He smiled and walked to the door.

She came up behind him and put her hand against his shoulder. "Ben, I can make this work."

CHAPTER 19

Brandy's Scheme

$\mathcal{T}$he police action in Vietnam was the big story on television every night. So naturally, nobody was happy about the war. Some people were very patriotic and supported the war. The rest of the people hated the establishment, especially the military.

Henry did not like the war, and his long hair drew more criticism because it identified him with draft dodgers and war protesters.

The following week, Bobby stopped Henry in the hallway. "Henry, some coaches and others will try to piss you off. Don't blow up for them, Rogue." Bobby patted Henry on the back.

Henry's English teacher stopped Henry. "The Athletic Director wants to see you in his office."

The door was open, and the seventy-eight-year-old Athletic Director, Coach Metzler, sat behind his desk.

Most of the school's coaches were there, including the Athletic director's assistant, Coach Anderson, and the baseball Coach.

Henry grimaced when he saw the Assistant Principal, Mr. Slinter. Henry tried to smile at Gordon Wells, a track team senior and captain.

The Athletic Director, the baseball coach, said, "Hello, Henry. Come on in and have a seat. Henry correctly acknowledged each of the other men in the room. He sat down and immediately knew what was up.

Coach Metzler spoke first. "Henry, did you know I went to school with your father?"

Henry remembered his father's stories of his high school friends; he did not remember him mentioning the name Metzler.

"My father never mentioned your name, Sir." Henry knew the drill. Each man would try to get Henry to see the need to capitulate and cut his hair. However, Henry had promised his father he would never cut his hair, and he knew it would break his mother's heart.

"Well, we were teammates, son. Your father was a hell of a ballplayer. Did you know he lettered in four sports?"

"Yes, Sir, I did because my dad shared many stories with me, plus he had a lot of trophies. Henry's suspicion was correct; his dad was not his friend.

Mr. Slinter was next. "Henry, your friends call you Henry. I don't think anyone calls you Hank, do they?" The Assistant Principal was a small man with small beady eyes, a small nose, and a small head. His features were thin and sickly. Yet, he made up for what Mr. Slinter lacked in physical prowess in harsh, unforgiving student policies.

"No sir, no one in school calls me Hank." Henry wanted to return to his classes; no good would come from this political pretense.

Mr. Slinter continued. "Henry, we think you have a lot of potential. You come from a good family and are a very bright student. All the teachers who have you in their classes are delighted with your effort and achievements. You're not a gang member anymore, are you?"

"The Rowdy Rogue has five members. Most of us are straight-A students. None of us have committed a crime. We do not have a plan to promote anything corruptible. Our small club is not open to the public. We have five members. Our logo depicts how the world is so unbalanced. We are not a gang that carries some evil connotation. So, yes, I am still a proud member of the Rowdy Rogues." Henry became irritated and obdurate. He counted to a hundred while the feeble little man continued.

"Barneyville High School has had a long, proud tradition of academic excellence. Hank, you are benefiting from the community; the citizens in our town contribute to your education, son. They pay their taxes every year. Without those taxes, we could not operate this institution. So, everyone follows the rules, Hank—everyone. Rules are needed to keep the peace; rules protect the citizenry. The rules are good, Hank. We want all our students to recognize how rules are beneficial."

"May I say something, please?" Henry cut him off just as he was about to continue. The toy-like man took great offense in being cut off. Henry saw hate and rage in his eyes.

"Please," he snapped.

Henry ignored the forced adulation and stayed the course. "May I speak freely?"

Mr. Slinter looked at the athletic director, then nodded. "Yes, we'll listen to you, young man."

Henry looked at all the men before he began. "First, only one person on this planet calls me Hank; she is extraordinary. Please, my name is Henry, not Hank. I know very well what you gentlemen want from me. I am not cutting my hair. It is not an aberration; it is long hair. It has no bugs; it is clean and not in disarray. It does not make me a communist or a drug addict. I am the son of a true American; I am America!

"America's forefathers wore long hair, or they wore a wig. Native Americans wore long hair. My father was eighty percent Chippewa. That means I am forty percent Chippewa. Why do you think it is so wrong? Why are you so quick to judge a person by his outward appearance? Even Jesus wore long hair, yet you remain stuck on your narrow-minded prejudices. Ozaawindib is my Chippewa name from the Ojibwa language. Its translation in English is Yellow Head. I am Chippewa. In the Chippewa nation, men and women are encouraged to grow their hair. Your biased view of the Native American is nothing new."

The room went quiet, and no one looked at Henry. The pause lasted a long time.

An older woman suddenly stood in the open doorway. "I've been listening to this conversation. Students and teachers benefit from my family contributions. I am forty percent Chippewa. My brother Ozaawindib has my blood in his veins. No one, except my husband, Thomas Kraneger, knows my heritage. Now you all know." Mrs. Kraneger explained.

Henry got up and said, "If this is all this meeting is about, I would like to return to my classes. You are right, Mr. Slinter. Barneyville is a wonderful academic experience, and I am extremely grateful to receive my education within its hallowed halls. I love this community."

The senior spoke up and was furious. "You are a Senior Henry; first- and second-year students look up to you. It would be best if you accepted the responsible lifestyle that comes with your age. These men have helped many students who had problems in the past. You are insulting them now, and if you walk out before you hear what they say, you are the problem, Henry, not them."

Henry became more obdurate, and he felt hatred for the upperclassman. "My intention is not to insult anyone. If you knew me, you would know I have never been belligerent to any of these men until today."

Mr. Slinter spoke up again. "Then you admit being belligerent and obtuse?" Mr. Slinter's face turned red, and he glared at Henry disgustedly.

"Why are you trying to twist my words? You do not listen to my words; you look at my hair. You have not understood anything I have said thus far because you have closed the door to your mind's eye. All you can see is my hair. May I leave?"

The men looked at each other, and no one said a word.

The athletic director said, "Henry, do you know what you're giving up? You're a gifted athlete, son, and your long hair will remain a problem in college."

Henry would not respond. He stood silently as the men became jittery. Finally, Mr. Splinter said, "Henry, thanks for coming, son. We are not your enemy, young man. Go back to your classes. Thank you for sharing your Native American heritage."

Henry shook each of their hands and realized their hate for him. Henry went back to his classes.

Henry and Barby went to the Flying Saucer Inn almost every Saturday night. "Barby, did you know about your mother's heritage?"

"No, I did not, Henry. But honestly, I was annoyed about why she hid her background. She talked to all of us at home when Brandy returned from college."

He walked with her up the large, open, box-like stairway.

"Your mom stole the show at school last week. I haven't thanked her, but I don't know what to say. I keep waiting for the correct explanation to surface in my mind."

"Henry, I wonder how high the outdoor lounge is in stories. Maybe six or more; what do you think winding its way up to the outdoor lounge."

"I don't know, Barby. You never sweat walking up here. It doesn't matter; the view takes your breath away."

"I don't know why, but I have wondered why your shirt is wet, Henry. Don't you use deodorizer?" A single table was located at each landing, surrounded by wooden benches. Traversing the ninety-two steps always made Henry sweat. He never understood how a girl could walk up without breaking into a sweat. Then, when they reached the roof, the view always took their breath away.

The old wooden structure, while safe, did move in the wind; standing on its deck, one might get the feeling of standing on a living organism.

The two teenagers talked as they slowly danced. "All I Have to Do is a Dream," by the Everly Brothers, was playing.

"Sweet seventeen," he whispered into her ear. She cuddled up closer to him as he led her across the floor.

Henry was an excellent dancer, and she loved dancing with him. So the song stopped, and they danced to "Yesterday" by the Beatles.

Henry noticed the star-filled sky. "Barby, do you ever feel like we are visitors? He looked deeply into her brown eyes. "Do you ever think about how tonight was yesterday?"

Barby thought for a moment; Henry was feeling a bit melancholy. How strange in such a romantic atmosphere, she thought.

"No, I don't. It would ruin the moment if we let ourselves think that way.

"Look to the east, Barby. Can you see the reflection of the moon on the Millpond?"

She was not tall enough to look over the parapet. "No, Henry. Is it beautiful?"

"Yeah, I wish you could see it."

She saw a hint of depression in his eyes. "Henry, do you recall what I told you when your father passed away? It was on the bus, you must remember."

He studied her features as he searched his memory. "Do you mean the night passed away?"

"Yes, I know, but I want you to tell me. Won't you please?" She pleaded.

He knew what she wanted but was unwilling to discuss it; he studied her delightful expression and relented. "You mean the night I cried, don't you?"

She saw the restrained effort in his demeanor but did not understand why he was reluctant to share his feelings. It was a memorable night for her, and she could not fathom his indifference.

"I remember the night," he added, hoping his admission would quell her concerns.

"Henry, do you recall what I told you?"

He tried hard, but the exact words were not coming to him.

Barby was becoming perturbed at his feeble-minded memory. "Henry, I told you you would be my first and last love, and I swore an oath to God above all the angels. I do not aspire to change such a virtuous statement."

"Barby, that sounds like something a politician would say, not a girlfriend."

She did not respond but became withdrawn and sad. Her nose was smiling, though. Whenever she was upset, Henry noticed the oddity.

"I'm sorry, Barby. I did remember. I couldn't remember the exact words, but I remembered the essence of your pledge, and it touched me deeply."

She kissed him quickly. Then, she would not look up at him; she was crying and did not want him to know. "Do you care for me, or are you just using me to see my sister?" Barby's voice was barely audible.

Henry could not believe his ears. "Barby, I thought we settled the hickey thing." But unfortunately, Henry did not like the emotional mood swings of the female species. He wanted to kiss her but became unresponsive and sad when he saw her tears.

"Barby, please forgive me. I'm a fool." She looked at him with a tear-stained eye shadow running down her cheeks. Henry kissed her wet lips and tasted her salty tears.

"Barby, we need to leave. It won't be long, and this place will be full of drunks."

Henry drove her home. They sat outside in the pavilion. Pink and white roses carpeted the sides of the white, park-like structure. They sat in the swing together—too close, much too close, but neither he nor she desired a more conservative embrace.

Barby wore a yellow silk blouse. It was a very prudent garment except for its luscious texture. Her breasts nipples were alarmingly firm, and the soft undergarment did little to disguise their arousal.

Henry struggled with his desire to touch her in her most private places. He rejected those feelings and kept his yearning in check. Barby leaned her Head on his shoulder as they swayed in the gentle breeze.

"Barbara, what are you doing, dear?"

The deep whisky voice of Mrs. Kraneger startled them both.

Barby slowly lifted her Head off his shoulder.

"We are just dancing and talking, Mom."

Mrs. Kraneger stepped out of the dark shadow. "I have talked with both of you. You know how I feel about the two of you being alone. Henry and Barby, you hold each other but not too close. Even married people are careful in public. I know Mr. Kraneger thinks you are above reproach, and in many respects, I agree with him, but I expect him to speak with you tomorrow, young man!"

"Yes, Ma'am. I understand how you and Mr. Kraneger feel, but I am honorable. I would never dishonor your daughter with any form of indecent exploitation."

"I understand you are an honorable young man, Ozaawindib, and Mr. Kraneger and I intend on helping you remain so. Get some rest; good night, Henry."

"Goodnight, Mrs. Kraneger. Wait a minute, if you don't mind— thank you for everything you said at school. Mrs. Kraneger, could you share your Chippewa name, please." Henry asked.

"Diindiisi, in the Ojibwe tongue, is Blackbird. Thank you for asking Ozaawindib." Mrs. Kraneger smiled.

Henry got up to go home; Barby grabbed his hand and whispered, "Henry, I need you to be more assertive." Her face pleaded with longing.

"Henry squeezed her hand and turned away.

Henry thought about the confrontation with Mrs. Kraneger. He thought about Barby, too. Henry wondered if he would ever understand women.

Later that night, Brandy slipped into Barby's room and climbed into her bed next to her baby sister. "Can we talk, sweetie?"

Barby was asleep and always enjoyed girl talking with her older sister. "Are you sleeping with me tonight, Brandy?" She enjoyed the nights her older sister slept with her. Brandy's closeness comforted and smoothed Barby. She loved her sister very much and knew she would soon be leaving for college again. Barby missed her terribly, and the nights they spent together served to reinforce their kindred spirit.

"I want to talk to you about Hank," Brandy said.

Barby sprang over on her back and became very attentive. "What about Henry?"

Brandy smiled and almost laughed; her sister was bonkers for the boy. "Barby, I know how much you like Hank; I do. But I also understand what it feels like to be seventeen. You are in love with everything, especially boys. However, the raging hormones will subside in about a year, and you will feel like a normal girl. In the meantime, I do not want you to get into a compromising situation that could damage your reputation. You know how Mother feels about a girl's reputation. I do not care, but I don't want you to hurt."

Barby knew her older sister adored her. Tonight would be one of the enlightened talks with special surreptitious feminine significance.

"Barby, believe me when I tell you Hank is the kind of guy that can hurt you." Brandy had her attention now, and Barby was all ears.

"Henry would never hurt me, Brandy. I know him, and he cannot hurt someone he loves." Barby smiled and was very sure of herself.

"Barby, Hank is a horny boy whose hormones are raging. Henry speaks honorably and has been virtuous. But listen honey, the guy is good-looking; he's cute, adorable, precious, kind, has manners, and wow, the hair and the eyes."

Barby smiled contentedly. "You forgot he is a beautiful young man," Barby said.

Brandy struggled with what she wanted to tell her sister. Brandy thought quickly. "Barby, open your eyes. If you think dating boys like Hank is what happiness is all about, you're in for a rude awakening."

"Why do you like him then?" Barby asked.

"Hank's the kind of guy that could be a lot of fun, and maybe he could make a girl feel like a woman. But, once he gets what he wants, all the charisma and charm will be a thing of the past. Barby, this is the most important lesson you can learn about guys. They quit being nice after they get in your pants. Hank won't be any different." Brandy said.

Barby looked sad. She studied her knees and rubbed them. "What do you want me to do with Henry?" she asked.

"He lives in a different world than we do, sweetie. Maybe he can change that, but I doubt it. Do you see me dating guys from Barneyville? Sweetie, listen to me. Hank is nice, but he will never leave this town. Look around you, honey. All the women are fat and enslaved to a lifestyle they hate. Most of them hate their husbands, and they hate this town." Brandy said.

"Henry's not a dumb hillbilly. He is as smart as I am. We are close, too, and you are just jealous. Brandy, your sights are set so high; all the boys think you are stuck. What's wrong with you?" Barby asked.

Barby was sulking; she did not want to give up on Henry. "So, what are you trying to do?" Barby cried.

Brandy smiled and lowered her Head like a snake.

Barby picked up her pillow and swung with all her might.

Brandy dodged the pillow but lost her balance and fell off the bed backward. Brandy landed on the square of her back and knocked the wind out of herself.

Barby clubbed her repeatedly, and Brandy held up her hands to fend her off. Then, finally, Barby jumped on her, but she realized she was hurt when she saw the terror in her sister's eyes.

Brandy could not catch her breath and passed out.

Barby did not realize the simplicity of her injury and interpreted her unconscious state with a frightening alarm. She screamed, "Brandy, wake up! Wake up, Brandy!"

Bobby burst into the room. He was getting out of the tub, and the towel he had positioned around himself fell to the floor. He was beside his older sister before Brandy. Barby was crying terrifyingly enormous sobs. Bobby shouted, "Barby, shut up!"

When Barby saw that Brandy was alert, she calmed down. She helped Bobby pick her up and deposit her on the bed.

It was about that time the sisters both noticed his lack of modesty. So, they stared at him or, instead, at his anatomy.

"Give me my pillow and quit touching my pillow with. . . Bobby, don't do that with my pillow!" She wailed.

"Are you hurt, stretch?" Bobby asked awkwardly, ignoring his twin.

Brandy did not answer, and both girls started giggling. But they did not turn their heads.

"Nothing like putting everything on display, huh, Pudge?" Brandy started smiling at her brother.

Bobby backed out of the room and picked up his towel during his retreat. Then, he tossed the pillow at his sisters and fled.

Barby smiled and realized again how terrified she had been just moments ago. "I'm sorry, Brandy; I didn't mean to hurt you." Barby started crying.

Brandy softened her disposition. She saw her sister's tears were genuine. She sat up and motioned to Barby to sit beside her. The sisters embraced, and Brandy whispered, "You didn't hurt me, honey; I knocked the wind out of myself, and then I must have passed out. I'm a fine sweetie."

Barby cried harder, unable to control her emotions.

Brandy scrutinized her sister.

Barby dried her eyes and kissed her sister on her cheek.

"Brandy, I love Henry, and he loves me."

The two sisters giggled, embraced, and flopped on Barby's bed.

Brandy could not tell her sister that she wanted to pursue Hank. Yet, she knew in her heart that if the opportunity presented itself, she would jump at the chance to be alone with him.

CHAPTER 20

Keeping Men Warm

"Henry, we need to spend more time together. I do not care what my mother thinks. I am going to ignore her bombastic insults. When she interrupts our private time, you cannot simply walk away. You need to be more assertive, honey. If both of us stand up against her, she will understand our relationship is more than a fickle high school teenage puppy love." Barby lamented.

"I understand why you feel this way, Barby. However, I need to respect your mother and your father. I feel this way about your entire family. I am not going to create a chasm against your parents. When we turn eighteen, we still need to respect our parents. We can gently persuade them to understand our relationship. Barby, we have many years to enjoy our lives together."

Barby loved Henry because he was a perfect gentleman. She understood his viewpoint and recognized his maturation. So why couldn't she understand how he understood everything?

Barby, Bobby, Gary, Terry, and Henry competed for the highest grades. They did not care who seemed to have the upper hand, but others in their class seemed to make a big deal out of it, much bigger than they ever did.

Henry and his mother spent the evening at the Kraneger's on a bitterly cold late January night. The holiday celebrations were long gone, and the typical cabin fever blahs had settled over the two families.

Red Skelton was entertaining the living room audience. Bobby sat in the oversized easy chair, and Sherry sat below him on the floor. Her bright red hair flowed down her back in large curls.

Henry laid his head in Barby's lap. She leaned up against the large sofa occupied by her sister and Jessica. Mr. and Mrs. Kraneger had one end of the small couch covered with handmade comforters.

A winter storm raged outside as the temperature plummeted. Snow was piling up, and the howling wind created huge drifts. The fireplace was roaring but could not keep the family room warm enough. Finally, Barby got up and distributed more comforters to everyone.

Consuela made a fresh pot of hot chocolate. Mr. Kraneger asked her to lace it with peppermint schnapps.

The warm, tainted drink delighted everyone.

Barby and Henry joined Brandy and Jessica on the large sofa. Henry sat between the two girls, to the delight of Brandy. Sherry joined Bobby in his chair, but Mrs. Kraneger kept a stern eye on them.

Henry sat up straight, and each girl leaned against him from either side. Jessica looked at her son, "Henry, you look like you're staying warm. Let me know if you two girls find it difficult to keep Henry warm."

Mrs. Kraneger said, "Well, Jessica. Come on over here and help me keep poor old Benjamin warm." So, Jessica slid in on the other side of Mr. Kraneger.

Henry added, "I'm still cold, Bobby, and I have two chicks to keep me warm. I don't know how you can remain warm with just one?" Brandy pulled Henry closer and readjusted the comforters.

Bobby howled, "Get up and go find me another girl, Sherry."

Sherry's mouth dropped open. "I will not; I can keep you plenty warm all by myself."

Mr. Kraneger said, "Gee, son, Henry may have a valid point. I'm still cold, and I have two lovely ladies trying to keep me warm,"

Jessica looked at Eileen. Mrs. Kraneger had consumed several cups of hot chocolate smothered with peppermint schnapps and felt frisky. Eileen pulled her arms inside the sleeves of Ben's flannel shirt she was wearing. She undid her bra, pulled it out of one of the shirtsleeves, and threw it into the middle of the room, to everyone's astonishment. The white B-cups landed with one cup open. "Now you have something with which to warm yourself, dear."

Bobby could not believe what he had just seen. He yelled, "Way to go, Mom!"

Barby's jaw dropped. "Mother, how could you?" she yelped.

Not to be outdone, Jessica unbuttoned her blouse under the cover of the comforter. Unfortunately, when she finally threw her bra into the middle of the room, the lacey D-cups landed with both cups open.

This time, Henry whined, "Mom?" He was embarrassed.

Brandy could not restrain herself. Her mother laughed when her black lacey B-cups landed in the middle of the room.

Jessica did not laugh. She said, "Henry Hershel, keep your hands to yourself."

Barby already had hers off but was afraid to throw it into the middle of the room.

Bobby tried to get Sherry to remove her bra, but she refused. Jessica saw them struggling and said to Sherry, "Go ahead, honey. Join the fun." When Sherry got her bra off, Bobby grabbed it from her and threw it into the middle of the room. The white, lacey B-cups landed with both cups down.

Mr. Kraneger yelled, "Way to go, Bobby!"

Mrs. Kraneger did not think this was funny, however. "Robert Thomas, you put her bra back on this instant."

Brandy yelled, "Way to go, Sherry!"

Barby laid her bra at the end of the couch, but now she retrieved it and flung it onto the pile.

Mrs. Rotyn could not believe what she had just seen. "Henry, let me see your hands. You keep them on top where Eileen and I can see them."

Brandy slipped her left hand into Henry's trousers. She had him hard before he could pull her arm out of his shorts. He leaned against Barby, trying to remove Brandy's arm.

Bobby looked at his father and silently lipped, "Trollops." Mr. Kraneger smiled but then realized the impact of Bobby's intent. Mr. Kraneger's smile turned into a frown. He held out his open hand, signaling for Bobby not to say anything.

Brandy saw the communication from the father to the son. She removed her arm in a hurry. "Pudge, don't ruin our evening." But it was too late.

Bobby exclaimed loudly, "You women are all a bunch of trollops."

Brandy threw her shoe at Bobby, just missing his head. Barby's shoe followed. Bobby caught it midair and threw it back, hitting Brandy in the neck below her left ear. The shoe struck with a wallop.

The incident happened too fast; Henry did not have a chance to put his hand up to block the shoe.

Bobby was up in an instant.

Brandy slumped over in Henry's lap, cringing in pain. Her left ear was burning and aching.

Jessica hurriedly finished buttoning her blouse. Mrs. Kraneger was at Brandy's side in a flash. There was a small amount of blood visible in her daughter's ear.

Sherry was phoning her uncle. He was a family doctor in Battle Creek.

Barby gathered up all the bras and returned them to the appropriate ladies.

Bobby and Mr. Kraneger were preparing to transport Brandy to the hospital.

Mrs. Kraneger was talking with the doctor after she examined Brandy.

Mrs. Kraneger spoke to everyone in the waiting room. "Brandy has a broken eardrum. The doctor wants to keep her overnight because she is in a lot of pain. She can control her pain best with a catheter."

The storm created severe problems and was deemed more hazardous than the broken eardrum. The Sheriff had already announced limited travel restrictions. The hospital was a few blocks away.

Everyone went in to see Brandy for a few minutes. Bobby was unimaginably distraught.

However, to everyone's astonishment, Brandy got up on the side of her bed and motioned for Bobby. He walked up to Brandy, and she embraced him. He stood still with his arms at his side.

"You can hug me, Pudge. I'm not a China doll." Brandy whispered.

"I don't want to mess up all the tubing. I am so sorry, Brandy." Bobby cried.

He had tears in his eyes afterward. He looked at his dad with tears streaming down his cheeks. His father gave him a disappointed look that pushed Bobby into further regret.

Henry helped Brandy back into bed. Brandy whispered to Henry. "I have something special for you, Hank."

Bobby located his twin and cried on her shoulder for a long time.

"Henry, we need to spend more time together. I do not care what my mother thinks. I am going to ignore her bombastic insults. When she interrupts our private time, you cannot simply walk away. You need to be more assertive, honey. If both of us stand up against her, she will understand our relationship is more than a fickle high school teenage puppy love." Barby lamented.

"I understand why you feel this way, Barby. However, I need to respect your mother and your father. I feel this way about your entire family. I am not going to create a chasm against your parents. When we turn eighteen, we still need to respect our parents. We can gently persuade them to understand our relationship. Barby, we have many years to enjoy our lives together."

Barby loved Henry because he was a perfect gentleman. She understood his viewpoint and recognized his maturation. So why couldn't she understand how he understood everything?

"Henry, I'm not supposed to tell you. All the ladies and girls carried another bra. No one was removing the real bra. That's funny, and we were not supposed to say anything." she smiled.

"I wondered how Mrs. Kraneger could pull that off. Everybody did this, Mom?"

"Everybody, honey. I'm sorry Brandy was hurt. I've never seen Bobby cry. Could you keep this to ourselves? The girls might tell you. Smile, dear."

CHAPTER 21

The Cascades

$\mathcal{H}$enry bought an old car from Mr. Kraneger; he got a great deal. The vehicle was a green and white two-tone 1963 Chevrolet Bel Air sedan. It had a 327 V-8 with an automatic transmission. It only had forty-two thousand miles, and the tires were brand new. It had dual glass pack mufflers with straight pipes and sounded very tough.

Barby and Henry went to Jackson on a Tuesday night in late April. He took her to dinner at Whimpy Burger; a colossal statue of Popeye's hamburger-eating friend stood out. The hamburgers were immense; consuming the meal took almost half an hour.

Afterward, they went to the Cascades. On Tuesday nights, the Cascades were free. There was no other place on earth like it.

The cascades were a series of nine ponds, three feet deep. The ponds were built like monumental stairs, rising almost seven stories high. All the ponds were exactly forty-foot in width, one-hundred-foot length, and seven-foot depth—each of the nine ponds allowed water to flow into the pond below. The lowest pond has pumps that push the water up to the top pond. The cascades are now operational. Each pond has seven feet of fall between ponds. The spill is one hundred feet wide and forty feet long. Lights installed under the dry side of the falls, Red, Blue, and Yellow, can create three other colors: Green, Violet, and Orange. The lights can create a mixture of seven lamps, too. On top of the hill was the first pond. Then, the water began rolling over a one-hundred-foot-wide pond below. This new pond filled with water until it rolled over evenly into the next pond. Nine ponds were filled higher than the pond could hold, creating nine falls 100 feet wide. When the bottom pond fills more than three feet deep, a large pump pushes the water to the top pond. The system keeps moving until an operator shuts it down.

A variety of different colored lights glowed under each of the waterfalls. The one-hundred-foot-wide cascading falls glistened three miles away. The colors changed from red to yellow to blue to green to orange and then into combinations of colors. The hues start light, then slowly become bolder until they become a full dark color. The program started at dusk and continued until eleven pm on weeknights and one in the morning on weekends.

Along the edge of the pools, stairs worked their way up, around the backside of the top pond. The opposing side stairs were a copy. Very tall, thick bushes lined the staircases' outer edge, creating a romantic, secretive, and secluded impression. These landings widened the pools, and benches lined the outer edges of the walkways.

Henry and Barby spent more than an hour walking all the way around. The pools, staircase, landing, and intermittent geysers rose into the heavens. A gentle breeze pushed the spray over the walkway at the upper levels.

Dusk was settling in, and dark shadows appeared along the stairwells; Henry and Barby looked back at the pools. Just then, the lights lit at the top, illuminating the falls and transforming into a broad belt of blue velvet. Slowly, each progressive waterfall lit up and took on the same bold blue hue. Henry kissed Barby and said, "I doubt there is another place on earth as beautiful."

Barby clung to Henry. "I love the Cascades too."

Later, they sat in the car, taking in the spectacle. "Henry, do you love your car more than you love me?" She put her head on his shoulder.

He looked into her probing brown eyes. "Probably, no, I'm wrong. Most certainly." She slugged him and bit his shoulder. "Ouch, I know someone who wants to walk home." He turned his face, raising his eyebrows.

"You wouldn't dare Henry." She clenched her teeth and displayed a sarcastic smile.

He smiled tenderly. "Bite me like that again, and I will forget I am a gentleman."

She kissed him for a long time.

"Are you looking forward to the University of California, Barby?"

"Henry, I am, but we will be 500 miles apart."

"I know, darling, but I will come up and see you every month, Barby."

Henry kissed her wet lips and sensed something different. Her hair gave off the fragrance of fresh lilacs.

Henry's trepidation regarding Brandy struck him solidly in his gut. Barby acted differently, too. Her kisses were romantic, and she flittered her tongue more intensely.

"Henry, you look sad, honey," she said.

Henry wrangled with his trepidation. She leaned against him while they quietly reflected on the colorful spectacle rolling down the hill. The rush of emotion passed in time, and he emerged from his stupor.

"You know my mom wanted me to go to Western. It's an excellent school for teachers."

She pushed his hair out of his face. "I know, Henry, but we can still see each other during the holidays. If we went to school together, how much studying do you think we would get done? We have less than a month of high school. Maybe we should concentrate on what time we have together, and as we mature, so will our love." Barby kissed him gently while she ran her fingers through his thick hair. Henry's kiss was much more intense. His technique became much more virile, and she enjoyed herself prodigiously. She regretted telling him their love could survive a lengthy separation. She would never be able to leave him if his kisses became more amative.

They pulled apart, and she kept her face against his shoulder. She was letting herself become too sensual. She trusted Henry totally, but she knew every man had his limits. A deep, powerful yearning spread over her flesh, and she struggled to gain control. She fought the urges, and the emotion began to subside. She wondered if a woman had a breaking point. Had she just visited hers?

"Barby, I need to explain some things to you." Henry was quiet.

Barby wondered what he was going to say.

He smiled and touched her hair.

"My mother is primarily Swedish, although her family has been in America for three generations. Surprise, I am blonde. My father was 20 percent Irish and 80 percent Chippewa Indian. I am 40 percent Chippewa Indian.

"The Chippewa is one of a few Native Americans who still live on the land natives lived on for thousands of years. Michigan sterilized thousands of male natives so that they couldn't father children. Rich people were behind this evil practice. Their reasoning was the Chippewa native was stupid and unhealthy. When Dad joined the Marines, he wrote he was a white man. He never joined his Chippewa Nation because he saw too many Chippewa sterilized by the State of Michigan. This evil practice continued until early 1950. I don't understand why my mother wanted me to have long hair. She wanted me to throw my heritage into the face of evil men. My hair is part of my heritage. How do you feel about having children who would be 20 percent Chippewa?"

"My god, Henry, this is horrible. We all need to stand up for our heritage. But, darling, I yearn to have our children. They would1950sal Americans too. I would feel so proud, honey."

"Native Americans have been slaughtered and tortured by generations of supposedly American Countries. Barby, more than 90 percent of the North and South American Indigenous Indians died by European nations. No one knows the true count in the USA. As independent Nations, Congress granted Native Americans the right to vote in every State three years ago. No ethnicity has suffered more in the USA than Native Americans. I learned all of this at the Pow Wow at my father's Memorial."

"I can feel your honor and devotion, honey. I am pleased that you have learned so much about your heritage. We need to raise our children to honor and respect their heritage. I love you so much, Henry."

"Barby, If I father children, they will become twenty percent Chippewa. The child you bear for us would have ten percent more from you. Our children would become thirty percent Chippewa.

"Henry, I want to have four children for you.

"Barby, you could have a Chippewa name. All you need to do is think about the time of the year you were born. Then, select something created to run on Mother Earth, fly in the sky, or swim in the water. You can also use the name of a plant, rock, or star. We can choose your character together, or you can create your name by studying creation.

"Can my mother help me?"

"Yes, she would be thrilled," Henry said.

"I cannot believe how much my life will change. Will my friends turn against me?

"Your mother is forty percent. Barby, this means you are twenty percent. We can look up a name for you. Please tell me right now, darling."

"Ozaawindib is my name. It means 'Yellow Head,' my love."

"It's a great name, Henry. Can we give our children Chippewa names, too?"

"Most certainly, silly girl." He exclaimed.

CHAPTER 22

Senior Year

*H*enry's problems with the athletic director continued. He still was not a member of the Varsity Club. Barby complained to him that all the other girls wore their boyfriends' school jackets. The only coat Henry wore was his Rowdy Rogue coat. Barby refused to wear it. Henry reasoned none of the other Rogues were members of the Varsity Club and had a varsity jacket, except Bobby.

A secret meeting in the athletic director's office convened in early May. The coaches agreed Henry did not represent the school's best interest because of his long hair and gang membership. Therefore, he should not be allowed to join the Varsity Club.

They decided to enlist the aid of several students to trick him. Several juniors took Henry off to the side at a school dance and told him they had some joints and wanted to know if he would join them. Henry told them he did not smoke and did not use pot. He did take a long drag from one, though. They offered him some beer, and he once again told them he usually did not drink but decided to have just one.

On the following Monday night, Henry went to a pre-induction meeting for the Varsity Club. He received the invitation in the mail the week before. One light bulb lit the area where the A.D. and his coaches sat. Henry could not see the students' faces because he didn't face them, and that part of the room was pitch black.

Bobby was at the University of Michigan doing a walk-through. Then, everyone stood and recited the pledge of allegiance.

The A.D. opened the meeting with a few questions. "Henry, have you ever smoked a cigarette?"

Henry knew right away what was happening. "No, not normally."

"Henry, are you admitting to smoking? Please answer yes or no."

"Well, now, Athletic Director, have you ever set a trap for a student because you didn't like a student?"

"Be a careful young man; that kind of talk can get you expelled from this school. Answer my question, and I will overlook your insult."

"Let's talk about the trophies you have in your cabinets from the State of Michigan. You cheated by offering me money to play on the football team for three years. I still have the cash. I didn't spend it."

"This is outrageous! How dare you accuse me of perpetrating such a horrible scheme. I will have you removed from this school immediately."

"Your face is pretty red, Athletic Director. How about I remove my last statement? Would you feel better? Entrapment is what you are trying to do to me. I'm not too fond of your guts. You were never a friend of my father. Most of the people in this school dislike you. Would you like to continue your game?"

"No, you have crossed the line, young man."

"I want to continue your game, Athletic Director. Who told you I smoke? Who told you I drink? These components were on city property, with coaches on your staff attending. Who gave the Juniors the beer and cigarettes? The school's Board of Directors will hear what happened here today. I don't need your coat. My Rowdy Rogue coat is the only coat I need.

Henry wanted to tell the coaches they could shove their sports programs to their asses. However, he did not.

Gary was waiting to go in next, but when he saw Henry leaving, looking like he wanted to kill someone, he did not go in. Instead, he followed Henry out of the building. Terry did not accept his invitation, but his twin brother Tom was there. However, Tom was in the bathroom when Henry came out. He wondered where Henry and Gary were and decided they must be in the meeting.

Tom was allowed to join, and he thought Henry and Gary were both there. Unfortunately, the light prevented him from seeing anyone except the coaches on the platform. When he found out what had happened to Henry, he immediately resigned. Tom talked to every varsity club member and told them what kind of idiots they had become.

The new football coach was from the Detroit area. Henry liked him because he never said a word to him about his hair.

Henry did not earn a letter or any awards for Barneyville.

Fred Rotyn met with the Board of Directors as he did for 15 years. He was the President of the Board for the past five years. He demanded the Board remove the Athletic Director and the Assistant Athletic Director. He also told them to draw up a new policy for determining which Student-athlete received the capital B and varsity club membership.

Bobby was going to play football at Michigan, and so was Gary. Barby was going to the University of California at Berkeley. Henry would go to San Diego State and live with his Uncle Fred on Coronado Island. Terry went to school in Central Michigan. Tom went to a two-year trade school in Florida.

Henry's mom told him, "You need to be content. You have a free ride for four years."

The Barneyville seniors felt incredibly special. During their last year of high school, they walked around like adults amongst children. All the Rowdy Rogues members wore their coats to school every Friday. They suffered terrific bouts of ambivalence. Whether they loved school or hated it, it did not matter. High school became a lifestyle. Each student was acutely aware of the social skills necessary to be comfortable. They knew how to climb up or down the scale of social acceptance. Their friends accepted them for who they were, not who they would or could become. Seniors understood all this; they assumed the strange dreams, the possibilities of success, the dread of disappointment, and the horror of failure.

The Rowdy Rogues wore their coats to school for the last time on the first Monday in June. After that, they decided it was time to give it up, but each would keep his icon for life.

CHAPTER 23

Senior Prom

*H*enry took Barby to the Junior-Senior Prom. Barby presided as queen and was busy all night.

Henry had to sit with Bobby, Terry, and Tom at a different table. Gary was the King.

Early in the evening, Mrs. Rotyn danced with her son. The entire auditorium stopped to focus on the fox-trotting mother and son act. Henry enjoyed himself immensely. He was never prouder of his mother, and she fairly bathed in his admiration. They practiced the dance for many hours until they mastered the athleticism and coordination required. They enjoyed a rousing adjuration from the crowd for an encore but declined amicably.

Terry managed to sneak a bottle of scotch into the auditorium, and Henry drank too much of it with orange juice. Finally, at about eleven, all the ceremonial presentations concluded, and Henry finally danced with Barby.

"I'm sorry, Henry. I did not intend to ignore you all night. But, hey, have you been drinking? You smell like my father." She noticed his red cheeks, rosy lips, and tired eyes. "This is our special night, Henry," she whined.

He wondered how special it was since she had ignored him until now. He did not speak to her, but he had something to say. She tucked her head into his shoulder and followed his lead silently while he lumbered across the floor. She knew she had ignored him all night and desperately wanted to make it up to him. Henry held her close, and Barby did not fight him.

Mrs. Rotyn was one of the chaperones, saw the intimate embrace on the dance floor, and had no intention of correcting matters. The senior prom was their night, and she thought no one should interfere if they kept their clothes on. Moreover, Jessica was popular with the students. As the senior secretary in the high school office, she knew every one of the students and treated them with dignity and empathy.

A few years ago, the seniors started a new tradition at the prom that she found entertaining. All the senior boys drew names from a lottery to have one or two dances with her. She was a stunning woman undaunted by youth, and her beauty radiated among even the prettiest junior/senior teens.

Mrs. Rotyn wore a brilliant yellow gown trimmed in silver. Her long blonde hair was piled high on her head like a twisted cone. She wore silver bracelets, anklets, earrings, and a necklace.

Henry blew a hair wisp near Barby's ear. She looked up into his eyes and saw his tenderness and sensitivity and his love for her.

Barby wore a bright burgundy gown closed tightly at the neck with white lace around her throat, wrists, waist, and hem. She, of course, wore a Queen's tiara and ribbon.

Bobby's date, Sherry, was a junior. The other girls in his class criticized him for his lack of style; many of them would have killed him to be his date. However, young Sherry McClanton was not intimidated; she was a brilliant student with a gorgeous redhead. She wore a dark green gown trimmed in gold. Her long red hair spilled down her back in flowing curls. She was a witty girl who, like Barby, was often all smiling. Bobby was really into her, and she adored him.

The Rowdy Rogues wore white tuxes, shoes, top hats, and gloves. They were the party's hit from start to finish, and each of their dates adored them.

Henry and Barby were inseparable now as the night wore on. "I love your hat, Henry. You look very debonair monsieur." His stupor had worn off now, and they danced with eager animation.

"You're gorgeous tonight, Barby." He was reluctant to tell her how he felt because Brandy was still in his brain. He wanted to drive off with Barby, far away from Barneyville. However, he was innocent; no man would have had the strength to avoid Brandy's trap.

"Barby, can you feel the excitement in the air?"

She looked at him, wondering what he was talking about now.

"Our future is like electricity. Can you feel it?" He wondered.

She smiled and cuddled into his chest. "Henry, you're such a romantic. I need Ozaawindib to carry me off to his Teepee."

They drove to Marshall and had a late dinner at Schuler's, an exclusive high-class restaurant. Barby conned her father into giving them the Chrysler for the evening. After dinner, he drove to the South Haven Municipal Marina North.

"Barby, it's a long walk to the beach. So why are we parking here, Honey?

"Jump in the back, Henry, and change your clothes, silly."

"You brought your swimming trunks, Henry?"

"Hey, don't take off your underwear. Instead, put on your blue jeans, Henry."

"Barby, we're on a beach; why do I have to wear blue jeans on a beach?"

"Someone is looking in your window, Henry."

"Ellen, hello again. What are you doing out here tonight?" Henry asked.

"Hello, Henry and Barby. How was the Prom? I thought I saw Barby driving. Oh my, Henry, you're drunk. Way to go, fellow. We might have one hell of a night," Ellen smiled.

"I'm tired now; how far is it to the boat, Ellen?" Barby asked.

"You cannot see it from here, but it's just around the corner behind this building," Ellen said.

"I guess we are spending the night on our sailboat. Do you have a ride home for the night, Ellen?" Barby asked.

"No, come on and follow me. Do you have much to carry?" Ellen asked.

"Not much, Ellen," Barby responded.

When they reached the boat, the hatch was already open.

"Dad was going to pick me up. Can I come back around noon? I could show you how to sail," Ellen said.

"Ellen, I was expecting some privacy on the boat," Barby complained.

"I understand completely. Just leave the boat. You need some privacy," Ellen giggled.

"Henry, I have some wonderful Acapulco Gold. You kids get high." Ellen urged.

Henry looked at Barby. They didn't say a word, and Ellen lit a joint in seconds and took a hit. She passed it to Barby, took a long hit, and passed it to Henry. In fifteen minutes, everyone was laughing.

Ellen left them a half bag of the Acapulco Gold.

The Summer of Love wouldn't end until the first day of summer 1968.

The following day, Barby was hungry. She started breakfast while Henry got up and took a shower. Barby needed help remembering how far things went last night. She wondered if Henry made love to her, but her underwear wasn't bloody. Barby thought they went only some of the way.

A light wind was blowing onshore. The June morning was warm. As the boat motored toward the lake, isolated fishermen dotted the north pier.

Barby was afraid she was losing Henry to her sister. So why didn't she let him make love to her? Wasn't it every boy's dream to get laid on prom night? She wondered again if Henry was as virtuous as he claimed. Maybe he was in love with her sister.

Henry was washing his hair when Barby helped wash it.

After breakfast, Barby was tired and dozed off. Henry was beside her in the V-berth. The sailboat began rocking back and forth from the waves created by the stiff breeze.

Henry was awake; he propped himself up on one elbow and watched Barby sleep. Her nostrils flared out gently with each exhale, and the sides of her nose sucked in ever so slightly when she inhaled. He studied her flawless face. Barby's peers had pitted faces from zits and blackheads, but Barby had no such flaws. Her red lips flickered as she slept. Henry wanted to touch the little valley that formed between her nose and lip. It twittered slightly when her lips fluttered. Her nose did smile, and Henry smiled when he remembered her reaction in the bungalow when he brought that to her attention.

Beneath them, long, sweeping, rolling waves sloshed gently against the boat. The two-foot swells split in two but continued moving toward shore. The slow, steady-flowing rhythm of the waves lulled Henry into a calm, peaceful sleep.

A thick, heavy fog moved off the lake, reducing visibility to about fifteen feet. Barby awoke when the foghorn sounded on the other pier. Henry was still sleeping, and the noise did not wake him.

"Take me home, Henry. I want to go home." Her voice startled him. Henry had slept for almost thirty minutes.

Barby raised and stretched while climbing to her feet. She leaned over and kissed Henry and then took the wheel.

'I'm sorry, Henry, but we cannot go out very far; this fog is too thick. You were exhausted. I started the engine, pulled in all the ropes, and put up all the sails. It's fine; I do this all by myself." Barby smiled.

Barby looked at him and smiled. She turned toward Henry, who was sneaking behind her. A large wave was crossing the opening between the two piers.

"Turn to Port Barby. Watch out for those rogue waves. They can push you into another boat or even the pier." Ellen advised from the pier.

Ellen dropped them off at the marina. Then, she whistled to them and turned upriver.

Henry and Barby found their car and headed for home.

Henry droves slowly in the fog as Barby cuddles next to him. It was almost four-thirty. "Henry, I love you."

He stared straight ahead in a heavy fog. The visibility was less than 20 feet.

She nudged him with her elbow. "Please talk to me, Henry. I planned on us being intimate tonight. A boy should never have to beg. What are you thinking about, and why won't you talk to me?"

Henry would not answer her, and she knew driving was difficult. So, she sat quietly, leaned against his arm, and waited for him to communicate.

He was not mad that he did not make love to her. He did not know the answer. As they drove, the fog evaporated further inland, and Barby slept most of the way.

He was sure Barby wanted to make love to him, but it didn't happen too.

Her parents were furious when Barby and Henry arrived at her home later that evening. Barby told them they should not have worried because she was with Henry. But Mrs. Kraneger was throwing a fit and accused Henry of improper conduct with her daughter.

Barby screamed at her, "Don't you get it? Henry and I are practically married."

Brandy was home from college. She was standing next to her mom. Henry caught her eye, and she gave him one of her cat-like looks. He had to bite his tongue to keep from laughing.

Mr. Kraneger took Henry into his study and ascertained his innocence. He did not ask Henry if he made love to his daughter. Instead, after a lengthy man-to-man discussion of proper etiquette when alone with the opposite sex, he embraced his virtually adopted son, wishing him well.

Mrs. Kraneger later asked Henry if anything happened; she needed to know about it. Henry assured her that nothing happened. His choice of words irritated her, but he used them anyhow.

School ended; Henry worked at the hardware store full-time. No onion fields, he kept his promise.

CHPATER 24

Jennifer

*B*randy graduated from college with a liberal arts degree. She started the summer working at her father's dealership. Henry saw Brandy on weekends and some evenings, but they spent little time together.

Henry, Barby, and Bobby graduated from Barneyville High School. The eighteen-year-old college-bound teenagers were excited to create and experience new dreams.

"Good morning, honey. What do you want for breakfast, dear?" Jessica asked Henry.

"I have been reading the paper. The moon landing is still a go. Do you think America can pull this off, Mom?"

"Yes, I do, Son. Breakfast?"

"French toast sounds good. Eggs over easy and some bacon. Mom, is that too much?"

"Let us go downtown; I'm all out of eggs. Do you have time for that, Henry?"

"Yes, Mom, but it will be my treat."

"Oh my, well, that is a surprise. I would love to spend the morning with you. I want to speak with you about something too. I am going to Kalamazoo tomorrow, and I would like to know if you can go with me. You have got your vacation with the Kraneger's coming up, and soon after that, you are leaving for California. So, I want to spend time with you, Henry."

"Mom, I can do that because I quit my job at the hardware store. I do not need the money. I was apprehensive. I look forward to college, but I have spent every morning with you for most of my life. I wish I could take you with me."

"You're going to make me cry, Henry. You might as well understand; I will cry the day you leave. But Ozaawindib, you are so special to me. I love you too, honey." Mrs. Rotyn said.

Barby spoke with Henry the night before he left. "You should go with your mom, Henry; she wants you to be with her."

"Well, you just settled the problem. Mom already asked me, and I said yes."

"I want you to know I will surprise you when you return. I promise you will not be disappointed this time." Barby assured.

"You're going to start a fire you cannot extinguish, Barby."

"I cannot deny you any longer, Ozaawindib. Your request to prove your bravery is now," she giggled.

"Yellow Head chooses to fulfill his tribal ceremony and conquer his maiden."

"Your maiden is on her period, goofy. So put it back in your pants, silly boy." Barby laughed.

"Trollip, you just ruined my impetus. Blue despair and agony on me, deep dark depression, excessive misery." Henry spoke comical words from a television comedian.

"Darling boy, I have all the tools to repair your despair, agony, depression, and misery," she laughed.

"I love you, silly girl."

"I love you, silly boy."

Henry kissed her and went home.

"Barby, I want to talk to you. Can you come into my room?" Brandy asked.

"Yep, let me finish putting these clothes away, and I'll be there in a minute," Barby replied.

"On your prom night, I hope you and Yellow Head used some protection?" Brandy chastised.

"Brandy, I won't tell you about my love life. You don't tell me about yours."

"Did you let Henry get into your pants, Barby?"

"No, I didn't, Brandy. I was remarkably close to removing all my clothes, but I knew better. So there, you happy now?"

"I don't mean to pry, honey. I have got some birth control pills for you. You need to take one every morning. Each packet is good for a month. Every day is listed here, and you cannot miss a day. These might make your period a little messy, but you get used to it, too. Do not have sex right away. Give the pills a few days to work, honey. Listen to me; I am not judging you, Barby. If you have sex with multiple partners, use a condom. Do not let strangers get your pants off, Barby." Brandy got the pills from a friend who worked at a drugstore. Barby had enough for six months.

Henry's aunt's house was an old Victorian with a large lot. Four large hardwood trees covered the property. A large stone fence ran along the front of the yard by the road—the home, while rundown, was still very appealing to the eye.

Henry was mowing his aunt's lawn when he saw a groovy-looking blonde sitting on the steps of the house next door, watching him. There was no fence between the two properties, and Henry noticed she looked lonely.

Henry waved hello after he finished mowing the front yard, and she waved back immediately. Then, he walked across the lawn where she sat and said, "Hello, my name is Henry."

She stood up and said, "Hello, Henry. My name is Jennifer. Jennifer Jenkins."

She was very tall and had a great figure. "Hi, Jennifer. These are big yards, aren't they?" he said as he wiped the sweat from his brow.

She smiled and said, "Yes, these are large lots, but they are so beautiful, don't you think?"

"Yes, I do," he replied.

"I can ask my sister if she wants her yard mowed if you want to make some more money," she said.

"Oh, I don't do this for the money," Henry chuckled.

"I'm sorry, I thought you were the hired man," she blushed.

"I was visiting my aunt and was bored," he smiled and poured on the charm.

She loved his blue eyes and long blonde hair but did not know him and would not let on that she found him attractive. "I'm visiting my older sister for a month. I am from Bremerton, Washington. Where do you live?"

Henry pointed east and said, "In a small village about sixty miles that way."

"I just graduated from high school. I have the summer off, then start college at San Diego State this fall," he said.

"I just graduated, too. I'm going to the University of Washington," she said.

Henry thought she was older than him. Jennifer was a tall blonde with long, slender legs. She was a few inches shorter than Henry. She had dark blue eyes and dressed modestly.

"I know what you mean about being bored. I haven't had one fun day yet, and this is my third week in Michigan." She complained.

Henry asked, "Why don't we go to the mall and see what's playing at the movies."

"Tell me you have a car," she asked, smiling from ear to ear.

"See the Belair?" he asked.

"That's my car," he said.

"Well, hello, Henry." She grabbed his hand and shook it excitedly.

They spent the day together, riding around in his car. They shared how college life would change their lives. Jennifer's father was a helicopter pilot. Her father died in Vietnam. Neither had a father, so they had that in a joint. Jennifer's mother was very well-to-do, though, unlike Henry's.

Jennifer bought Henry a new watch and a nice ring. He was reluctant to have a girl buy him things, but she insisted. Every time she bought him something, she broke a fifty-dollar bill. Henry thought the Kraneger's had money, but this girl made them seem like paupers.

They spent all their time together—except evenings. One day, while they were alone in the backyard, she asked, "Do you smoke, Henry?"

Henry shook his head no.

Jennifer asked, "Have you ever tried pot?"

Henry looked at her funny. "I have smoked a few joints," he replied.

"Would you like to try some?" She smiled with a naughty girl look on her face.

Henry asked, "Have you tried it?"

She said, "Yes!"

"I took a puff maybe twice but didn't seem to do anything," he remarked.

Jennifer said, "I have excellent Mexican marijuana. You probably had marijuana that thinned out with tobacco. The best way to find out is to try it for yourself." She had some in her purse but wanted to ensure he would be cool.

She moved closer to him and whispered, "Is there somewhere we can be alone, maybe in your aunt's house?"

His whole disposition changed. "Yes, we can go up in the attic. See the tower in the center? It is a room with windows that open wide. I like to read up there. Come on, I'll show you," he motioned for her to follow him.

When they arrived at the watchtower, he told her how his aunt's house's hidden room used to hide enslaved people during the underground railroad.

It was hot in the attic, so they opened several windows. She lit up a joint, took a big hit, and passed it to Henry.

Jennifer took long drags and then held her breath. He copied her, but he laughed at everything.

She kissed him tenderly. She moved away before he could put his arms around her. "That was far out," he said.

Henry leaned out the window and spread his arms wide, pretending to fly. A light wind seemed to carry him into the clouds. He got carried away with his goofiness.

He looked for her, but she was gone. He looked out the window. He saw her running across the lawn to her sister's.

The following day, Henry took a long hot bath. Afterward, he walked over to Jennifer's and knocked on her door.

He waited a long time, but she never came to the door. He figured she was not home and returned to his aunt's house and napped on the couch.

After about ten minutes, someone knocked at the door. When Henry opened the door, Jennifer was standing there smiling. "Can I come in?" she asked. Her beauty mesmerized Henry.

"Yes, please. I am sorry, Jennifer."

He looked lovely, and she wanted to hug him but fought the urge.

"You look like I woke you?" she asked.

"Yeah, I came over earlier, but I guess you weren't home."

"Can we spend the day together?" he asked.

"Yes, I would like that very much," she said.

"No one's home, so we have the house to ourselves. Would you like to play some cards?" He asked.

"Sure, have you ever played strip poker?" she asked.

"Strip poker?" Henry did not know what to say.

"Why, Henry, you're blushing. Haven't you ever played strip poker with a girl before?"

"No way. You don't cheat, do you?" he laughed.

"Yes, I do, but you can cheat too if you like," she said.

"Oh, I like to cheat; boy, do I like to cheat," he said.

She stepped up, touched his cheek, and kissed him lightly. "We can skip the card game if you like?" she asked.

Henry picked her up and cradled her in his arms. "I don't like to play games," he said. He carried her up the open staircase to his room and lowered her onto the bed.

"She wiped the sweat from his brow, "That was very romantic. What other surprises do you have in mind?" she asked.

He kissed her, and she rolled over on top of him. She loosened his shirt, pulled it over his head, and worked frantically to remove his pants.

He had her blouse off, and she pushed him back on the bed. "It's my turn first; lay still," she said.

She jumped up, removed her bra, pants, and panties all in one move, and jumped back on top of him. She leaned over and kissed him and then slid down to his crotch. She pulled down his shorts. "Henry, oh my goodness. Henry, you're more than a girl can take, honey," she whispered.

"Yeah, I'm sorry, Jennifer," he said.

"Boy, aren't we full of bologna? Henry, you are not more than any girl could take. My thoughts were not literal. I do like what I see, sweety," she giggled and tossed his shorts off.

"I like what I see, too, Jennifer."

"Do you want to fool around before we get serious?" she said.

"I need to come clean, Jennifer," he lamented.

"Henry, what's going on, honey?" she wondered.

"I've never done this before today," he surrendered.

Jennifer smiled brightly. "Henry, you haven't done anything yet."

"Yeah, I know, but I want to do something," he said.

"Just what do you want to do? I don't believe you're a virgin."

"Yeah. I'm sorry," Henry blushed.

"Henry, you're not telling the truth, huh?"

"Jennifer, this is embarrassing as hell."

"Do you want to stop Henry?"

"No, honey, but I don't want to lie to you," he admitted.

"Awe, honey, are you sure? You were excited about strip poker. I would love to teach you. Will you let me?" she stared into his eyes.

"You cannot tell anyone. I have a girlfriend. Maybe two girlfriends. In the same family. I think they both know about each other. Should I stop talking about other girls?" he asked.

"Yeah, I don't want to hear about your love life, even if it is not real."

"Oh, it's real, Jennifer."

"No, it's not real if you're telling me the truth, Henry.

"Oh, yeah. I get it now. I am telling you the truth, Jennifer! I have two girlfriends but have never done this with them."

"Henry, you talk too much," she said.

"Henry, what did you do? You ejaculated all over my belly."

Henry was embarrassed. "We need to get out of here. My mom will be home in a few minutes," he said.

"Henry, you did not last more than a few seconds. What the hell, baby? I got cum all over my belly. She began dressing; she smiled at him. She grinned, and then she laughed. Oh, Henry, do not get upset. However, this is funny, honey."

Henry did not want to talk. He tried to grin, but he was embarrassed.

He watched her put her clothes on, and she was stunning. "Did I do something wrong?"

"Sweetheart, we need to talk. I have never met a man like you, darling. The first thing is this, honey. You did not do anything wrong. You sure as heck surprised me, dear. You did prove something, though. Henry, you were a virgin for sure," she grinned.

"Why am I so tired? I did not do anything?" Henry said.

"I need to get home and take a shower. Then, take a bath and take a nap. Then, I will show you what to do so you do not wear out quickly. We have all week, sweety. You are a stud lover, boy.

She kissed him and left in a hurry.

She came back amazingly fast. "Honey, could we have breakfast together," she asked.

"I'd love to, and maybe we could spend all day together?" Henry asked.

She kissed him, opened his door, and hurried down the stairs.

The next day, after breakfast, they shared a bath. Then she crawled into his bed and taught him all the secrets of making love to a woman. He stumbled around at first but learned quickly. Later, he slept for two hours.

It was hot the next day, and thunderstorms moved in. It rained all evening. Late that night, he walked her home in the muggy rain. It was so warm it felt good to get wet.

"Henry, can we spend the night in the backyard together? Can you sneak out?"

"Yeah, I think I can. What time?" Henry asked.

"Twelve-thirty," she purred.

Henry spoke with his aunt and discovered she had an old tent in the garage. Henry informed his aunt that he loved sleeping in a tent in the rain. He received permission and set it up in the location Jennifer selected.

Jennifer found him asleep in the tent shortly after midnight. A warm, mild drizzle soaked everything. She disrobed and climbed into his sleeping bag.

"Henry, can we go out into the rain?"

"Jennifer, I like it right here, and I need to do a little better tonight."

"It smells in here. Besides, I want to do it in the rain. I have always wanted to do it in the rain. Please?"

They crawled out into the rain. Jennifer sprawled out on the wet grass where the lawn was thick and luxuriant.

They did not notice the lightning, the deluge, or the wind. Jennifer wrapped her legs around him. They were both naked on a dark lawn.

They went swimming the next day at a park downtown. Jennifer was an outstanding swimmer. She said she was on the swim team at her school. While resting beside the pool, she confided in him. "I'm glad I decided to have sex with you, Henry. You were amazing. I turned eighteen last week."

The following morning, Jennifer left for Washington.

Henry and his mother went home the next day. He knew his relationship with Barby could no longer remain platonic; Barby wanted assertiveness, and Henry would not ignore her needs.

CHAPTER 25

Aphrodite

Henry and the Kraneger's went to Ludington State Park on the 4th of July. Mr. Kraneger docked the ski boat at Hamlin Lake. Hamlin Lake was a large inland lake just inside the shoreline of Lake Michigan but at a higher elevation. Lake Hamlin was about the seventh lake in size that drained into Lake Michigan.

A bridge over the stream ran down from Hamlin Lake into Lake Michigan. The bridge was twenty-five feet above the water. Henry and Bobby jumped off the bridge into the swift stream. The narrow stream quickly pushed a swimmer out toward Lake Michigan. Even the most capable swimmer could find it difficult to crawl up the bank. The bank was never more than just a few strokes away, but it took a lot of strength to get out of the racing waterway.

All the kids were standing around watching, thinking Henry and Bobby were so brave, but it was nothing compared to thunder jumping. So, no one believed that story whenever Bobby and Henry discussed it.

Bobby and Henry were on the bridge, hanging their legs over the edge and talking. "I wonder if we can get Stretch to do this. What do you think, Henry?"

Henry thought for a moment. "I think she would, but I owe her one, and I may use this to my advantage somehow."

Bobby looked at the queer look on his friend's face; Bobby had not seen this one before. "What did she do now?" Bobby asked excitedly.

Henry smiled and thought about telling Bobby, but his male ego took hold, and he could not do that to himself. Bobby was a good friend, but he had a big mouth. Henry wanted this kind of thing to be private. "You don't want to know, trust me!"

"Barby would never do this, not in a million years," Bobby stated.

"I don't think Barby is the petite and dainty doll your family has her dressed up to be," Henry said in a severe tone.

"You have a thing for both of my sisters, don't you, Henry?"

"Bullshit, I do not have a thing for your older sister, Bobby. Brandy is much older than me, but she does not let that stop her from teasing me. She would take advantage of my innocence if she had the opportunity."

Bobby couldn't believe his ears, "Bullshit back to you, Rogue. You're not innocent, Henry!"

Henry smiled. "Hey, you know I haven't gotten laid yet. Besides, it would have to be her idea, not mine."

"Damn, you know what, Henry. Barby would never talk to you again if you let that happen. Do you think Brandy would do that, or is this another wet dream you fantasize about?"

Henry looked at Bobby and smiled. "Bobby, there are mysteries beyond your knowledge. Women like men with long hair, are well-dressed, have great hygiene, are muscular, quick-witted, smart, and have thick wallets. You, my good friend, could fulfill most of those seven items. However, throwing them all in a pot of accomplishment can become tough. Good luck, Rogue."

Bobby said, "You got that silly-ass, double-dimpled, dip-shit grin on your face again, Rogue."

The two young men returned to the camp. After dinner, they sat around the campfire, singing songs and telling stories until late in the evening; it was a magical time.

Later that night, at about midnight, everyone had gone to bed. Henry went across the street to the bathroom and took a long, hot shower. On his way back to his tent, someone called out his name from the bushes. He was initially uneasy, but then he realized only Brandy called him Hank. Then he saw her deep in the trees. She raised her hand and waved to him. Henry went through the bushes and around some trees where Brandy was, but she was not there when he arrived at that location.

He knew something was up then; she called his name again. She was just over the rise toward the water in the sand at the tree break. Henry kept his eye on her as he climbed the dune, walked over the logs, and climbed the steep wooded hill. He ducked under the thickets and veered around several trees, always keeping his eye on her. Then, finally, she disappeared over the rise as the dune fell sharply toward the water. There was only a quarter moon, and the night was dark this far from the camp. He noticed the pink blanket she had spread on the sand under a thicket of bushes as he approached her. The spot was uniquely secluded; it could not be seen from the top or bottom of the hill because it sat into the dune about the halfway point.

"Nice spot, Brandy."

The pink blanket glowed in the dim moonlight. "Hello, handsome Hank." she half-whispered in a silly, giddy way.

Henry asked her, "What's up, mysterious lady of the night, Brandy?"

"I wonder if I could top that euphemism or synonym?" she giggled.

"I like what I see, beautiful. You take my breath away, lady. There is not another woman on this planet that can compete with your beauty."

"Nice honey, but we need to talk, Hank."

"Cute, charming, and adorable," he said.

Brandy sat on the blanket, patted it with her hand, and said, "Sit down."

Henry sat next to her. "You look fabulous in the moonlight," he said.

She smiled, "Hank, my sweetheart, prince of castles, robber of hearts, the chateau of lovers, please join the lady of the night."

The moon shone on the lake, and the reflected light sparkled in her eyes as she leaned over and kissed him. Brandy's lips were wet, and she pushed her tongue into his mouth and caressed his. She tasted sensational, but he was not letting his guard down.

Brandy pushed him over and lay beside him. "Isn't this splendid? We have the surf crashing softly in the distance, an exciting college junior, and an excited high school senior." She slid over closer to him.

Henry reached over her shoulder and pulled her sleek, long, dark hair over his face. "This is nice," he said.

"Do you remember when we were in Traverse City last summer? I told you if you behave, you might get lucky," she said.

"Yeah, I haven't forgotten what happened," Henry said lugubriously. His heart started racing. What was she going to do? She had that same look in her eye.

She gave him a quick kiss. "Don't be like that; be yourself," she said seductively. "I have big plans for tonight." She put her hand on his cheek. "I want to teach you how a boy could make a girl feel like a woman. Do you remember asking me how it felt to make love?" She gently kissed his cheek.

Henry was dumbfounded and speechless and needed to pretend he was still a virgin.

She pressed up against him. He could smell her perfume and her hair.

"There, that's not so bad, is it?" she whispered. Brandy pushed her groin up against his.

Henry looked into her intriguing dark green eyes. "You are so beautiful," he mumbled deliriously.

Brandy smiled brightly. "Tonight, I'm going to be your Aphrodite." She whispered. She slid her finger down his cheek, onto his chest, down to his navel. She moved her finger in circles, and she kissed him gently.

Henry put his arm around her. He thought about Barby. He wanted to say something, but his virtue let him down. She pressed his free hand against her blouse. Henry squeezed gently; she was not wearing a bra, and he could feel her nipple, which felt uncomfortably hard.

She slid her hand down his trunks. Henry grabbed her wrist with his free hand. He pulled away from her kiss, looked into her eyes, and said, "Don't play with me, Brandy. I'm not the foolish kid I was last summer."

"I already told you I'm giving you something special; cool it and let go of my arm. Brandy kissed his bare chest.

Henry felt weak and nervous; Brandy nibbled on his nipples, and Henry felt uneasy.

She looked up at him. "Still a virgin?" she asked.

He nodded yes.

She kissed him again. "Lift your ass, Henry."

She pulled his swimming trunks off before he could put his hand in position to stop her.

She slid her shorts off, and then Brandy fell on his chest.

Brandy found his hands and held them firmly pinned to the ground above his head. She perched over him and wiggled. "Hank, oh my god, darling." She was a woman, and he was almost a man; indeed, she could handle him, but she was hesitant.

Henry tried to hang on to her hands to steady himself, but she had a firm grip on his wrists. He let her win over his senses. He recalled his first thunder jump at the Millpond, vertigo, and nervousness.

Henry submitted to her perceptive powers, and every second floundered on and off deliriously.

"Hank, you poor baby, this is too much for you. Maybe I should stop," she said playfully. She kissed him while he fell into never-never land.

Waves crashed on the shoreline, and a warm offshore breeze transported the humid air over their bodies. Brandy continued her sincere and passionate assault.

Henry fought off the urges and submitted to the woman he adored.

Brandy had a frantic, innocent, wanting look; Henry stared into her eyes; she captivated him with her body.

"You sure you were a virgin?" She whispered.

Henry nodded yes and remembered Jennifer.

The crashing waves obscured their moaning and taunting responses. Physical strength and fervent passion deprived them of their endurance.

Brandy frantically woke him when the eastern sky brightened. Then, finally, they returned to camp, showered, returned to their tents, and slept until mid-morning.

Henry took a long, hot shower. He turned the cold water off, allowing only the steamy water to blanch his body. His thoughts condemned his lack of virtue. However, his heart wrangled with a desire of immense proportions. He was both cheerful and depressed, emancipated and immure.

The significant abnormality had been erased twice and replaced with elucidation. The affair, however endearing, left Henry with despair and abject ambivalence. His love for Barby suffered a devastating setback. How could he ever look her in the eye? He could not tell her about the sexual events. Would Brandy keep her silence, or would she obdurately expose him for becoming such a lecherous scoundrel? The weakened remnant of virtuousness he held onto dissolved and compelled him to approach Barby on his knees and beg for forgiveness. Henry had to speak with Brandy beforehand. Indeed, he could appeal to her sense of sibling affection. He meant to confront Brandy immediately.

Later that day, they finally met alone in the water while bodysurfing. He looked into her eyes and tried to find the passion that was there the night before.

Brandy saw the lovesick look. She felt uncomfortable but did not want to hurt him. "How was your date last night?" she asked.

He wanted to say something important.

Henry grinned, and she saw him perk up a bit. "Hank, you made me sore."

He wanted to impress her with some witty, carefree, happy thoughts. But unfortunately, Henry could not formulate what he wanted to say or how he wanted to say it.

Then Brandy's facial expression changed. "We can never do that again, Hank!"

Henry could not believe it. He did not want to talk about that. "What about tonight? Just one more night?" He suddenly ached all over. Then he realized how bad his reaction had been.

Brandy kissed him quickly and said, "I'm too old for you, Hank. I am twenty-one; you are barely eighteen. We had some fun together, honey. Leave it at that. You'll make Barby incredibly happy, but she can never know about last night."

Henry pouted like a little boy. The emotional trauma he suffered earlier resurfaced. However, this time, it wore a different face. Why couldn't he feel elation and indifference? Brandy removed all his worries in one sentence. Why didn't he feel better? His ambivalence made him physically ill.

"Oh, and Hank, Barbara is much too young for what we did last night. Give her a few years, okay?"

"Sure," the word popped out of his mouth briskly. Brandy ducked under the water, and he supposed Brandy would reach out for him, but he did not feel her touch. He waited tensely, not knowing what to expect, but she was not there.

She came out of the water fifty feet away, swimming toward shore. He felt so empty and helpless.

Henry lay back, floating on the water, looking into the deep blue sky; he was alone with his thoughts again, struggling with his enlightened knowledge of the female species.

Brandy did not get pregnant. She was taking birth control pills, but Henry did not know.

For the next several weeks, Henry dreamed about the night he spent on the beach with Brandy. He did not go to bed thinking about it, but the dream ignited a burning deep in his loin every night.

CHAPTER 26

First Love

*H*enry and Barby drove to South Haven on a hot Saturday in mid-July. They parked the car in the municipal parking after unloading all their supplies for the weekend.

He walked with her together, down to the marina. Barby helped Henry store the goods and started the engine. Then, Barby left to make a phone call.

A soft, steady breeze was blowing off the lake. Ellen brought the boat up from the farm. Henry pulled in all the lines, and Barby motored down steam between the piers and out onto the lake. She set a course for due west and continued that heading. Henry removed the sail covers while she piloted the boat, and then he steered the Sailboat while she set the headsail.

The sun was hot, and Henry went below and peeled off all his clothes. Then, he made his entrance on deck.

"Henry, oh my god. People will see you. I see you. Henry!"

Henry took the wheel. "Aye, Captain. She feels fresh as a jolly Roger. Make yourself an indecent woman. Then we can sail on to eternity."

"I will do no such thing, you animal, you pirate." She giggled and watched him sway. "Henry, you're uncouth."

"Nobody can see us, can they?" He looked for other boats, but they were far away.

"We are not that far from shore, Henry."

"Do ye have the skull and crossbones so that we can fly our colors?"

She walked through the companion's way but kept one eye on him. "Are you sure you want to see me naked?" She giggled.

"I do not have time to look at you. I have a boat to care for, lady."

"Look, you are a low-ranking sailor. I'm the Skipper Henry and the Captain, too, buddy." She wiggled out of her clothes.

"Captain, she deserves all my attention. Skipper, can you raise the main? Your duties await you. Remember the halyards and sheets and mains and mizzens. Shiver me timbers, woman; the first mate requires instruction and training. Why do you dally, Captain?"

Barby stepped up through the companionway several minutes later with one hand between her legs and crossing an arm over her breasts. She looked over the water, and no other boat was in sight. The land was still visible, but they were way out on the lake. "Henry, you cannot look at me, and you must promise to be a gentleman."

"Aye, Captain, the first mate, will keep one eye on the horizon and the other on his vessel, but women of refinement will rule the neigh. The first mate is the progeny of one of the most feared Caribbean pirates, but alas, he has virtues and honor. He might also desperately need to find the love of an island maiden."

Barby dropped her hands, and Henry tried not to look, but she was gorgeous.

She slid next to him and covered his eyes with her hands. "You cannot look. If you look, you will want me, and you cannot have me yet."

"The first mate needs his vision to read navigational charts and the ship's compass."

She kissed him, and her hair blew over their faces. Henry took a rubber band out of his hair, pulled it into a ponytail, and fastened the rubber band in place.

Henry tried to lock the steering.

"What are you doing? She asked.

"I want to talk, Barby. Can you lock the steering wheel?"

"Yes, turn that knob clockwise."

Henry locked the wheel in place. "Will it sail with only the head sail?"

"Yes, now what do you want to talk about." She noticed his third leg was growing.

Henry was about to spill his guts. He wanted to make love to Barby, but he could not do it without telling her about his mistake with her sister. So, instead, he looked into her lovely brown eyes and got a lump in his throat.

Barby loved Henry; she wanted him to take her into his arms and never let her go.

The boat shifted, and she fell against him. When her breast touched his chest, he could no longer fight off the urge. He kissed her and wrapped himself around her in every way he could. Finally, he descended the ladder, and she followed and fell into his arms. He carried her to the V-Berth. She lay back on the bed and guided him into her arms.

She wrapped her legs around him with no reluctance. She was his woman, and such a glorious sensation flooded her senses.

Barby held on to his neck and enjoyed his intensity. "Oh Henry, my darling Henry!"

Henry kissed her for a long time. The boat rolled back and forth as he lost himself in her femininity.

"Earth to Henry. Wake up, silly boy. You slept for over an hour. Let's check the boat, honey," she giggled.

"I love you, Barby; I'm sorry," he whispered into her ear.

"Henry, look at me. I am not a doll. I am a woman. I wanted you as much as you wanted me. We made love, Henry. You and I, together, it was glorious for me."

When he saw the blood, he panicked. "Barby, what did I do to you?"

She sat up and wrapped herself around him. "Silly boy, a virgin always bleeds the first time. I bought an old sheet. We can get rid of this later. I'm fine, Henry." Secretly, she was worried that she might be pregnant. She had been on the pill for over six months but was still concerned.

They dropped the sail and bathed on deck. Then Henry and Barby jumped in the water and swam together.

Later, they put up all the sails and set a course off the wind. Then, finally, the boat heeled over and sped off into the setting sun.

This is called close-hauled; it's the closest point of sail to the wind. Henry, I want to stay out on the lake overnight. I want to sleep with you tonight. Can we? My parents will be furious, but this is our special occasion."

"We should call first Barby. It would not be fair for our parents to worry about us."

"I already did that, Henry." She blushed and bowed away from him.

"Oh, so now the truth comes out. Did you plan this whole thing? Barby! I have been beating myself over the head, making myself physically sick because I took advantage of you.

"Well, guess what, Don Juan. We have been a thing for many years. It is a beautiful morning, darling. The coffee is ready. Please get some for us?"

Two weeks later, the two lovers were out on Lake Michigan again. They sailed for four hours. Neither could quelch the happiness.

It was getting dark when he dropped anchor two miles north of Holland. They were two hundred feet off the coast in 35 feet of water close to Holland State Park.

They had a nice dinner and took a quick swim.

It was a warm night, but a steady breeze dried their naked bodies. She crawled into the V-birth first. She kissed him first.

They made love until after midnight. They slept all tangled up together. It was warm for a long time until Barby opened the forward hatch. Then, just before dawn, a quick-moving storm blew in and disturbed their sleep.

"Barby, wake up. The boat is bouncing all over the place."

She grabbed him and pulled his head down to hers. She kissed him.

"Barby, a storm is coming; I hear the thunder."

"No, make it go away. Henry, I'm ready for you, silly."

"Barby, can you hear the wind? It is going to rain soon. This storm could push us up onto the beach. What happened to the shoreline? We could have swum in last night."

"No, it won't. The weatherman said it was going to be a nice day. So, Henry, kiss me."

The waves grew to ten feet while they slept. Henry forgot all about the storm. A storm brewed outside, but a cyclone had struck below deck.

"Henry!" Barby yelled at him from the companionway.

Henry had fallen asleep. The boat flopped every which way. He sat up and realized he was still naked. He leaned over to step onto the floor and fell out of the berth. He landed squarely on his ass. He looked around sheepishly. She did not see the incident, and he was not hurt, so he jumped up quickly. He found his swimming trunks and sneakers.

Barby had the motor going and was steering the boat east. She could not see land and did not know how much they drifted overnight or which way. The waves were ten feet high every six seconds, and the boat had difficulty tracking east because the storm came out of the southwest. The wind was blowing from the lake to the shore.

Henry came up through the companionway. "What can I do?"

"Go down below and look under the cushions. There are hatches, and one will have the Yankee in it."

"What's a Yankee?" he asked.

"It's a storm sail. We need to get it up on the forestay."

"What's a forestay?"

"Go get it, silly, and I'll show you."

Henry came back with a light blue sail. "This is not noticeably big. What good can this do?"

"Take the wheel, Henry."

Barby took the storm sail and made her way up to the bow. Unfortunately, she forgot to retrieve the halyard from the mast and had to make a desperate lunge for it. The boat dropped suddenly, and she fell to the deck hard. Water splashed over her and made the deck slippery.

"Henry yelled for her."

She waved her hand, got up, and retrieved the halyard. She had to undo the line at the mast, then drop to the deck and crawl out to the forestay. She connected the halyard hanked on the Yankee and attached the foot of the sail to the bow pulpit. She crawled back to the mast and used the winch to raise the sail. The boat immediately steadied and quit bouncing around out of control.

"Hey, sweet Barby, you go, girl, way to go, Captain!" Henry yelled.

Barby made her way back to the cockpit. "What a difference, huh," she said.

"Barby, what happened to our anchor last night?" he asked.

"This is complicated. We had a nice leeward blow toward the beach when we turned in. Later in the night, the wind quit. Then, the wind began to go from the shore to the boat. The anchor line on a Leeward blow drag against a shallower shore the closer it gets to the beach. It would help if you had a heavy anchor to prevent the boat from reaching the beach. We did have a good anchor. The boat's anchor position was backward when the wind shifted to a windward blow. When the boat turned every few inches, it could pull the boat into deeper water. Eventually, the anchor could break free of the bottom, and here we go. The blow can carry us across the lake. You usually will only sleep that short. Skippers usually yell at one another, allowing everybody to reset their anchors in deeper water."

"I think I got it. Is that a fog bank toward the east?"

"Yeah, I am watching it, honey."

They kept on an easterly course for two hours.

"Barby, do you see what I see?"

She smiled and kissed him. "Yep, land ho." She yelled.

"Barby, I don't see a pier. Do you?"

"We're too far out, Henry. We need to get closer. Some binoculars are hanging above the sink. Better get them."

Henry began searching the coast but could not find a pier anywhere. Then, a violent lightning bolt struck the water about a mile away. The wind picked up, and the boat heeled over slightly.

"We need to get off the lake, Henry. What should we do?"

"Can we call for help?" he asked.

A boat came into view from the south.

"Henry, we've got flares down below. Take the wheel."

Barby came up with a flare gun, pointed it into the sky, and pulled the trigger. A bright orange trail lit the sky above them like a giant rainbow.

She took the wheel, and Henry identified the boat. "It's the Coast Guard Barby."

She smiled and touched his face. "Skippers take good care of her crew."

Henry waved to the Coast Guard Cutter when he could make out crewmen on the deck. The Cutter turned quickly and came alongside. A sailor with a bullhorn yelled instructions.

"Is your boat the Sparrow?" he asked.

Henry turned to Barby. "Is it?"

"Yes, that's the name of our boat, Henry."

"I didn't know. There isn't a name on it, is there?"

Barby pointed to the Cutter. "Talk to them, Henry."

"Yes, this is the sparrow," Henry yelled.

"Do you have a medical emergency?" The sailor asked.

"No, we are fine," Henry yelled.

"Is your boat in peril?"

"No, the boat's fine too. But we were lost."

"Are you wearing your life vest?"

"Yes, we have them on."

"Can you follow us into South Haven Harbor?"

"Yes," Henry yelled.

The Cutter turned away to the south, and Barby followed. When they reached the opening of the channel, the storm was raging. Lightning flashed all around them but did not hit the boat. The stiff wind subsided when they motored further up the track, but a cold gust popped up occasionally.

When they pulled into the marina, Mr. Kraneger and Henry's mother were waiting. They had spent the night in a nearby motel and were both incredibly happy. Of course, they wanted to stand firmly against their rebel son and daughter, but their joy ruled the day.

Henry loved Barby. He knew she was the real thing. But unfortunately, Brandy was just a mistake. He wondered if he could ever tell Barby.

Henry loved his mother, too. She was cool about everything, and Mr. Kraneger was not nearly as mad as Henry had imagined.

CHAPTER 27

"The Summer of Love"

In early August 1968, the Kranegers and Henry were off on another vacation. This time, they traveled in a large recreational vehicle. They left Michigan early on Sunday morning, headed toward Chicago.

They spent Monday at the Museum of Natural History. They did a lot of walking. Brandy was humorous, Barby was sexy, Bobby was hilarious, and Henry was constantly stuporous. His love for Barby dominated his waking hours, but he kept dreaming about Brandy. She did not help matters much. She took it upon herself to poke and rub against him at the most inopportune times.

Henry was not shaving, and his face became yellow from the thick stubble. It made him feel older and more mature.

On Tuesday, they went north into Wisconsin. They visited the Dells, a series of lakes with limestone cliffs and rocky-sided islands. They cruised in a rented boat all day and picnicked on a sandstone shelf twenty feet above the water. The sunny summer days were endless.

Early the following day, they went on the road again.

Thursday, they crossed the upper Mississippi and drove southwest across Iowa and parts of Nebraska. Friday, they went south into Kansas, then west again into Colorado. Mr. Kraneger stopped at the state line, and they camped on Friday night.

Saturday, Bobby drove into Denver. Everyone went to a real rodeo and ate huge beefsteaks. Mr. Kraneger bought some local beer called Coors in that part of the country; he let his children drink one, including Henry. Brandy smoked a lot of dope in college. She turned Barby on to marijuana. Barby loved getting high and sprang a joint on Henry during a private moment later that night at the campsite. Henry pretended not to know much about it. They got high together, and he wanted to make love to her, but she refused him.

It was tough for him to maintain his presence of mind. He wanted to make love to both Barby and Brandy, but he had to suppress his desires. Henry knew his innocence was on trial, but his virtue was illusive. He kept arguing with himself and wondered if he was going crazy.

Henry and Bobby slept in a tent. During the night, Brandy snuck over to Henry's bunk. He dreamed he felt her hands in his boxers. When he finally realized it was not a dream, he pulled her under him.

"You're in big trouble, lady."

Brandy asked him quietly, "I'll bet you don't have the nerve, fuzzy face."

Henry reached out for her, but she would not let him touch her. "Come closer, you trollop."

Brandy gave him her cat-like look. "Are you making my sister happy?"

Henry grinned and thought it was weird of her to bring up something so personal. "I don't know, Brandy. I don't know."

He turned away from her, and she kissed his neck and bit him lightly. Then, she walked out of the tent and closed the zipper. She snuck back to the RV and quietly climbed in next to Barby.

Monday, they left Denver and climbed into the mountains. It took all day to get to the top, a place called Vail. There was snow along the roadside—in July, no less.

Mrs. Kraneger had made reservations at a remote chateau; it was immense. The entry had ceilings fifty feet high, and everything was marble. They have three rooms:

- Bobby and Henry shared one.
- Brandy and Barby shared one.
- Mr. and Mrs. Kraneger were in the other.

After a nice dinner, they sat and talked about how they would spend the rest of the vacation.

Barby and Henry sat alone in the scenic overlook room. People came and went, but they kept their distance.

"Henry, are you having a good time?"

"Yes, I am Barby, but I wish we could be together."

"Little miracles amaze people every day, Ozaawindib." Barby smiled.

"You seem to enjoy my Chippewa name, Barby."

"I like everything about you, Henry."

"How do you feel about being so far apart?"

"Henry, please try to enjoy our time together. You seem so distant at times. What are you worried about, honey?"

"Silly things, maybe; I worry about Mom and you and me. I'm sorry I've turned into such a worrywart."

"Maybe you need to relax more, honey. But, Henry, my love for you is never going to waver. So please don't worry about me."

"This is nice, Barby. You make me happy, honey. Do you think the next four years will pass as fast as our high school years?"

"I hope not, Henry. I want to have some fun in college."

"Look at the time, Barby. We are getting up early. I'll walk you to your room, sweetheart."

"Will you kiss me goodnight, lover boy?"

They strolled to their room. Henry took her into his arms and kissed her goodnight.

Henry fiddled with the door key. Bobby opened it before the key worked. "Henry, why don't you shower first? I want to fill out some postcards. I will be gone for a while. Plus, I need to call Sherry."

When Henry got out of the shower, he went through his usual hygiene habits; fifteen minutes later, he went to his bed stark naked, and Bobby was still gone.

He flopped onto his bed and closed his eyes. A few minutes later, he heard the door open. He opened his eyes and found Barby staring at his exposure.

"Bobby is spending the night in Brandy's room. What do you think? Can you handle me, Hank?"

Henry smiled, jumped up, and stood erect; Barby was staring at him. He nervously looked down, and something was imitating his stance. "I didn't do that, Barby." It was not his intention to flaunt his lack of modesty. "Barby, could you turn your head or close your eyes?"

"Why should I?" she teased.

She called him Hank. Barby never called him Hank. He continued lamenting over whether she knew about Brandy. He quickly decided to play dumb.

"I hope you've been dreaming about, my dear?" she scolded seductively.

He stood dumbfounded until Barby turned on the radio, and "December 63," by the Four Seasons, was playing. Henry felt the song was appropriate for the occasion.

"Henry, you are naked; cover yourself. Don't you have any virtue?"

She quickly removed her robe and climbed under the covers. Henry slipped in next to her. Barby turned on a small black light on her bedside table just before Henry turned off his lamp. Her white nightgown glowed in the dark, along with her teeth and the whites of her eyes.

"Barby, you smell incredible." She came into his arms. "I'm wearing Brandy's perfume. Do you recognize it?" Again, he wondered.

"I thought I recognized it, but it smells wonderful on you."

"I thought you'd like it. Oh, by the way, do not worry; I am on the pill. Brandy got them for me, but Mom and Dad do not know."

He kissed her gently, and she wrapped her legs around his and pulled herself against him.

"I have wanted this to happen for a long time. But unfortunately, it has been too long since you made me a woman's fuzzy face."

"Why did you call me fuzzy face?" he lamented.

"I heard Brandy call you fuzzy face the other night."

Henry worried about what else she heard. He capriciously agonized about what she would say next and braced himself for the emotional damage he sensed would follow.

"Henry, have you been intimate with anyone else?"

"Well, there was this one girl." Henry talked without thinking and was highly uncomfortable.

"Who, Henry?" she asked wildly.

Oops, he blew it. "The woman was much older than me. It was a long time ago."

"When Henry? I have known you all my life. Where is Henry? Do I know her?" Barby knew Henry; he was about to confess his secret liaison with a girl he was inventing. She would have to act upset at first, and she may cry a little, but when he begged for forgiveness, she would accept his apology, but only with suffering and much remorse. He was taking too long, though, and she was getting impatient. Finally, Barby grabbed his face with both of her hands.

"Henry, who did you screw?"

Henry quickly ignored that one and decided to pull a Tennessee two-step. He would tell the truth but not about Brandy. He could tell the truth to avoid a lie.

"It happened while I was in Kalamazoo. She was from Washington State; you do not know her. She got me high on marijuana, and then she seduced me."

Barby was furious. She never thought Henry would stoop so low. He was lying to her.

"She was about twenty-six; I didn't even get her name. I was going to tell you I am sorry and do not love her. I'm not even writing to her; I love you, Barby." Henry hoped she would remain disconnected from Brandy.

"Is this what you'll do if we get married?" she complained. "You cannot jump any strange girl you want." Barby wanted to make him squirm.

"I know I shouldn't have done it. The lady told me she could teach me how to make love to a woman. I fell for her trap, but she taught me a lot, Barby. That's the only reason I went along with her."

She started to calm down a bit. "So, you did it for me, fuzzy face?"

Henry nodded.

She kissed him quickly. "Henry, you better never push this on me again. Instead, I will show you how to fulfill my sexual needs. Do you understand me, Henry Rotyn?

Henry stood still and hung his head.

"Who else have you been fucking?" she asked rudely.

Henry thought about Brandy but was afraid to come clean. Finally, he decided a lie was better than the truth this time. "Yes, there have been many, too many. I do not remember them all."

Her blood began to boil, "You liar!"

Henry loved Barby, and his love for her conquered his apprehensive attitude.

"Barby, I'm not from an affluent family like you. I sometimes wonder if you care for me. Sometimes, you are considerate and kind because you feel sorry for me. Are you going to California to get away from me? I want you to love me, but sometimes I get these feelings. Please understand, though, that I live for your love. I am apprehensive because I'm afraid of losing you."

Barby stared into his eyes, and her anxiety melted. Passionate, pent-up hours of longing and desire burst into a fiery lust. "Henry, I have never felt that way about you. I love you because you have beautiful hair and are bright, witty, handsome, polite, loving, loyal, and cute. You are a wonderful person. I love you, Henry, and I don't care how much money you have."

Barby remembered the conversation she had had with her older sister. When Henry shared his most intimate feelings, the truth came out. He was not from an affluent family. He may never have the kind of money Barby enjoys. Cash is essential; was Brandy correct in assessing his motives?

Henry stretched his finger out and flipped her bottom lip down. "Flip a lip."

She smiled and fell into his arms. Barby pouted.

"I'll be a gentleman, pretty girl."

She kissed him. He was very tender, and she kissed him for a long time. Barby slid her hand down over him. She poked, pushed, petted, and stroked.

"I want to look at it," she stated boldly, pointing her face to his.

Henry laughed sarcastically. "You have seen it before," he said.

"I want to see it up close," she whined.

"Why?" Henry figured he had a good enough reason to feel apprehensive, given his history with Brandy and Barby.

"It's bigger, too big. It's huge." She pulled the sheet off him. She stared at it up close. She pushed it over, and it snapped back. "What do you call it?" she asked.

"Silly girl, I don't call it anything," he said and laughed.

"You have to give it a name. Every boy has a name for his penis, don't they?"

"I don't go around asking my friends what the name of their dick is, silly." Henry was hysterical.

"We have to give it a name," she laughed.

"Barby, you're so bad!" He could barely get the words out because of his giggle.

Barby stared while she poked at it. "It has an eye; that's where the expression cockeyed comes from.

Henry could not talk; he tried not to laugh and pushed at her shoulder.

"Can we call it Cyclops Henry? It has only one eye, and it's big and mean-looking."

She looked into his eyes imploringly. "Cyclops is bigger now." Her voice was teasing and sensual.

Henry slid up on top of her. He came up to her and kissed her.

Henry was her most kindred spirit. Her love for him had never been stronger.

She put her hands on his cheeks and kissed him. "You're making me feel so marvelous; why have we waited so long? I love you, Henry."

They kissed again. Henry was feeling very guilty. He loved Barby, but he had not been faithful. "I love you so much, Barby."

"Be quiet, silly boy. Quit teasing me, Ozaawindib."

They made love until the wee hours of the morning. Sleep won the night.

She woke him around four, and they climbed out of bed and bathed together.

Barby told him, "The story about the girl from Washington was cute." She studied his face to judge his reaction.

Henry played dumb again and forced his most demure expression.

Later, he held her naked body against him in bed and asked, "Do you still love me, Barby?"

She smiled and kissed his dimples. "Get some rest, Ozaawindib."

Barby leaned her head on his shoulder and stared at his face until he fell asleep.

She returned to her room, but Bobby would not wake up.

Barby crawled into bed with Brandy. Brandy smiled at her. Barby turned over with her back against Brandy's tummy.

Brandy put her arm around her little sister, kissed her cheek, and stroked her hair gently. "I love you, Barby."

Barby reached back and touched her sister's hand tenderly.

Brandy whispered, "Barby, is he wonderful or what?"

Barby spun over and faced her sister. An unimaginable, powerful emotion struck her. She began crying softly and mumbled almost incoherently, "I love him, Brandy. I love Henry. Brandy, I love him. Why can't I be with Henry?" Barby wanted to be with Henry now, tonight, tomorrow, and forever.

Brandy held her sister tenderly while Barby cried herself to sleep.

In the morning, Mrs. Kraneger wanted to know why Bobby slept with the girls, and he told her Henry suffered from flatulence. When Henry discovered what Bobby told his mother, he wondered how even his best friend could smear his name. It seemed only fitting.

Henry loved Barby, but he did not feel good about it. Now he had two women in his life he should marry. His heart desired something he knew was impossible.

They crossed the Rocky Mountains and drove across Utah into Nevada, pressing on late into the night until they reached Las Vegas. The glitter, glamour, and lights lit up everything around them. They decided to gamble just fifty dollars each and win what they could.

When they saw Elvis perform live, Henry thought Mrs. Kraneger would lose it; she went nuts over the guy. Mr. and Mrs. Kraneger rented a hotel room that night instead of staying in the RV. Mr. Kraneger was going to get a workout. Mrs. Kraneger was all over Mr. Kraneger and completely ignored her children. It could have been more comfortable.

Barby and Henry slept at one end of the RV. Brandy slept on a couch. Bobby slept on the other couch. Barby wanted to sleep with Henry, but her menstrual cycle had begun. No sex or necking; she needed to sleep in his arms.

On the way to San Diego, Henry and Barby told their parents they would get married after college.

The following day, they went to San Diego. That evening, they saw the sunset over the Pacific Ocean.

The RV Park they found overlooking the ocean. The village was called La Jolla. The sea looked just like Lake Michigan, except the water was salty, the waves were further apart, and kelp and jellyfish.

The ocean was majestic, and Barby loved the sunsets. At Sea World, they saw a man ride a killer whale, sea lion shows, dolphins, and fun rides. It was a long day; they only left the Park once it closed.

One night, they crossed the border and had a late dinner at a Mexican restaurant on an open veranda, where they danced and listened to a mariachi band on the south side of Tijuana.

The San Diego Zoo was the largest in America. It took them four days to see everything.

They spent several days on the Beach. Brandy, Barby, Bobby, and Henry had a blast. The surf was up one day, and they bodysurfed on five to eight-foot waves.

Brandy spoke with Henry while they were in the water. "I want us to spend the night together. I have a natural obsession with you. We must work something out, or I will tell Barby everything." Henry smiled and held up the peace symbol.

On the last day in San Diego, they visited the Scripps Institute of Oceanography and toured the World-Renowned Aquarium.

They were supposed to leave for Disneyland the following day, but Mr. Kraneger called his business every Monday. He learned his business manager had a massive heart attack and died. Mr. and Mrs. Kraneger booked a flight to Michigan. They thought it was best if Barby went with them. Barby was angry. She told them she wanted to go to Disneyland too. Barby got on the plane, but she was furious.

Bobby, Brandy, and Henry drove the RV. Brandy was to call home to call Michigan every night.

Bobby needed to learn about the relationship between Brandy and Henry. Henry worried about Brandy. If Bobby found out, he was confident there would be hell to pay. So, Brandy and Henry cooled it for a while.

They took the northern route up to San Francisco. They were not supposed to be in San Francisco, but Brandy threw a fit one night on the trip north. She called her parents and told them she had forced Bobby and Henry into the San Francisco trip. She insisted that she have this last fling before going back to Michigan. Her parents gave in. Bobby and Henry followed her wishes, secretly hoping she could pull it off.

Henry and Brandy blended in with the anti-war crowd in the city. Bobby's short hair put him at odds. Nevertheless, he remained close to the RV.

Henry and Brandy went to a sit-in with many hippies at Haight-Ashbury. It was groovy, far out, hip, cool, psychedelic, and dangerous, but everyone smoked pot in the open. The cops circled the sit-in with loudspeakers threatening to break up the so-called illegal assembly. Some people threw trash and rocks at the peaceful demonstrators.

Henry and Brandy dressed alike. They wore paisley shirts and blue jeans. They wore leather thongs and leather bandanas. They bought two prominent peace symbols hung from their necks, love beads, and pieces of seashell. Brandy wore a pink carnation in her hair, and Henry wore a blue one. They wore matching sunglasses that were very dark. Henry still had not shaved and was sporting a nice beard.

Bobby noticed Brandy hung all over Henry. He practically carried her everywhere they went. Finally, they sat in the crowd, holding up the peace symbol. Brandy kissed him passionately, and they shared huge joints with other hippies in between kisses. Several pipes of hashish were being circulated through the crowd, too.

They heard about a free concert in Golden Gate Park later that night. Brandy wanted to go. So did Henry, but he did not get all excited like Brandy.

Bobby met a young hippie; her name was Penelope. She wore leather pants and a leather vest. She had a brutal and petite figure, and Bobby forgot all about Sherry. Instead, he asked Brandy and Henry to let him have the RV alone. After some mild teasing, Bobby told them to set the tent up in the Park. After a reflective protest, they agreed.

At the free concert, the Four Seasons sang "December 63." The standing-room-only crowd sang along, arm-in-arm, swaying back and forth.

Later, while walking through Golden Gate Park, Henry and Brandy sang, "Late December 1963, what a lady when she came to me, what a lady what a night."

At twilight, they found a secluded spot in Golden Gate Park, where they set up the tent. Brandy made a bed out of sleeping bags.

The Park was full of hippies setting up make-shift accommodations. There was a community bonfire nearby. They went over and sat with the other long-haired, peace-loving flower children.

Brandy had saved a special bottle of blackberry brandy, and Henry helped her drink every drop. Then, they lit some joints and tripped out on the blazing fire.

Later, they staggered back to their tent. Henry opened the flap that allowed them to see the stars. He also needed some fresh air.

He stumbled around while she stripped him. "Henry, I want Ozaawindib to go on the warpath and conquer this maiden. I want to spend the night in your arms," she said.

They drove into the sleeping bags and removed all their clothes. Henry kissed her incredible thighs until she could take no more.

Brandy tried to make him forget about Barby. Her gracefulness and sleek, silky touch put him into orbit. Henry noticed the tent was spinning in circles. Brandy continued her assault while poor, helpless Henry submitted to her needs.

He lost all sense of time while he tripped out on her love. The spirit of the night dwindled as two hearts became one. The summer of love psyche engendered a cherished time. They both interpreted their emotions with a yearning passion. Their relationship struggled for freedom to mature, but their love for Barby made them afraid to be free. They slept soundly, cuddled in a maze of appendages.

The summer of love occurred in 1967. The lovers tried to copy the summer of love in 1968. On a late July night, Brandy and Henry became more than lovers: they fell deeply in love with one another, though she would not admit it to herself or him, nor would he.

Henry suffered in his dreams. His love for Brandy gnawed at his virtuous ideals. He knew he could never live without Barby, but now he could also not without Brandy. His ambivalence made him physically sick at times, and he hated himself, but then his love for Brandy and Barby made him incredibly happy. He had no clear way to solve his problem but reasoned it was free love. Everyone talked about free love all the time. He smiled and realized he was living the life all the hippies promoted. He adopted a peaceful feeling, and his nerves calmed day by day. He was a sixties man and fulfilled his end of the bargain. The summer of love was real, and he was living it up.

Penelope ran away from home to escape an abusive stepfather. He had raped her ever since she was fourteen. Bobby talked her into going home and confronting her mother. Penelope lived in Chicago before she ran away. Penelope wanted to get back at her stepfather but was afraid of him. Bobby told her she needed to overcome her fears and report the jerk to the authorities. She agreed after many tears and supportive encouragement from Bobby and Brandy.

Later, they drove across the Golden Gate Bridge, turned around at the scenic Park, returned through San Francisco, and crossed the Bay Bridge. Finally, they moved to Berkeley, where Penelope had stayed. They picked up some of her things. They left and made it to Reno the first night; Bobby and Penelope were in the rear, and they shook the RV. It made Brandy mad. Henry did not know why she was furious; he thought it was neat. Brandy came and slept in Henry's bunk since it was toward the front end of the RV.

Bobby woke Henry at six in the morning. He spoke softly. "Henry, what's up with you and Stretch?" Bobby pointed to Brandy. Henry was on his right side, but her right arm poked out from under his chin. Brandy was still sleeping and had her right leg stuck between Henry's.

"Gee, I guess she must have gotten cold during the night, Bobby. She has her clothes on, though." Henry noticed her bra lying on the table and hoped Bobby did not see it.

"Damn, man, are you taking on both of my sisters, Rogue? That is not right, Henry."

Brandy was listening quietly, and she had had enough. "What was all the noise about last night, Pudge? Do you think we cannot hear or feel the blasted RV shake? You listen to me, you oversized walking refrigerator. Do not ever accuse Henry of being immodest. I was trying to get away from your nasty sex. Henry let me sleep here, and he kept me warm. Another thing, he did not grope me or act indecently in any way. So back off, Pudge. Back the hell off."

The next night, they stopped at Salt Lake City. Brandy and Henry did not behave themselves. While Bobby rocked the RV from one end, Henry and Brandy rocked it from the other.

In the morning, Bobby found them together again. He sat looking at them as they slept. Their clothes were strewn all over the RV as if they had thrown them about on purpose. His sister was in his best friend's arms, tangled in knots. They covered up with a sheet, but Henry's bare ass hung out on the far side.

Bobby got up and started the RV. He rolled it out of the Park and snaked out onto Interstate 80. He looked back, and they had not budged.

Penelope staggered up through the maze of clothing. "Far out, Bobby. It looks like your sister had some fun last night." He gave her a dirty look. "Chill out, Bobby. I think it is cool. I wonder what time they got to sleep."

"Hank, wake up. We're moving," Brandy said.

Penelope caught Brandy's eye and showed the peace symbol. Brandy flipped Penelope the finger. She turned her head away, and Henry pulled her into his embrace. Penelope could hear them whispering but could not understand what they were saying. Brandy's arm came out of the tangled mess, and her fingers formed the peace symbol. Penelope smiled and returned the signal.

"Bobby, they are awake," she said.

He looked back and could see movement but did not say a word. The two bodies wrapped in one sheet struggled to retrieve the articles of apparel strewn about the shifting RV. They disappeared into the rear bedroom and closed the door behind them; over an hour elapsed before anyone came out of the bedroom. Bobby pulled into a truck stop when the two emerged.

After refueling, the two couples enjoyed a quiet breakfast together. Bobby looked at his sister.

She smiled with a slightly embarrassed look on her face. "I love you, Bobby. You may have wondered about that over the years, but I love you. I hate how tall you are now, but I still love you. I love Hank, too, Bobby. I have loved him for a long time." She looked at Henry. "I don't know if he's aware just how much I love him." She reached out and touched Henry's face.

Bobby filled his face with food and chewed while staring at his sister and best friend. He took a big swig of coffee, cleared his throat, and said, "So, Henry, what the hell are you up to?"

Henry did not say anything. Instead, he looked at his friend and put his arm around Brandy. "You can't possibly be any more confused than I am, Bobby. Yes, I am sleeping with both of your sisters. Yes, I am in love with both of your sisters. I'll marry one, but I don't know which one."

In a more civil tone, Bobby asked, "Does Barby know about you two?"

Brandy was about to spill the beans when Henry cut her off.

"No, Bobby. But I'm going to tell her when we get back."

Brandy put her hand over Henry's mouth. She looked at her brother, half pleading but primarily bewildered. "Bobby, we need to maintain some civility. There is another matter of great importance. Do you remember the Four Seasons song you like so well?"

Bobby realized what she was getting at. Sherry, so now it was time for a bit of blackmail. "Yeah, sure. 'December 63?'" he asked.

Brandy smiled at her brother. "Yes, silly, that is the one." She had his attention and was very sincere. "Sometimes we get carried away with life, and things get a little crazy. Give us some time, Bobby; we can sort things out and devise a solution we can all live with amicably." Brandy gave her sibling an undeserved smile.

During the rest of the meal, Brandy conversed with her brother and Penelope and tried to get on his good side. "You two were having a good time last night. But, of course, Henry was getting his kicks out of listening to you. He had been behaving until she started ripping his clothes off. Well, I guess you saw the results."

"We need to drive all night to get home on time. How about Penelope and I drive until dark? Then you two can drive tonight?" Bobby watched for Henry and Brandy's reactions.

Henry said, "Sure, but we need to get some sleep." He looked at Brandy to get her opinion.

Brandy said, "Bobby, can we have some privacy while you two drive today? I mean, we need to get some sack time in. We'll drive tonight, but we need some sleep, if you know what I mean."

Bobby looked at Henry, "You shithead, you think I am going to drive down the highway while you're throwing the bone at my sister."

Henry smiled at him, and Bobby could not keep a straight face. Henry smiled at his best friend and added, "Keep her between the ditches, and I'll keep it in my britches."

Everyone laughed.

Brandy whispered to Henry, "Not if I have anything to say about it."

Bobby did not know what to think; he was no longer mad, but he told Henry privately he had to make up his mind; he could not have his sisters. He did not care, but he supposed a brother should say something in a situation like that.

Bobby drove during the day; Henry and Brandy drove during the night. The RV rocked its way through Wyoming and Nebraska.

When they stopped for a meal in Iowa, Penelope called her mother and informed her of the incidents. Penelope's stepfather still lived in the house. Penelope's mother had almost given up on her daughter. When she learned about the allegations, she confronted her husband. Then she turned him into the authorities. The next day, around dusk, Bobby dropped Penelope off on the near north side. Penelope said she was only a few blocks from her house and did not want Bobby involved in the mess she was about to create. A tearful departure ensued, and Bobby begged her to let them meet her mother, but Penelope stood fast on the issue.

When Penelope arrived home, her mother, brother, and many other family members welcomed her home in a very emotional celebration. Her stepfather was in jail. He made a full confession about the abuse. Penelope was not going to have to testify. She was so delighted.

Several months later, Bobby received a letter from Penelope saying she was pregnant with his baby. Bobby showed the letter to his father, and they went to Chicago the next day.

Mr. Kraneger set up a meeting with Penelope's mother. He said he would instead work out a settlement without involving Bobby as the father. Penelope's mother was so happy to have her daughter back she was glad to work out a compromise.

Mr. Kraneger arranged to pay for all of Penelope's medical expenses. He set up an account for her to draw from to finish high school and attend a good university. He insisted on having visitation rights for himself and Bobby. Bobby saw his father in a new light. He became closer to his father as a result. Mrs. Kraneger would never learn of the secret grandchild.

CHAPTER 28

Brandy's Parting Gift

When he got up Sunday morning, Brandy was sleeping on the couch. Henry showered, but before he finished, Brandy joined him.

"Move over, Hank. I hope you're feeling frisky," she said.

"Brandy, I hope you locked the front door?" he asked.

"Front door and back door. I turned the lights off everywhere and left a note saying you were with your mom. You are mine for the day, buddy." She gave him a cat-like look.

Brandy helped Henry dry off. Then she shaved him and combed his hair. He brushed her hair, and then he went into his bedroom. She came in a few moments later, wearing a towel. He was in bed, covered by a sheet. She dropped her towel and slid in next to him.

Brandy slithered over him and kissed him hungrily. "Hello, my tender lover. Should I say hello, Ozaawindib? I want you to relax and take this like a grown-up."

She brushed his hair off his face and kissed him. "We need to talk, sugar. Am I making you uncomfortable?"

He looked up at her, smiled, and shook his head no.

"Hank, I'm going to marry a boy from college." She moved but watched for his reaction. "You and I had a good thing going, sugar. Hey, we can still spend time together. We will need to be discreet."

Henry wanted to tell her not to do this. Her words hurt so much. She saw the look on his face and knew what he was thinking. "I know Hank, but we never really had a chance. I mean, really. I'll always love you."

Brandy started to cry. She buried her head into his shoulder. "I love you, Hank. I love you so much, but this idea would never work. It is better this way."

She was in love with him, and he liked that a lot. Henry wrapped his arms around her and pulled her closer while he slid back and forth over her breasts.

They took another shower together, but his mother arrived before they got out. Henry heard her come in the front door. He warned

Brandy. She dressed quickly and threw a towel over her head. Henry greeted his mother and helped her bring her luggage from the car.

Jessica went into the bathroom as soon as she got home. Brandy was in Henry's room hiding and came out on the run. She got as far as the front door when Henry's mom saw her. Brandy felt awkward. She pretended to have just arrived, but Jessica looked at her suspiciously and went into her room without saying anything.

Jessica made chicken and dumplings for Henry. Brandy stayed long enough to feed him. After Brandy left, Jessica talked with her son. "Is there anything going on between you and Brandy that I should know about?"

Henry looked at her funny; she seemed to accept that as his answer. He had had enough emotional trauma for one day, and he was hoping to avoid any more.

Brandy married Doctor Quinn.

CHAPTER 29

Henry's Ambivalence

In time, Henry settled in and concentrated on his classes. Then, finally, his uncle offered him a part-time job in the refrigeration and air conditioning business. He changed air filters, washed condensers, checked temperatures, and replaced worn-out electrical parts. He liked the work, and the money was very nice too.

In early February, Henry received an airline ticket to go to Atlanta. Brandy talked her dad into a short family reunion. Barby, Bobby, Sherry, Brandy, Henry, Jessica, and Mr. and Mrs. Kraneger would spend a week together in Florida. Everyone would meet in St. Petersburg.

Henry ran two miles on the beach every day. Surfers often yelled at him to give up running and get wet. "Where is your board, dude?" They waved at him and cried. "Hey, Yellow Hair! Any guy with hair like yours has to learn to be a surfer."

The surfer's learned Henry was going to Florida. "Hey man, a Californian wouldn't be caught dead on a Florida beach if he couldn't surf."

The surfing school began with quick lessons. They called Henry a Kook until he learned to surf. He began to learn on an eight-foot board. He started on small waves first. Then, he learned to stand on the giant board on small waves. Then he tried some two-footers standing. Then he took on the five-foot waves, but he crashed every time. Eventually, he rode one to the beach.

A friend gave him a shortboard. After that, he became a good surfer because his friends were excellent surfers.

His hair was too long, so one of his female classmates trimmed it for him. But unfortunately, it was still way past his shoulders.

His grades were good. Winter in Coronado was mild. It was the first time he experienced winter with no snow. One weekend, his uncle Fred took Henry into the mountains and found snow at about 5000 feet. It made Henry homesick for about two or three days.

On March thirtieth, Henry flew from San Diego to LA. He looked around for Barby at his arrival gate. She was sitting next to a young man who looked like he was still in high school. Barby was reading a book but did not notice Henry. Henry could sneak up behind her on the opposing seat without giving himself away. A very nice-looking woman looked up at him and moved a few of her things to make more room for Henry before he sat down. She was reading the Chicago Tribune. The lady dressed like upper management.

"Thank you very much." He told the lovely lady and smiled.

Barby still did not notice him.

"Do you live in Chicago?" The question took the woman by surprise. She put down the newspaper. She must have realized he was trying to be friendly without coming on to her. She seemed to drop her business-like disposition. She responded politely.

"No, I live here in LA. I'm a college student at UCLA."

Henry could not believe Barby; she had her nose stuck in her book.

"This is my girlfriend, but I don't think she knows I'm here." Henry pointed at Barby.

"Very pretty, but it seems as though she may be preoccupied. Can I buy you a drink when we board? Oh, where are you going to school?" she asked.

Henry said. "San Diego State."

"Are you a surfer?" she asked.

"Yeah, but how did you know?"

"I saw you pushing your board on the baggage cart."

"She is my girlfriend, no kidding." Henry tapped Barby's shoulder. She turned and looked at him with no expression.

"Henry? When did you arrive? I am sorry, darling, but I was distracted by this book. I have been waiting forever. She climbed up on her knees and leaned over. "Kiss me now. I can't wait another minute."

Barby wore a hot pink top with white jeans. She was wearing perfume her mom had ordered for her from France. Barby removed her bra and stuffed it down his shirt. Henry glanced down at her blouse, and it drove Henry crazy.

Barby knew it, too, as she cooed into his ear, "Silly boy."

They boarded the plane and clung to each other. Barby kept kissing him, stopping the flow of passengers trying to get to their seats. She pretended to touch his crotch accidentally. Each time she made contact, she let out a little squeal. Henry thought he was going to go blind from desire.

Barby had her hair done up in a honey bun and looked lovely. Barby and Henry were very intimate on the plane. The stewardess threatened to sit between them. As a result, many passengers thought they were newlyweds coming home from a honeymoon.

Henry's mother met them at the Atlanta airport. They found the rental agency and drove to central Florida. They talked about all the things they needed to catch up on.

Saturday night, they checked into the hotel. It was nice and modern, but it needed the Hotel Del Coronado's luxury and charm.

Brandy's flight was not due until the next day, so Barby had Henry all to herself. But she still needed to sneak into his room. So, long after midnight, Barby knocked at his door. She kissed Henry as they stumbled across the room. When they finally separated, she whispered, "Hello, Silly boy. I hope Ozaawindib is energetic and horny."

Barby took her time, and Henry watched her undress from the bed. "I like your hair like that, Barby. It makes you look taller and thinner."

She stared at him, wondering if he knew what he had said. "So, you think I'm fat?" She raised her eyebrows and put her hands on her hips, waiting for his response. She had yet to remove her slip and was going to unless he had some excellent explanation.

Henry did not understand why she was so pissed off. All he said was she looked taller and thinner. "Oh, no, I didn't mean it that way. I do not think you are fat. I think your hair makes you look more like Brandy's physique. You know what I mean, don't you?"

"No! I do not have any idea. Do you think I'm fat, Henry?" She was mad now and wanted to hear the truth.

"Barby, you're petite, not fat. If a petite person looks taller, then she looks taller. She's still petite, but she looks taller and thinner." He knew he was in trouble now. "I'm talking too much, huh."

"Do you like it that I look more like my sister?"

"Honey, look, I'm sorry. I should not have made that comment. I hurt your feelings, and I am sorry. I'm guilty here, and I can say nothing to fix this."

"I'm not trying to look like my sister. If that turns you on, though, I need help. Does it turn you on?"

"You turn me on. I do not care how you wear your hair. You turn me on, sweetie, with your cute buns and your unbelievable cleavage."

Henry climbed out of bed while he talked. "You have legs to die for, lady. Your nose smiles, and you have the perfect philtrum I have ever seen." He waited for the question he knew would come.

She smiled and began laughing. "What in the hell is a philtrum?"

Henry guided her into his arms, but she was still tense. "I would like to show you where it is on your body if you permit me."

"Where is it?"

Henry kissed her upper lip and then sucked on it. Then he flittered his tongue above her lip. "It is right there. It is that little valley under your nose. Your philtrum is beautiful."

"It's not fat?"

"Oh, no. There is not a speck of fat on you, pretty girl."

"Do you want to make love to me?" she asked coyly.

"Oh yeah. I wanted to make love to you on the plane."

"Well, we could try, but you don't have to if I'm too fat."

Later in bed, she sat in his lap, fully connected; she purred in his ear.

"Tell Cyclops to stand up and take it like a grown-up."

Barby was horny. So was Henry.

Henry and Barby were supposed to meet the family for breakfast at nine. Everyone was looking for Barby because she was not in her room. She finally made her entrance at nine-thirty. Henry discreetly arrived at nine forty-five.

Brandy arrived minutes earlier, and everyone was still buzzing about seeing her.

Barby sat on one side of Henry; Brandy sat on the other. Quinn sat beside Bobby at the far end of the table. Henry did not know the guy that sat next to Bobby. He thought he was Bobby's friend from college.

Henry and Barby looked very tired. Henry drank a lot of coffee; he needed to be in command of his senses. During the meal, Barby identified the stranger when she kicked Henry and addressed Quinn. "This is Henry; we grew up together in Michigan." Her voice was terse and nervous.

"No, but I believe you must be Henry. You do have unbelievable hair. I understand you are attending San Diego State. How's your golf game, Henry?"

Henry immediately hated the jerk. "I do not play much. I like the game, but it takes a lot of money to be good." Henry said.

"You need to join a Country Club. Think of it as an investment. Brandy and I are members of a prestigious club on Perry Winkle Point, north of Boston. We could play a few rounds if you ever get out of our way. Brandy talks about you all the time."

Bobby stood up and held his drink up high. "Here's a toast to the Maize and Blue."

Everybody stood but Quinn.

"I understand they have a new coach with a difficult name to pronounce, and he was a coach at Ohio State. How is the University of Michigan going to make that work?"

"Quinn, come on, man. I play for the coach with the difficult name to pronounce." Bobby said.

Brandy remained standing. "Do you have to be an ass, Quinn? Bobby, ignore Quinn. I hope you kick the ever-loving Maize and Blue out of Ohio State, Bobby!"

After they ate, Henry reluctantly shook his hand, but Quinn would not have survived if looks could kill.

The family sat and talked for several hours. It was almost noon before the separation took place. After that, the women all went shopping and saw a movie together.

Mr. Kraneger reserved a tee time, and the men left for the golf course.

Bobby told Henry Quinn, and Brandy was trying to make amends. However, the whole thing was Mr. Kraneger's idea, and Brandy wanted to be happier about the arrangement.

Henry did not like the prick. He was about Bobby's height but very slim, dark-headed with a dark complexion. He was very polite and spoke a very polished Bostonian. Bobby and Henry shared a cart, and Henry only spent a little time with Quinn except on the tees and greens.

Henry played about as well as he could but was eight over, Bobby was six over, Mr. Kraneger was five over, and Quinn was four over par.

Henry saw the guy was hard to like, and something was not right; Henry felt it in his bones.

The late dinner was very casual, and Henry sat with his mother on one side and Barby on the other. Brandy sat with her brother and Sherry; she still refused to sit with Quinn.

After spending some time at the bar, the family separated and went to their rooms around midnight. It was not long before someone was at Henry's door. It was Quinn. "Great golf game, Henry. Do you get to play much in California?"

"Yeah, about once a week. What do you want, Quinn?" Henry was trying hard to control his anger; Quinn was the last person he wanted to consider a friend.

"I'd like to chat a bit. I understand you and Brandy have been great friends. Unfortunately, our relationship is a bit precarious; I would like your advice. Would you mind terribly?"

Henry was not impressed with his pretentious concern. "Let's go down to the bar."

"What's on your mind, Quinn?"

"I love Brandy very much, Henry, but I have had some personal problems."

Henry could tell the son-of-a-bitch was putting on an act. How did someone as savvy as Brandy ever fall for his sick demeanor?

"Well, let me ask you a question, Quinn. Have you ever hit Brandy?" (Henry noticed his wince.) Henry was fuming and secretly hoped the prick would affirm his suspicions.

Quinn stammered and said, "No, my god, man, I'm not the person who would brutalize his wife. I am in anger management therapy, and I know I can find a solution to this problem. Then I can make Brandy happy—incredibly happy. However, you must understand I did not come to you to discuss our private affairs. So let me get to the point, older man. Would you be so kind as to speak with Brandy on my behalf? I believe she would listen to you."

"We grew up together, Quinn. I'm exhausted, but I'll give it some thought."

Brandy walked into the room. The smile on her face evaporated when she saw Quinn.

Brandy turned and fled down the hallway.

Henry pushed Quinn out of the way and ran after her.

"Brandy, come back with me. I'll get rid of him." When she looked at him, he saw distrust in her expression.

"Why are you talking to that sorry excuse of a man, Hank?"

"I will explain later, Brandy."

She walked beside him toward his room. She leaned against him and said, "I'm not talking to him, Hank."

Quinn stood at the end of the corridor and demanded, "What in the hell are you doing here?" His terse statement was both nasty and vicious.

Henry was about to knock him on his ass, but he saw the terror in Brandy's eyes. So, Henry guided Brandy into his room.

Henry looked back at Quinn. He was walking toward his door. "The exit is just around the corner, slick. You found your way in; you can find your way out." Henry wanted Quinn to take a poke at him. He would not need much of a reason to kick his ass.

Quinn tacitly grimaced, then shoved past Henry, who was holding his door. Then, after walking several paces down the hall, he turned and remarked maliciously, "I fully expect to continue this conversation later."

Henry did not say a word. Instead, he turned and saw the hurt in Brandy's eyes. Her expression was doleful and saturated in misery. He closed the door and set the lock.

Henry took her in his arms and held her gently. She tucked her face into his shoulder, and they stood quietly and absorbed the moment's calm.

"Can I stay with you tonight, Hank? I can sleep on the other bed."

Henry lifted her chin and kissed her very tenderly. "You can sleep in either bed, but you will sleep here tonight. Barby was supposed to come up, but I'll make up some excuse."

"She's not coming, Hank. I spoke with her, and she was not feeling well. I told her I would tell her. She knows I am here, Hank. Don't worry; she only knows that we're good friends."

"Why is Quinn here, Brandy? Do you want to work things out with him?"

She swayed her head no; it crushed her that he would even suggest such a thing. She buried her head against him again and started to cry quietly. He picked her up and carried her to his bed. He sat her on the bed. He took off her high heels and sat beside her.

She cried off and on for a long time. Henry wondered how a woman so strong could tremble in his arms. He had not come to grips with his deep feelings for Brandy. Their relationship changed after she was married, but he was happy to have her in his arms again. She was no longer the free-spirited woman teaching a young man all about the pleasures of life. Brandy needed emotional and physical protection, and as the young apprentice of her romantic escapades, Henry intended to provide her with that comfort.

Henry and Brandy talked for hours. She told him about the physical abuse. "I have some photos; I had a black eye here. Here are the black and blue broken ribs. He tried to rape me the last night he was in our house. I cannot call the police because his uncle is a captain in the city police."

Henry was boiling inside. He wanted to kill Quinn. However, he noticed how fragile Brandy had become. His blatant hostility only seemed to make her more uncomfortable. Henry understood what she needed now: caring, wholesome love, some security, and a kind man.

Brandy slept quietly, and Henry did not touch her romantically, but he did hold her. She slept cuddled in his embrace. Brandy woke up once during the night screaming. Henry calmed her nerves with hugs and kisses and reassured her that she existed safe in his arms. The last time Henry looked at the clock, it was almost three.

The next day, Brandy stayed in his room. Instead, she stayed in bed most of the day.

At breakfast, Henry discovered Barby already knew what he had just learned about Quinn.

Barby joined them for lunch. "Henry, I need you to stay with Brandy. I knew about the physical abuse but did not tell you because I did not want you in jail. I am sorry, Honey. Henry, this could be better, but we need to help Brandy. Barby spoke frankly, and Henry understood her concern. Deep down, he knew she was correct.

Barby and Henry covered for Brandy, telling her parents she was exhausted and needed to rest.

That night, Henry and Brandy shared very tender, passionate expressions. But then, Henry became aware of a significant change sometimes at night. Brandy was becoming more like Barby, and Barby had become more like Brandy. Or was it just that they were sisters and some were in the other? Is that why he loved Brandy so much? Henry thought about it as he fell asleep with Brandy in his arms.

In the morning, someone woke them by pounding on the door. Brandy got up and went to the door. It was Barby, and she barged in. When Henry heard her voice, he pulled his pillow over his head.

Barby chided emotionally, "Is that my boyfriend in your bed?"

Brandy replied playfully, "Yes, I think he's just a darling, right?"

Henry knew this day would eventually come. Barby and Brandy talked as if he were not even in the room. Henry wanted to crawl into an exceedingly small, dark, distant private hole. Forever!

Slowly, he slid off the backside of the bed. They ignored him when he slipped into the bathroom and showered. When he came out, the two sisters were on the veranda. Barby was still doing all the talking. He quietly made his way over to the bed. Henry wanted to gather his clothes, but they were not there anymore. All he had on was a towel. Then Brandy saw him.

"Hank, Barby, and I need to talk with you. Honey, you look like the little boy who got caught with his hand in the cookie jar."

Henry was a loser. He never intended to allow his relationship with the two sisters to get so far out of control. His innocence was elusive.

He got down on his knees and looked under the bed, but nothing. Then, he felt a soft and warm body come up behind him.

"Silly boy. I love you, Henry. I know this must be hard for you."

Henry spun around, and Barby trapped him against the bed. He sat on the floor and buried his head in her tummy.

She whispered, "Henry, look at me, please." He wrapped his arms around her and held his face against her belly. She felt his hot tears through her blouse, and she knew he was in emotional agony. Barby caressed his hair and neck while he cried.

Henry's pain intensified. He thought his chest would explode from the agony.

Brandy looked over at Barby to see what was happening. When she saw the painful expression on her sister's face, she hurried over and kneeled beside Henry.

"Darling, listen to me, Henry; this is not your fault; you are not bad. On the contrary, we both love you and want your children. But, Hank, we didn't mean to hurt you."

Brandy stepped over and kneeled next to him. She started to cry, and Brandy clung to his side. She could not bear to see Hank suffering.

Barby put her palms on his cheeks and slowly lifted his head. She kissed his eyebrows and his cheeks. When she found his lips, they were wet, and she tasted the salt from his tears.

While Barby kissed him, Brandy whispered, "Hank, you can love both of us. Find a room in your heart. Put me on one side and Barby on the other."

Henry wrapped his arms around the two sisters, but he could not get control of his emotions.

"Poor baby, this has been hard on you. Brandy and I did not realize the extent of the emotional torture we have been putting you through. We're sorry, Henry." Barby kissed him hungrily, twisting her lips against his expressively. Then she got up and walked away.

Brandy took her place; she was still sobbing. "I love you, Hank. I love you more than life itself. I am sorry I hurt you. It is my fault; please do not blame Barby. We both love you, Hank; we had no cruel intentions. We both want to have your babies." She kissed him tenderly.

Barby rejoined them and was shaking. When her eyes met him, she felt her heart sink in her chest, and she somewhat threw herself on him, sobbing convulsively.

Brandy sat against the bed and wiped her eyes. "Oh no, Barby. We have surely made a mess of this, Honey." She put one arm around her sister and the other on Henry's shoulder. "Okay, from now on, we will share everything. We are so sorry, Hank; come on, you two. Let us get dressed and have some lunch. We have a lot to share. Come on, Barby. We have shed enough tears. It's time to heal."

They helped Henry stand up, but his knees were shaky, and he had no energy. Finally, Henry shook like a leaf, and the women allowed him to sit on the bed. Brandy sat on his left, and Barby sat on his right.

"Henry, we are so sorry. Please try to forgive us. But, my god, Brandy, what have we done?" She looked bewildered at her older sister. Henry began to get hold of his emotions. He took some deep breaths and tried to hold his head up.

Brandy nuzzled against him. She whispered into his ear. "Hank, I know you are strong enough to handle this. Concentrate on our love for you, darling. You know we both love you."

Henry was feeling better. The color returned to his face, his head cleared, and his mental faculties stabilized. "I don't know what hit me. I thought you were mad at me, Barby, and I couldn't handle that emotion." Large tears fell on his cheeks, and he could not continue.

The two sisters hugged him, cuddled against him, and stroked his arms, chest, face, and hair.

Then, they both got up and walked out onto the veranda. Henry still had the towel wrapped around him. Brandy looked at him and admonished, "Go make yourself presentable, you bum. We do have a guest."

Henry kissed Brandy. Henry intended to kiss Barby, too, but she grabbed his towel and pulled him onto her lap.

"Get up, you brute!" She pushed at him until he stood up. She jumped up, pushed him into the chair, and jumped into his lap. Barby kissed him passionately. When she felt his arousal, she wiggled her butt against him, furthering his state of ecstasy. She put her forehead against his and touched his nose with hers.

She whispered, "What is that? Are Cyclops waking up?"

He smiled, and she kissed him again. "Brandy, Henry has a problem between his legs. Have you had your shower yet?"

Brandy started to laugh. "You wouldn't dare, would you?"

Barby looked at her sister and nodded yes. "Brandy, go take a long, hot, sultry bath. I hoped you could close the door and not come out until I knocked on the bathroom door. Please be nice, Brandy!"

Barby kissed him while Brandy got up, went into the bathroom, and closed the door.

"Are you up for this, silly boy?" Barby was hot to trot. Henry stood with her in his arms and walked to the bed, losing his towel.

A loud knock on the door brought him to his senses, but she was still in want.

"No, do not answer the door, Henry. Ignore them, Honey; they will go away."

Bobby stood beside Sherry out in the hallway. He yelled, "Hey, open the door. Come on, Stretch. Open the door. I know you're in there."

Barby tugged at Henry, "Stay here, silly."

"Barby, I need to answer the door." She pushed him off her, jumped out of bed, and ran to the door. She engaged the safety chain and cracked the door open.

"Hello, children. Unless you have earth-shattering news, please go away. Come back in an hour." She removed her blouse as she leaned around the door. She looked back at Henry and said, "Thirty minutes, please?" She slammed the door and was naked before she reached the bed.

She leaped over him and shouted, "Cyclops to the rescue!"

Brandy yelled from the tub, "Are your children finished yet?"

"Barby, what made all the ecstasy explode?"

She nuzzled into his chest. "Henry, we need to spend some serious time together. I cannot go months on end without you. A girl has her needs, silly boy."

Brandy came out and slapped his butt. "There's nothing quite like sweet serenity."

Barby looked up at her and smiled contentedly. "I feel better."

"I ran you a fresh tub of water. Take lover boy with you. Who was at the door?" Brandy walked out onto the veranda to give them some privacy.

"It was Bobby and Sherry. I may have been rude, but lust does that to you." Barby giggled.

Brandy went to the door after Henry and Barby went into the bathroom. She was surprised to find Sherry pinned against the wall. Her brother let go of her when he realized he had an audience. "Do you two need to use the bed now?"

Sherry's face became as red as her hair. She cringed away from making eye contact with Brandy.

"I'm game." Bobby's words slipped out before he had a chance to think.

Sherry pushed him away, "We can wait, unlike some people!"

The rude comment caught Brandy by surprise. She looked at Bobby, and he showed her a strong jaw. Then, she looked back at Sherry. "Well, we need to remain civil. Barby meant no disrespect. She was suffering from a touch of lust."

Sherry's natural smile returned, and she walked over and hugged Brandy. "I understand, no disrespect taken." Sherry was shorter than Brandy but taller than Barby, and her brilliant red hair was immaculate.

"Come on in, you two. Henry and Barby are freshening up in the bathroom."

Bobby gave his sister a big hug.

Brandy smiled and stood back a bit. "Wow, are we developing a sibling relationship?"

Bobby ignored her and pushed Sherry down on the bed. He kissed her, and she pushed him off.

"Robert Thomas, you're a flirt. Brandy, how did you put up with him all these years?" Sherry asked.

"I had my room. The door had a lock on it. My stereo had headphones. I went away to college as far as I could go on dry land. Need I say more?" Brandy said.

Sherry grinned at Brandy, "Those are some great ideas."

Bobby was pretending not to hear them. Instead, he turned on the television and listened to a game show.

CHAPTER 30

Quitting Quinn

*L*ater that morning, Bobby, Sherry, Brandy, Barby, and Henry left to join the parents for breakfast.

Brandy and Barby took Henry off to the side before they reached the restaurant. Brandy saw Bobby ahead of her. "Bobby, tell Mom and Dad we'll be there in a few minutes."

The three young adults sat in the parlor by themselves. Barby looked at her sister and started the conversation. "Henry, we wanted to talk with you. We both love you. Honey, we did not plan it like this, but here we are. Brandy told me all about the private moments you two have shared. We think you're gorgeous and want to have a baby with you."

Henry started to say something, but Brandy cut him off. "Hank, this was all my idea. Barby is not responsible. You should marry one of us; it is the only decent thing to do. We never intended to hurt you, Hank; we greatly love you. I love you, Hank, but I won't stand in the way if you decide to marry Barby."

Henry held up a hand. "May I get a word in, please?"

Brandy looked at Barby, and then they both looked at Henry. He saw that they were not going to interrupt, so he continued. "Am I getting the full picture here? Brandy, you told Barby all about us?"

"She's my sister, Hank. Yes, I told her everything, every minute detail." Brandy smiled at her sister.

Henry swirled his head around, "You too? Barby?"

Barby touched his face and kissed him tenderly. "She's my sister, Henry; I tell her everything. It would help if you decided which of us you will marry. We want you to finish college first, though. There, now, you have lots of time to decide."

Henry looked at Brandy, "Then Quinn is out of the picture?"

"Yes, I filed for a divorce before I left Boston; Quinn hasn't received his papers yet. So, it's finished, Hank."

Henry tried but could not find the right words; his feelings were so profound for each of them. He was genuinely perplexed.

Barby took his hand, and Brandy grabbed his other one. They pulled him up and walked arm-in-arm to breakfast.

When they arrived at their table, Henry sat between Brandy and Barby. They ordered coffee and talked about old times. But, unfortunately, Quinn and the Kraneger parents and Mrs. Rotyn had not arrived yet.

Eventually, the conversation turned back to Quinn.

Barby asked Brandy. "Please go to Dad and ask him to tell Quinn to leave because his presence makes us all uncomfortable,"

Henry said, "I'll go to Quinn and tell him myself."

Brandy disagreed vehemently, "No, Hank! My father needs to tell him, not you."

"I told Bobby about the abuse. Bobby was livid, Brandy." Henry replied forcefully.

Brandy asked Sherry, "Can you control him at all."

Sherry looked at Bobby and shook her head no.

"Let us go talk to Quinn, Henry. You girls stay put. Quinn is going to slip and fall." Bobby was already mad.

Brandy protested, but Bobby would not listen to her.

Henry left with Bobby. While they walked, Bobby asked, "How long have you known about this, Henry?"

Henry stopped him in his tracks. "Yesterday. I had some clues earlier, but I dismissed them as jealousy. Calm down, Bobby. So, you hurt him. If you go to jail, Bobby, who will protect me then." Brandy appealed.

"This is how innocent people wind up in jail. Quinn's the criminal; do not lower yourself to his level. All we will do is order him out of our lives forever. Do you understand? We do it for Brandy, not for us." Barby said.

Quinn was not in his room.

Bobby and Henry went back and joined the girls.

The parents arrived while Bobby and Henry were gone.

Barby addressed Bobby and Henry: "Dad says Quinn will join us in a few minutes." She pursed her lips at the two young men, desperately trying to persuade them to avoid a scene.

Quinn finally made his late appearance. His smooth demeanor won over the parents, but everyone else looked like they had suffered some debilitating injury.

Brandy leaned against Henry. She kissed him and cuddled him.

Quinn's face was beet red.

Bobby gave Quinn dirty looks, but Quinn did not notice. He had watched Brandy from the time he sat down. Henry could see Brandy made her parents uneasy, but Brandy did not let up until Barby gave her a dirty look.

Quinn left with Mr. Kraneger after the meal. Mr. Kraneger returned a few moments later, and he was upset by the conduct of his oldest daughter. Mrs. Kraneger tried to calm him down, but he was obdurate.

Jessica was upset with her son, and Brandy, for that matter. She intended to get to the bottom of this but would not publicly pursue it.

Mr. Kraneger spoke directly to Henry. "I'm very disappointed in your conduct, young man!"

Henry addressed him, "Mr. Kraneger, there are things about Quinn you just don't understand."

Mr. Kraneger was livid now. He had never spoken harshly to Henry, but now that bubble broke. "Young man, I know more than you could ever imagine. Don't you ever address me in public in a condescending manner?"

The outburst made Bobby hot; he stood up and pointed at his father. "You can't see further than the end of your nose, Dad."

Mr. Kraneger was shocked; his son had never spoken to him with such disrespect.

Bobby was encouraged to continue, but he saw his father sit back in his chair. "Where the hell is that son of a bitch, Quinn?" Bobby asked.

Mrs. Kraneger was appalled. "Robert Thomas, you sit down this instant. How dare you address your father with such disrespect? I said, sit down, Robert!"

Bobby sat down, but he was upset. Sherry tried to calm him but to no avail.

Everyone except Barby overlooked Brandy. She had covered her face with her hands in apparent anguish.

Barby went to her sister and held her. Brandy bent over and cried.

Henry got up and went around the table to Brandy's parents. He knelt on one knee in front of them. "You both have been like parents to me. I would never insult either of you. I love you like you were my parents. But some things are going on here that you need to understand."

Mr. Kraneger spoke with a tense, restrained voice, "Henry, I know all about Quinn and Brandy's problems. Quinn came to me and told me that Brandy had a lover, and that was the reason they broke up." Then, in a profoundly severe tone, he asked Henry. "Are you having an affair with Brandy?"

Henry needed to be incredibly careful with his answer. "No, she was married. I love Brandy very much, but that is not the issue. Other things are going on here you need to know about."

Henry saw the hurt in their eyes. Then, finally, Mrs. Kraneger asked, "What about Barby?" She looked over at her youngest daughter, who was still attending to Brandy.

Henry continued, "Have you had a serious private conversation with Brandy?" The parents looked at each other and then indicated they had not.

Mr. Kraneger stood up and walked to the side of the room, and Henry went with him. "I know about verbal abuse. Quinn came to me several weeks ago and told me about the problem. He asked me to help him by encouraging Brandy not to divorce him. Quinn is in counseling and has the support of his family. He is a very apologetic man, I think. He deserves an opportunity to better himself, Henry."

"Please speak with your daughter. I have seen direct evidence that the abuse is much more than verbal. But you should get this from your daughter, not me."

Henry walked away from him and joined his mother. He tried to explain to her what he knew, but as it was, he still did not have the whole story.

Later that day, Mr. and Mrs. Kraneger called Henry and asked him to join them at dinner.

When Henry arrived, the entire Kraneger family, Jessica and Sherry, were seated in a private room. When he entered, Mrs. Kraneger came over to him and embraced him. Henry was uncomfortable. Her embrace was very physical, and she held him tightly for several moments.

"Henry, please accept our apology. We did not know, dear. We didn't know."

Mr. Kraneger walked up to him and shook his hand. "Your father would be proud of you, son. I want you to know that I had a heated conversation with Quinn. Unfortunately, he is no longer a member of this family." Mr. Kraneger slapped him on the back.

Henry went to take his seat but kissed his mother first. Then he kissed both Brandy and Barby and sat down between them. Brandy slid her chair over and leaned her head on his shoulder. She looked like she had been crying for a long time.

Bobby announced his engagement to Sherry. She was stunning and glowed all evening.

Barby whispered to Henry, "Brandy and I flipped a coin. You're mine for the night."

Henry sat tall in his chair. Barby grabbed at him every chance she got. Then, with Brandy on his shoulder, Barby kissed him several times. Her kisses were not discreet, gracious, or subtle. Conversation breakers: that is what her kisses were like every time.

Henry never once embraced her, but he whimsically waved his hand in front of his face, fanning himself several times. The symbolism brought bright smiles from onlookers who, with jaws gaping open, were undoubtedly confused.

Brandy contributed to their confusion with her facial expressions and gestures. After each of Barby's kisses, Brandy pursed her lips and held up either one, two, or three fingers, depending on how she rated the kiss.

Once, Sherry chirped, "Upgrade that one, Brandy. It was a solid three."

Brandy whispered to Henry, "Thank you."

He looked down into her eyes. She was at ease now and cuddled into his shoulder again.

Mrs. Kraneger said, "If I didn't know better, Henry, I'd swear both of my daughters want to get their claws into you."

Bobby added, "Yeah, Henry. You better listen to my mother."

Henry tried to see the humor in their comments, but secretly, he was terrified. He loved them both.

Barby interpreted the occasion as a need for another kiss. The champagne on her lips wet Henry's. He did not know how much more of her prodding he could resist.

Brandy held up three fingers before her sister released him.

Jessica sat silently across from her son and enjoyed the show; she had seen the signs that her son was in love with both sisters. However, Jessica could not imagine how such a thing was possible until she reasoned on her predicament.

They discussed the activities to pursue the next day, and everyone retired for the evening.

Barby went to Henry's room at about midnight. Bobby was spending the night with Sherry. Jessica spent the evening with Brandy because she was terrified of being alone.

Barby was very physical and demanding. Henry did everything he could to satisfy her needs, but she was too much for him. Henry was not sure if it was his physical virility or his heart that let her down. As it was, they only slept shortly before two.

The mixed families spent six days at the theme parks. Of course, they drank too much wine and spent too much time in the sun, but they had a wonderful time together.

Barby told him to spend the rest of his time with Brandy because she would have him all to herself in California.

Brandy slept in Henry's bed every night after that. She was beginning to fixate on their relationship. Brandy needed Henry in her bed every night, not just for the lovemaking. She required his companionship, his kindness, and tender affection.

"Henry, when I was at Dartmouth, I opened my boutique. I named the boutique 'Brandy's.' The business is a huge success, and I have counted on my manager to staff the store seven days a week. In the divorce, I walked away from the house. I bought a small Tudor on the north side of Boston. I want you to fly out and spend a holiday with my honey. Will you think about it, Ozaawindib?"

On several occasions, Mr. and Mrs. Kraneger mentioned they had not seen Brandy so happy and full of life in a long time.

Mr. and Mrs. Kraneger met Henry. They gave him incredibly unique expressions of their love. He knew Brandy was the object of their affection.

Barby and Henry left for California.

CHAPTER 31

The Accident

On a dark, moonless November night in Michigan, an intoxicated and tired truck driver lost control of his rig on M60 east of Tekonsha. He crashed into an oncoming late-model sedan, destroying the car and killing its passengers.

Bobby called Henry from Ann Arbor at about bedtime. "Henry, I am glad I caught you."

"Bobby, what's up?"

The line went silent.

"Bobby, you there?" Henry got a sick feeling in his stomach.

"I got some real bad news, Henry." The line went silent again.

"Bobby, what's wrong, Rogue?" Henry asked.

"Henry, my mom and dad are dead."

The sick feeling suddenly became a dreadful fear. "Bobby, did you say your parents are dead?"

"They were killed in an automobile accident tonight near Tekonsha." The line went silent again.

"Damn, Bobby. I am sorry, old friend. What happened, Bobby? Do you know?"

Bobby described the dark November night. Henry imagined Bobby was in shock. "Brandy called me with the bad news. The state police contacted Consuela, and she and your mom went to identify the bodies. I guess they did not want to say anything until they were certain. Your mom is taking it hard, according to Consuela. Consuela called Brandy; Brandy wanted me to call you because she had to leave for the airport. She is flying into Detroit from Boston tonight. I will pick her up at the airport and drive to Barneyville in the morning. She needed to leave as soon as possible to catch her flight."

Bobby was in Minneapolis; he played in the game that Michigan won. Bobby gave Henry an 800 number because the airlines were still working on his flights.

"Barby doesn't know yet, Henry. I want you to fly to San Francisco in the morning, and I want you to tell Barby in person. I do not want to say to her over the phone. She is going to take it hard. So take care of her, Rogue. Brandy and I will pick you up in Detroit. You can pick up your tickets at the San Francisco airport. I'll pay for the tickets.

"Your flight leaves San Diego at about noon. We need your support, Henry. I know we can count on you. Love you, Rogue." Bobby hung up.

Henry was frightened for the second time in his life. He called his mother in Barneyville, but She did not answer her phone. Henry needed to think clearly. What night was it? Wednesday, it is Wednesday night. His mother must be home. He tried it again. He let it ring, and she finally answered.

"Hello."

"Mom, are you alright?"

"Henry, thank god. Have you heard what's happened?"

"Yes, Mom, are you alright?"

"No, I need you here, Henry. I spoke with Brandy about twenty minutes ago. She was getting ready to board her flight. I wanted to call you but thought I'd wait until you were home."

"It's awful, Mom. I feel so bad."

"I know, dear; I loved both of them desperately. More than you will ever imagine."

"I'll be home tomorrow night, Mom. We can talk then. I am flying to San Francisco early tomorrow. I will meet Barby when I get there. Losing both is going to be extremely hard, Mom. Bobby and Brandy will pick us up in Detroit. We will be home late. I love you, Mom."

"Honey, the neighborhood is shocked, but we're all meeting for breakfast. I'm looking forward to seeing you, dear."

"Okay, Mom. See you tomorrow night."

"I love you, Henry." She hung up.

Henry caught his flight in the morning and was in a rental car at the San Francisco airport before 9:30. He crossed the Bay Bridge in light traffic. He was in Berkeley in twenty minutes. Barby was away from her sorority house, and one of her sisters said she had classes until four.

Henry located the building where Barby was working on some project in a lab. He talked to a fellow student and learned that Barby had just stepped out for a cigarette. Henry did not know she smoked.

Barby walked into the lab at the other end of the building. She saw the guy with the hair that looked like Henry, but she did not make the connection.

He had his back on her when she realized it was not someone who looked like Henry. "Henry. My god, what a nice surprise." Henry did not smile, and when it was apparent to her that he would not smile, her glee evaporated. She approached him and tentatively asked, "Why are you here, Henry?"

He did not say a word. Henry reached out for Barby.

One of her colleagues jumped in front of him as if she were going to protect her from him.

"Hello, I'm her boyfriend. My name is Henry. What is your name?

She smiled at him. "Pepper. My name is Pepper."

"Pepper, I need to talk with Barby. We need some privacy, somewhere quiet." Henry patiently waited for her.

Pepper looked at Barby, then at Henry. "Yeah, sure. There is a quiet terrace outback. I want to accompany you."

"Please, I think that would be very helpful," Henry added.

"Barby, let us go out to the terrace. I need to talk with you."

She was looking into his eyes; her beautiful brown eyes were searching his face for a clue. Barby whined, "Henry?"

They walked out into the courtyard. "Pepper is my roommate, Henry. Why are you here?"

He put his arm around her. "We need to be alone for a few minutes, sweetie."

He sat her on a bench under a tulip tree. They were in a secluded corner, and Henry thought the spot was about as good as he could do. She was almost in tears, and her whole body was shaking.

Henry dropped to one knee in front of her. He whispered to her, Barby, I have some horrible news. Hang on to me, darling."

She lowered her head and raised it to face him; her tear-filled eyes studied his face. "I'm all right, Henry."

He brushed a hair wisp off of her face. Henry bit his lip and felt his heart skip a beat. "It's your parents, Barby. They're both gone."

Barby tried to smile, "What exactly do you mean, Henry?"

"Bobby said they died in a terrible automobile accident, Honey."

Barby fell forward and fainted in his arms. She was out cold.

Henry held Barby while Pepper and another friend helped gently lower her to the grass. Then, Henry asked Pepper to get a wet towel.

He sat down and held Barby's head in his lap. She was breathing gently. Another girl elevated her feet and treated the moment with quiet dignity. Henry took off his jacket and put it on the grass. He lowered Barby's head to his coat.

Pepper ran up with a wet washcloth, applied it to Barby's forehead, and began to stir.

Pepper was very slim. She had a dark complexion, and her short blue hair stuck out straight as if she had just been frightened at a horror movie. Nevertheless, she was gorgeous, and the spiked hairdo did little to complement her beauty.

Barby opened her eyes and immediately buried her face in Henry's chest. "No, it can't be true. It can't be true."

Then came the tears, no sound, just tears. She clung to him closely while she cried silently. Henry wiped his eyes several times, and then his tears flowed freely.

Barby's anguish increased, and she cried heart-wrenching sobs of sorrow.

Students crowded around and wondered what was going on.

Henry asked Pepper if she could go and pack some of her things because they had a flight to catch in a few hours.

Barby struggled to whisper, "Does Brandy know?" Finally, she lost her composure and started crying before he could answer.

Barby reached up and grabbed Henry's ponytail and pulled his face to hers. She looked at him closely and kissed him. "Thank you for being here. I love you so much!" Henry wiped her face with another towel.

"When are we leaving, Henry?"

"Soon, sweetie. Real soon. Our flight leaves at four this afternoon."

Pepper helped Barby get to her room and take a shower. Pepper had a Volkswagen van. She and some friends were taking Henry and Barby to the airport.

Some of Barby's friends began asking questions. Henry told them what he knew. Barby was immensely popular in Berkeley, just like she was in Barneyville. Some of her friends took up a collection. Henry did not think they were aware of the money in her family.

Barby tried to be strong, but Henry could tell she was shocked. However, her friends were terrific and did many things to console her.

Barby slept most of the flight. She slumped against Henry and cried occasionally. The plane finally landed in Chicago; Barby's tears and sweat made her uncomfortable. They had a two-hour layover and finally landed in Detroit around two in the morning.

Bobby and Brandy were waiting for them at the airport. Barby was hanging onto Henry's arm through the arrival gate. When she saw Brandy, she ran crying into her sister's arms. Bobby was at least three inches taller than Henry now. The two men embraced and slapped each other on the back.

"Thanks, Henry. I knew I could count on you, Rogue."

Barby fell into Bobby's arms next, and Henry hugged Brandy.

Brandy mumbled hysterically and cried. Henry picked her up and carried her to the seats. An attendant who witnessed her reaction cleared a spot to lay her down. But Henry decided to hold her. He sat down with Brandy in his lap.

"I hurt so much, Hank; I hurt too much," Brandy wept.

Barby cried hard in her brother's arms.

Hank stood up and let Brandy catch her balance. Then, they walked to the baggage area. Brandy cried intermittently briefly, then whispered lovesick innuendoes into his ear.

Brandy, Bobby, Barby, and Henry cried their hearts out most of the way to Barneyville. They shared loving memories of their parents. They made promises of allegiance and support to each other, desperately trying to calm their shared fears and anxieties. It was a particular time for them to reaffirm their love for one another.

The Kraneger's ceremony was on Saturday morning, November 29, 1969.

Before the accident, Bobby's team won the Ohio State Game; it was a huge upset.

Bobby took over the dealership. The rest of their parents' estate was divided evenly between the three children. The family will keep the home in the family.

Mr. Kraneger made a generous contribution to Henry's education and left his mom enough money to remodel the old home completely. He also gave Jessica Rotyn a new car and an unusually liberal sum of cash separate from what she needed to remodel the house.

Brandy wanted Henry to go to Boston with her. But she was reluctant to ask him.

CHAPTER 32

Christmas 1969

$\mathscr{B}$arby and Henry arranged to share a room in the Claremont Hotel Tuesday night in Berkeley. They wanted to spend one night together before traveling east.

Henry arrived after seven in the evening; she had been waiting for him since five. He drove up from San Diego and ran into traffic in Los Angeles.

He knew he was late but was glad to return to the Bay Area. Although Henry was tired from the long drive, the valet told him to let the Concierge know when he arrived. Henry walked up to the desk wearily.

"Good evening, Sir. You must be Mr. Rotyn." The Concierge smiled.

"Too much traffic in Los Angeles and Oakland." Henry gave her a half-smile.

"I'll have your luggage brought up to your room. The lady waiting for you has called every ten minutes asking for you."

"Don't let her know I'm here." Henry arranged flowers and champagne.

Barby was unusually antsy and worried sick. She was half-afraid to answer when the doorbell sounded because she had instructed the front desk to announce Mr. Rotyn's arrival.

She was sure she had heard his voice and swung the door open. Henry stood there with his double-dimpled big smile. When he saw the state of her anxiety, it was only then that he realized he should have called to inform her about his tardiness.

Barby broke down and fell into his arms. She cried and mumbled the incoherent, hysterical imaginations of doom she had conceived.

"Barby, I'm sorry. I should have called you. It was very insensitive to me. Please forgive me," he said.

Barby beat her fists against his chest; she was so upset with him. Then, finally, she grabbed him, threw her arms around his neck, and clung to him quietly.

Henry picked her up, kicked off his shoes, and carried her into the bedroom. Henry lowered her onto the bed and stretched beside her; Barby snuggled into his arms and wept.

Barby finally calmed down and cuddled into his arms.

She whispered, "Henry, oh god, Henry; I was so scared. I had the most horrible thoughts. But, Henry, I want you to promise me something—Henry, are you listening?"

Henry was sound asleep.

Barby slumped off his shoulder; she daintily kissed his cheek and whispered, "Silly boy. Sweet dreams, darling."

Barby slipped out of bed and ordered their dinner. The flowers and champagne Henry ordered arrived a few minutes later.

She drank half the champagne and took a bubble bath while he slept. She woke him at nine.

"Brandy, is that you?"

She grabbed a pillow and clubbed him. "Cute. Just keep it up, buddy. Now, get up and take a shower. You smell." He sat up, and she gave him a glass of bubbly. He drank it like water and reached for her, but she backed away.

Barby pointed to the bathroom, "Shower!"

He headed for the bath, removing his clothes as he walked. She smiled but was not impressed.

Barby put on some relaxing music. Then, finally, their dinner arrived, and she arranged the table, lit some candles, and shut off the lights.

Henry took a long, steamy shower. Then, he yelled to her, "Barby, did you order some coffee?"

"Yes, hurry up. I'm hungry," Barby said.

She had laid out some clothes on the bed for him. He dressed and joined her in the candlelight. He walked over to her and kissed her. "Nice touch, very romantic. I'm sorry I made you worry."

"Are you hungry, Henry?"

"Famished, undernourished, and in need of some feminine wiles. Viva la difference," he said.

"Typical man; you want to fill your belly and get laid!"

"Man cannot live on bread alone," he said.

"Henry, I think you're confused on that one. It's not love, and it's life."

"Live to love, love to live. What's the difference?"

"Eat, and I'll give you a demonstration, silly boy!"

Near midnight, he lay on her, coupled and spent. "Henry, darling, promise me you will live near me the rest of your life. Even if we marry but divorce, promise me you will always be near me, please."

"Barby, you're so pretty tonight." He kissed her neck, and then he nibbled on her left nipple. Finally, he kissed her passionately, taking her tongue into his mouth and caressing it.

"Henry, oh, you bad, bad boy. Cyclops is alive and well." She clung to him while he smothered her body.

She rolled him over and snuggled into his chest. "Oh, Henry. That was splendid. You make me feel so wonderful. Hold me, darling." He took her in his arms. She pulled the sheets up over them. "Go to sleep, Henry. You need your rest; the poor baby isn't used to making love."

When she woke up, she had hot coffee and donuts waiting for him. She smiled at him. "Viva la difference." She kissed him and sat looking at him. She could not take her eyes off him.

"Hello, pretty girl. I love you, too. Come over here." She got up and sat in his lap. "I'll consider putting my hat at your feet a privilege. My door will be your door. My heart will cling close to your heart. Our world will enlighten our children; our children will enlighten the world."

Her face lit up. "Henry, that was beautiful; I thought you didn't hear me."

"Don't think I haven't thought about it because I think about you daily. I have loved you since the third grade." She kissed him, but he had not shaved yet, and she did not like his beard.

"You need to shave before I kiss you again."

"Oh, all right, our flight leaves at eleven, so we must move on."

On the plane, she talked about school and her best friend, Pepper. "Pepper is a Chinese Hawaiian, Henry. She is so much fun."

They behaved themselves on this trip. Barby was a charmed, contented woman. Henry was happy in her company, but his anxiety began to brew again as they came closer to the source of his concern.

Bobby and Sherry picked them up in Detroit. They arrived in Barneyville at nine pm.

Brandy and Jessica met them at the door. They all spent a few hours together, and then Barby went with Bobby and Sherry to Battle Creek. Brandy stayed at Henry's.

As they talked around the kitchen table, Jessica served freshly baked cookies and milk.

"How are you holding up, Brandy?" Henry asked. He noticed a quirky distortion in her expression.

She smiled at him, "I hold on to my good thoughts, try not to dwell on the bad. I miss you terribly. But I think a lot of people miss you." She looked at Jessica, reached out, and held her hand.

"You two are the most beautiful women I know. I'm thrilled to be here with you."

"Henry, our families to be spread out nationwide. Please consider our need to be near you. I did not raise a son to see him move thousands of miles away," Jessica said.

"Mom, as soon as I complete my education, we'll be together, I promise. I am going to take care of you. You wait and see."

"Brandy, are you safe living by yourself? Are you ever afraid?" Henry asked.

Brandy touched his face. Then she leaned over and kissed him tenderly. "I have some concerns, but so far, so good. My employees at work and my neighbors are very protective. I feel safe and loved."

"Mom, how are you doing? Is there anything I can do to help while I'm home? Mother, you are positively glowing."

Jessica was reluctant to mention her secret but could no longer contain her glee. "I have an announcement. You better get a grip, Henry. you're going to have a sibling." She turned her head away from them, covering her face with her hands. The baby was Benjamin's; she could never reveal that to anyone.

Henry looked at Brandy; they both were stunned. "Mother? What do you mean? How can you be pregnant?"

"Henry, don't act so prudish. My god, you must know how a woman gets impregnated."

"Mom, I didn't mean it that way. It is wonderful. Who is the father? Anyone I know?"

"Henry and Brandy, you must never ask that question again; I mean never!"

"Mom?"

"I'm going to raise this child alone; Henry and I may need your help. Will you help me, dear?" Jessica's emotions were out of control again.

"Sure, Mom. You can count on it. But, Mom, do not cry, please. I do not care if Santa Clause is the father. Mom, I'm sorry."

"Jessica, we will never judge you. I would love to call you Mom." Brandy said.

Henry talked with his mother and Brandy until midnight, then retired for the evening.

Brandy was supposed to sleep in the spare bedroom, but she crawled into bed with Henry before dawn without waking him. Jessica was up first and caught them in bed together, but she did not say a word.

Brandy woke up before Henry and quietly went downstairs. Jessica was already sitting at the dining room table.

"Merry Christmas, Jessica." Brandy saw the worry in her eyes.

"Merry Christmas, dear. Where did you sleep?" Her remark was sharp, cutting.

"I love him, Jessica. He loves me too!" Brandy lowered her head and did not look at Jessica.

"Yes, I can tell. It would take a fool not to notice. But Henry also loves your sister, and I believe she loves him?"

"Yes. It's a frightful conundrum." Brandy held her head up proudly.

"Well, we are not Mormons, Brandy. What does Barby think about all of this, or doesn't she know?" Jessica's voice was stern and unkind.

"It's complicated, but things have a way of working themselves out." Brandy smiled.

"Well, are you and Henry serious, or is this just some cheap fling?" Jessica asked rudely.

"Jessica, I have the utmost respect for you. I'll never question your morals if you don't question mine." Brandy tried to quell her mounting rage.

"Brandy, I'm Henry's mother. I do not see anything but problems. But, my god, what were you thinking?" she scolded.

Brandy loved Henry and did not want to debate the issue with his mother. Brandy loved Jessica, too, but she would sacrifice their friendship if it meant giving up Henry.

"My father didn't think anyone knew about his secret. I stumbled onto some evidence and confronted him last summer. We talked long, but I kept quiet because I knew my mother was a cold bitch at times.

Also, I genuinely love you, Jessica. Please, I do not want to go down this road with you," she pleaded.

Jessica felt a stabbing pain in her chest. She dropped her cup of coffee, and the cup shattered into tiny fragments. Jessica lurched back in her chair and hung her head. She could not look at Brandy. "I'm sorry, Brandy, I should not have pried; it won't happen again." Jessica paused and sat quietly. Then she asked the question she most feared. "Does Henry or anyone else know?"

Brandy spoke calmly and with reverence. "I think my mother knew he was seeing someone, but I don't think she ever suspected it was you. Jessica, I am not going to hold this over your head. Regardless of how you feel about Hank and me, I will never reveal this to anyone. You made my father incredibly happy, Jessica. You were very dear to him. He was not much of a family man until the last few years. My mother refused to sleep with him after returning from our California trip. My parents almost divorced, but I think your companionship prevented that from happening. Dad told me he loved Mom, but he also needed the love of a woman. I will be eternally grateful, Jessica, because he told me he loved you, and you motivated him to continue. Look at me, Jessica, please? My dad is the father of your baby, isn't he?"

Brandy picked up the shattered pieces. Then she wiped up the spill.

Jessica began to cry. She put both of her hands over her face and wept.

Brandy came back to the table and knelt in front of Jessica. "No, don't do that to yourself. Hank will be down soon. We do not want to upset him, Jessica."

Jessica examined Brandy's beautiful face and realized she was sincere. "Can you ever forgive me, dear?"

"There's nothing to forgive. You are the mother of my father's child. I am going to have another brother or sister. We are more than simply good friends now; we're family. I need a mom, and so does Barby. So, let us let things work out, and we will embrace the result. Can we do that, Jessica?"

"Yes, Brandy, we can. I like the way you think, dear. You're such a positive woman."

"Merry Christmas, Jessica. If you ever need to talk, I am a good listener. I am going to have another sibling, too. I love you. How far along are you?"

"Thank you, dear; I'll try. I am glad you know. I want you to know I loved your father very much. The doctor says I am four months old. I told your father I would not wreck his marriage. We were both happy with our relationship."

"I know, Jessica. It would take a fool not to notice." Jessica smiled and laughed, "That's good, dear."

"Let's make breakfast, Jessica."

They woke Henry up, fed, mothered, and loved him.

The drive to Battle Creek allowed the three adults to discuss the mature theme that had presented itself.

"So, dear, how long have you and Brandy been an item?"

Henry was driving, and his mother sat behind him. He looked at his mother in the mirror. She had a crooked expression on her face. "Mom, look out the window and be quiet." She slapped the back of his head and then pulled his ponytail hard. "Ouch. Will you look at the scenery and behave yourself?" Brandy sat next to him, laughing. "What have you two wenches been up to this morning?"

"Answer my question, Henry." She yanked his head back again.

"She took advantage of my innocence when I turned eighteen, Mom."

"Bullshit, he was never innocent, Jessica. On the contrary, he's the most virile man I have ever known!"

"Who are you going to marry, Henry? Brandy or Barby?"

"Mom, we do not have to get married; maybe you should just look out the window," he said slowly.

"Hank, your mother is worried about you. She loves you and wants you to be happy. I'll make him happy, Jessica!"

"Henry, I'm going to look out the window even though there isn't a thing to see; I'm looking."

"Mom, we don't discuss our relationship around Barby. Of course, she knows about everything, but avoiding the subject is helpful."

"Henry, I will not say a word," Jessica said.

Bobby and Sherry's estate sat on a bluff overlooking Goguac Lake. The two-story limestone architecture stood alone; the nearest neighbor was hundreds of yards away. An eight-foot hurricane fence surrounded the property, which measured fourteen acres. A row of blue spruce trees lined the long driveway leading to the park-like yard in front of the house.

Henry pulled up to the main entry and shut off the car. Sherry and Barby ran out of the house, smiling and waving. "Merry Christmas. Hello, family. Brandy, Jessica, and Henry." Bobby stood in the doorway waving. Henry caught his eye, looked around, and flipped him off. Bobby pointed at him with one finger and smiled.

Henry asked, "How did you find this place, Bobby?"

Barby gave Henry a coy smile. Henry tried to ignore her, but she wore a low-cut blouse and a tight pair of black pants. She wiggled her stuff for him. Bobby was talking, and Henry missed most of what he said.

Sherry was watching Henry and noticed his preoccupation with Barby. She kindly reworded everything her husband related. Henry made eye contact with her, and she made a slight quirk, acknowledging his appreciation.

The estate had been on the market for years. Sherry's uncle helped them find it when they got married. Bobby had been leasing it but was now in the process of buying it.

Bobby said, "So, stretch, are you returning to Michigan?" Barby turned and kicked Bobby. "I'm sorry, Brandy. Are you coming back to Michigan?" Bobby asked politely.

"I don't know, Pudge, I mean Bobby," Brandy said.

Sherry winked at Brandy.

"I have my home and business in Boston. So, if I move, I do not think it will be back to Michigan. But I don't know," Brandy said.

Bobby asked, "Where are you going to live, Henry?"

Jessica looked at her son; "I'd like to know the answer to that question, Henry."

"Well, there's this girl I know; she lives out on the coast. I'm thinking about joining her in the future."

Barby and Brandy, in unison, said, "Which coast?"

"I don't know. Which way is the coast from here?" Henry asked.

Barby pointed one way, and Brandy told the other way. When they realized what he was doing, they put their arms down and smiled curtly at each other.

"How's business, Bobby? Are you making any money?" Henry asked.

"If I could get more cars from Detroit, it would make things a lot easier, but yeah, we're profitable, Henry," Bobby said.

Later, while Henry was alone in the kitchen with Sherry, she approached him and said, "Henry, sisters?"

"It's a long, complicated, long story," Henry said.

"We need to talk long, Henry, just you and me. How about I call you sometime, or better yet, you call me. Bobby wants me to get more involved in his family. I think you're a project."

Henry remembered what Bobby had told him earlier, "Sherry wanted to major in psychology. Although only a freshman, she already thought she could fix men."

Sherry arranged the rooming. Henry was sleeping by himself. Jessica smiled at her son;

Celibacy can have its rewards, dear."

Everyone met at the Flying Saucer Inn the following day for lunch. Afterward, Brandy needed to leave for New England. Henry drove her to the airport, and Brandy cried to Detroit. Henry was beside himself with grief. She did not talk about why she was so upset, and she declined when he tried to engage her in conversation.

She still had not said a word when he escorted her to her gate. Brandy clung to him desperately, kissed him firmly, and walked away without looking back.

On the trip back to Barneyville, Henry cried several times. Brandy was constantly on his mind. His chest ached from the anxiety he suffered. Henry wanted to go to Boston with her but was reluctant to pursue her. She was very vulnerable, and he did not want to exploit her. While he drove, he reasoned his love for her was much more than the physical attraction. He missed her wit and confidence. She made him feel like he could do anything in life and be extraordinarily successful. When she was in his presence, exciting aura-like electricity filled the air. He thought about how he reacted in her presence and realized how delighted he was with her.

Henry wanted to call her when he knew she would be home and tell her he was moving to Boston to be near her. But did she want him? On the contrary, she seemed to want to stay in New England. Was there a reason? What could it be?

He came upon the exit for Barneyville and drove into town. He was still pondering his dilemma.

Barby was taking a nap in his room when he arrived. His mother met him at the door.

"Henry, I'm worried about you. I can tell you have been crying. I have some fresh coffee brewing. Let us talk, dear."

They sat down together in the kitchen. "Mom, I don't have any answers, and I know you want to know what I will do. Well, I do not know. I don't know."

She reached over and put her hand on his shoulder. "You love them both, don't you?"

"Yes, Mom, I do. I cannot live without them both. It is not right. I know it is wrong. But my heart won't let go."

"Henry, you need to be fair. It will not be easy, but you must choose—the sooner, the better. It is not fair to Brandy Ba,rby, or you. It may be the most difficult decision you will ever have to make, but you need to do it, and it needs to be permanent."

"I know, Mom and I will seriously consider this. I will make my decision by summer, I promise."

"I love you, Henry. I know you will make a fair choice. But I need to tell you something. Brandy is head over heels in love with you. I think Barby loves you, too, but her passion is more intense than Brandy's. Brandy needs you, Henry.

"Barby in your room. I will turn the television on low. I was young once, too!"

"Mom, you're still a wonderful woman. Is there any future with your baby's father? I'm not asking who, Mom."

"Go to your room, dear. Don't worry about me." She ran her fingers through his long hair. He was much too tall now, but she still enjoyed the ritual. Then, finally, he broke out in a sizeable double-dimpled smile.

She asked, "What? Go ahead and say it. I know it's coming." He held her against him.

"Way to go, Mom. It is wonderful. I hope you'll let me help you."

"Go to your room, but don't make any babies. You're too young."

Henry thought about calling Brandy; he knew he needed someone to care for her, and he knew he could fill the role, but now he worried about Barby. She was never as strong as Brandy in the past, but their roles seem to be reversing. Henry was in a dither. Free love. There is nothing free about love. How could he allow himself to get involved with two sisters? Free love? It did not work anymore; sublimating his relationship with the two sisters was wrong.

Henry knew his mother was correct; he needed to be a grown-up about things and make the difficult decision to make things right. Moreover, he needed to be a kind man.

Jessica knew she was pushing Henry toward Brandy, but she felt the two were a match. She questioned her resolve to wonder if she was more worried about Brandy because she knew about Benjamin but dismissed it as nonsense.

Bobby and Sherry took Barby and Henry to Detroit Sunday morning. Bobby stayed in Ann Arbor, but Sherry went back to Battle Creek. After that, they would only see each other on weekends until he graduated.

Brandy was divorced from the monster she had married in the early spring. She intended to stay in Boston.

Henry was going to be a sophomore at San Diego State. He received a letter from Brandy in early May inviting him to Boston for the summer. Barby expected him in Berkeley, and he had promised to spend most of the summer with her.

Things had worked out by the end of May so that he would spend the first three weeks of June with Barby in Berkeley. After that, everyone met in Barneyville in the last week of June. Jessica was due that week. Henry would be in Boston with Brandy in the previous three weeks in July. Then, in August, he would be in Barneyville with his mom.

CHAPTER 33

Barby's Berkeley

The drive from San Diego was a long one. Henry drove five hundred miles in thirteen hours.

The Berkeley hills were still green in early June.

Pepper, her best friend and one of her sorority sisters went to Europe for the summer with her parents. Barby was house-sitting for them in June. The house was a large multi-story home overlooking north Berkeley.

The early evening sun was very intense in northern California. Henry had difficulty navigating the turns as brilliant sunlight appeared from the shadows at almost every turn.

Barby was outside taking groceries into the house when Henry arrived. She waved and smiled and ran into his arms. "Hello, silly boy. You took your sweet time getting here. I have been on pins and needles for hours. You look nice, very handsome. Are you hungry?" she asked.

"You look fabulous, Barby. You smell even better. Yes, I am starving. When do we eat?"

She helped him get his things into her bedroom. "Now, take off your clothes while I draw you a bath. You smell. Dinner will be ready in an hour."

She joined him in the garden tub twenty minutes later. The bathroom was in the center of an atrium. There were hanging plants dangling down the walls, and a lush, thick vine covered the ceiling.

Barby scrubbed him from head to toe. She shaved him, trimmed his hair, cut his toenails, and cleaned his ears.

Barby purchased some apparel for Henry because she did not like his taste in clothing. So Barby bought Henry light summer clothing, a pale green polo shirt, white Bermuda shorts, and white sneakers designed for the deck of a sailboat.

Barby wore a white satin blouse, a white pleated skirt with large red and purple flowers, and red pumps.

They went into the rear patio to watch the sunset over Marin County. Barby prepared fresh lemon-lime fruit drinks drenched with Jim

Beam. They ate, and then she broke some weed and called a cab while they shared several righteous joints.

They went into the city to her favorite underground nightclub. The place was noisy and crowded.

"How long have you been coming here, Barby?" Henry asked.

"Pepper turned me on to it. So, we come here together on Saturday nights." He looked at the girl he thought he knew. His jaw-dropping gesture made him look like a little boy.

"We always go home together, so don't get all puffed up like a toad." He held her close while they danced, but his step was charisma, and she thought he was too macho.

By midnight, she had pumped him full of whisky and Marijuana. His old personality resurfaced, and he danced more as she remembered.

It was past two before they returned to their lodging. Henry and Barby were trying to remember how they got back.

Henry woke up and was cold. He did not know where he was, but someone was warm beside him. She looked like an angel, a brunette beauty. Her eyes cracked open, and a kind, loving smile followed.

Henry peeked through crusted eyelids, "I've seen those eyes before. So, what are we doing this week, sweetie?"

"We're going to work at propinquity," she said.

Henry smiled, "What the hell is propinquity?"

She leaned over and kissed him. "We're going to re-ignite our fire." She kissed him again. "Get to know each other as if we were related. You know, kinship." She rolled over and lay on his chest. "Make love to me, Henry."

She did not have to ask him twice. They wrestled with one another for over an hour. He could not get enough of her, and she responded the same way. Unlike Brandy's athletic slenderness, her body was still incredibly soft and pliant.

Barby egged him to be more aggressive, coaxing him to be virile and masculine with his technique.

They took another long bath together and talked while they teased each other.

"I missed you, Henry. I wish we lived closer. Don't you?" She was sitting in front of him, leaning back and kissing him.

"You're turning me on again, pretty girl. You're playing with fire, you know." He kissed the nape of her neck and pulled her bottom against his waking virility.

She leaned back again and met his eyes. "No, you can wait a while, can't you? But, my goodness, Henry, you will wear me out. Look at you; you're ready to suck the life out of my body."

"Barby, you turn me on. I cannot help it. It's not like a switch you can turn off."

She reached up with her finger and pushed his nose sideways. "There, I turned you off. I will turn you on again when I am ready. Come on; we're going for a drive."

Barby rented a Porsche for the week. Then, they drove up to Napa, stopping for brunch.

Afterward, she drove Highway 101 to Willits, a small town on the edge of Redwood Forest. She was a little girl the last time she read about it in a book. A nine-hole golf course in the middle of the redwoods took your breath away. So they rented clubs and went out to the golf course.

The immense trees were bare of branches for over one hundred feet, making a golfer navigate several stately trees. Henry and Barby felt like leprechauns playing in a whimsical fairy tale.

The scenery was breathtaking. The lighting created an illusion of grandeur. Light and dark purple, peach, green, yellow, red, and brown shaded the mythical fairways. Ribbons of high fog interlaced the two-thousand-year-old living legends. Bright, thin beams of sunlight gleamed hundreds of feet down through the canopy and landed on moss-covered rocks.

The first tee was between two twin trees. Barby's ball bounced off the left tree and ran onto the fairway.

Henry's shot split the two giants but hit a rock and bounded off to the left out of play. Barby shouted, "See what you get for showing off!"

"How did you find this place, Barby?"

"Pepper told me about it. I came here with her last month. Isn't this grand Henry?"

The holes played quickly, and the round was over too soon. The golf course was busy with golfers. Barby and Henry only stood a chance of playing another game after dark.

She drove south across the country over the coastal range to Highway 1. They had dinner at Bodega Bay.

They crossed the Golden Gate Bridge around midnight. It became cold quickly, so they stopped along with the Marina District and had some coffee.

"It's nice to be together again, Barby. I've missed you something awful." He put his arm around her as they sat together in the booth.

"Hasn't it been a beautiful day, Henry?" She sipped her coffee and snuggled against him.

"How are you doing in school?" he asked.

"I'm carrying a 3.85 GPA. Some of my classes are difficult, but you know me, all work and no play."

Henry let her perfume seep into his nostrils and whispered; I will not hide my feelings for you. I want to marry you, Barby, and I want to do something other than three or four years. So we do not have to have children right away. But I want you to know several girls at San Diego State are pregnant. They are going to school full-time. So, I'm saying that if you got pregnant, you wouldn't have to quit school."

Her smile was the casual one she wore most of the time. Unfortunately, it did little to encourage Henry.

"Henry, I love you. I do. I cannot marry you now, silly boy. I want to marry you, but I must still be twenty-one, Honey. Please, Henry, my education has to come first."

Henry knew she would not say yes, but he had to try. "How long do you expect me to wait for you?"

"I don't have an answer for you. You know I do not. I can only promise that if you wait, I will marry you, Henry. I've wanted to be your wife since I was a little girl."

He sat quietly, trying to formulate a better argument.

"Henry, can we talk about something else? This subject is making me uncomfortable."

Henry was trying to convince himself that she was correct. First, however, they needed to wait until they both completed their education. Barby touched his face, "Do you miss the snow, darling?"

His warm smile replaced his grimace, "Yes, I do. But, no, I do not. Sometimes, I guess."

Barby was surprised by his quick response. She needed to be optimistic now, and as she studied his face, she was not convincing herself. Henry was not falling for it either.

"How many girlfriends do you have in San Diego?" She felt her smile enlivened and hoped it would affect him.

"I only have two girlfriends. Not one is in San Diego, though. I wish I were born in Utah."

She reached over and held his hand. "That would never work, Honey. It would help if you made a choice.

"This is not easy for me to say, darling. But it needs to be said. Of course, Brandy loves you as much, maybe as much or more than I do. Nevertheless, I want you to decide before you return to Berkeley. You must do this, Henry, for your sake, Brandy's, and mine."

The waitress came over and filled their cups again.

"Henry, Brandy needs you to tell her about your intentions toward her. I want to get married when I am twenty-five. After that, I want to go to medical school, Henry. Brandy needs to get on with her life now. You must tell her if you are not a part of it."

He gazed at her and looked confused. "Look, silly boy. I want to enjoy life for a while and not be tied down. Don't you understand?"

"No, it doesn't make sense, but I am trying to understand." Henry was sharp with her at first, then his voice trailed off, and he became contrite. He was dumbfounded. His innocence was lost a long time ago.

Barby clarified, "Even if I got married, Henry, I won't change my name. I'm not going to have any children until I'm thirty." Barby's voice was tender and supportive.

"I'm almost twenty-one years old; you won't be twenty-one until October; we have a lot of time. I don't know how you can say you want to wait until you're thirsty to have children." Henry was losing her, and it was his greatest fear.

"I want kids when I want them: four children, two boys and two girls," she said.

Henry tried to smile and told her, "I'm sure you will get what you want."

The drive back to the house in the clouds was cold but quick. Then, finally, they were in each other's arms again, and all the emotional pain evaporated.

The following day, they left for Monterey. They rented a room overlooking Pebble Beach. They slept in until ten am the first morning. Then, they had a late brunch and played eighteen holes of golf.

They ate at the most excellent restaurants and then danced until midnight every night.

Barby and Henry spent six days in Monterey golfing, sightseeing, sailing, and dancing until the wee hours of the morning.

The week passed by quickly, and they were on their way back to Berkeley.

"I will love you until the day I die, Barby."

He was not teasing, and she knew it. "I know how to fix a broken heart." She smiled.

When they arrived in Berkeley, Barby promptly set to the task of making Henry realize that he would never forget those nights, those precious Berkeley nights.

CHAPTER 34

Jessica's Baby

*H*enry and Barby arrived in Barneyville on a bright summer day. Bobby decided for them to drive a new Mustang convertible. The next day, Henry and Barby picked up Brandy in Detroit. Together, they stayed at Henry's house with his mother. Jessica was due to have her baby in four days.

Brandy, Henry, and Barby walked over to Millpond the following day. Barby was running in California with her friend Pepper. Barby asked them, "Want to go for a run?"

They went back to the house and dressed to run.

Brandy said, "Well, kids, this is a surprise."

Barby was touching her toes. She grimaced and said, "I've never run around the entire trail. How hard is it?"

Henry was doing deep knee bends. "We'll go easy on you, Barby." Henry looked at Brandy, "Short legs; she'll never keep up."

Brandy giggled. Henry never heard Brandy giggle. Instead, he had a warm, excellent feeling wash over him, and he took in a deep breath.

Henry walked down the trail. He was ducking under the willow tree that covered the dirt path before the footbridge.

The late July morning was cool and damp, and mud puddles were everywhere. It rained nearly every day the past week. A deep blue sky brightened the morning.

Brandy walked behind him and gasped, "Barby, look at the tulips. Oh, aren't they pretty? Do you remember going to the Tulip Festival in Holland, sweetie? I have not been to the Tulip Festival in years. Do you remember Honey?"

"Yep, I remember the fit Bobby threw. So, brandy, we should go to Holland on a warm spring day. Hey, you two, I'm ready to run."

Barby blew past Henry, and Brandy was hot on her heels.

Brandy yelled, "Come on, Hank. Where did she get all this energy?"

Henry was laughing, Barby's little butt wiggled around the corner, and Brandy was stretching out and trying to catch up to her.

When Henry made the turn, the cat-o-nine-tails blocked his view of the footbridge, but he heard the girl's footsteps romping over the wooden walkway. His laughter gave him a side ache, and he could not get into a rhythm. He broke into a hard sprint but knew he could not keep up that pace for awfully long.

The women were off the bridge before he got there. When he crossed the peak, he saw Barby in front of her sister. They were climbing the highest hill on the trail. Henry slowed to a steady pace, but it was still too fast.

Henry came down the big hill and could not believe his eyes. Barby and Brandy were off the trail and heading for the highway bridge. There were a dozen kids lined up to make the thunder jump. Barby pushed through the kids and leaped before Henry arrived at the bridge. Brandy leaped and turned to wave at Henry; down, she fell into the abyss.

Henry was in the pipe ten seconds later. When he surfaced, the two sisters splashed him. Brandy was behind him. She ducked under and pulled his shorts off.

Brandy surfaced and threw the shorts at her sister. Barby's eyes were bulging, and she grabbed his shorts before he could retrieve them. Finally, Barby yelled, "Wow, Henry, I am so out of breath. Did I kick your ass or what?"

Brandy came up behind him and wrapped herself around him. Henry stood on a hollow tree trunk. The water was almost over his shoulders, and Brandy could barely touch the log.

"Hank, turn around and stay on the log."

"Hello, beautiful." He kissed her tenderly.

She reached down and caressed him while they kissed. He trembled from surprise. He steadied himself while she kissed him.

Barby was treading water fifteen feet away. When she first recognized what her sister was doing, she swam behind Henry and hung his shorts over his head. Then, Barby swam for the shore. She turned toward them when she touched the bottom and yelled. "You two are unbelievable."

Brandy pulled away from Henry's lips. "Don't move; kiss me. Henry held her upper body still, but she had her way underwater in the unseen depths.

Later that evening, after helping Jessica, Barby teased Henry and Brandy about what they did in public. "You two have no shame. I swear you both should be for indecent behavior. There were little kids there today."

The three of them were sitting together on the couch, watching television. Henry was in the middle.

Brandy smiled and gave her sister a wrinkled nose. "You're just jealous because you didn't think of it."

Henry held out his palm, and Brandy slapped it hard.

Barby shoved Henry and said, "I'd never jump him in public like that, Brandy."

Brandy came right back, "Define public."

Barby thought for a moment, "More than two people."

Brandy smiled and gave Henry her patented cat-like look.

"I remember a time in Florida when you jumped him in public." Barby looked at her and smiled. She formed her mouth to make a reply, but her lips could not follow the confusion her brain was sending them. So, her mouth looked like a baby when it wanted to say something but could not decide. It formed a word, then changed and reformed back and forth. Finally, she said, "Uh, uh!"

Brandy looked at Henry. "Is that what you learn in college in California?"

The three young adults enjoyed their evening together. Henry slept by himself.

Brandy and Barby left together on the third day and were gone most of the afternoon.

Henry sat talking with his mother.

"Henry, get me the pillow behind you, dear. I need it for my back." Henry took the pillow over to his mom. "Put it behind me, dear."

"Mom, you look ready to have a baby."

She smiled at him. "This baby is much bigger than you were, and I don't remember having this much trouble with you. I cannot get comfortable, Honey. I think I may need to go lie down." She saw his reaction and realized he was, in many ways, still just a boy.

"Mom, do you need to go to the hospital?"

She knew that was coming; it was written all over his face. "No, Henry. I need to get comfortable. I'm fine."

He wanted to do something to help her. She seemed so helpless. He had never been around a pregnant woman before and had no idea what was happening. The front door opened, and Brandy and Barby walked in.

"Help. I do not know what I am doing." Brandy smiled at Barby.

"Typical male, what do you think?" Brandy teased.

"We better go rescue him. He looks like he is the one about to have a baby. But, Brandy, this requires a woman's touch."

The sisters set about arranging the couch so that Jessica could relax. They sat and talked for an hour, and then Barby left for Battle Creek.

Henry and Brandy put his mom in bed and went to the Flying Saucer together.

They were dancing on top of the outdoor lounge. Henry noticed Brandy had a sublime glow about her. She looked at him with a glib expression. Slowly, her facial expression transformed into a warm, loving grin.

"You look extraordinary tonight, Brandy."

She raised her chin, slightly twisted her face, and gave him a pursed-lip lost-in-thought look. "Hank, do you love me?"

He started to reply, but she put her fingers over his lips.

"Think before you say anything. Do you love me?"

Henry realized she was looking for a mature answer, not a giggling teenage response.

"When I took you to the airport after the funeral, you cried most of the way to Detroit. I could not empathize with your feelings. I wanted to know why you were crying and did not understand your pain. "On the way back to Barneyville, it finally hit me. I imagine you were sad because you had just lost your parents. I also reasoned that your marriage did not work out, and the emotional baggage was heavy on your heart. Last, I pondered your pain, possibly due to your love for me. I dismissed the last one because I did not love you. I thought I did, but I did not know love—not real love," he said.

The music ended, and they went to their table.

"When you were here for the funeral, we were not intimate. Do you remember Brandy?"

She held his hands and sat before him on the table's edge. "I remember Hank. You were very considerate."

"Brandy, I realized on the way home that my love for you was not just some primal sexual pleasure. I wanted to call you and beg you to let me come to Boston and live with you, and then I woke up. I asked myself, 'What woman will want you to shack up with her and not be able to support her?' Then I thought you had a secret lover, which appeased my pain. But unfortunately, it did not last long, and I was hurting again. I came to understand there is no such thing as free love. There is nothing free about love. I have not been virtuous with you. I have used you to satisfy my own carnal needs. "As I drove to Barneyville, I was overwhelmed by grief. Brandy, I cried so hard I stopped the car. I was so ashamed of myself." He looked at the floor, unable to go on.

She whispered, "Let us go home, Hank. Please, darling, let me take you home."

Henry managed to get up. He was thankful for the cover of darkness and poor lighting. He knew his face was wet with tears, but he was ashamed to wipe them off, thinking someone might see him.

He could not look at her, and even when they arrived home, he avoided her eyes until they were in his bedroom. Brandy undressed him and tucked him into bed. She went to check on his mother. When Brandy came back, he was crying into his pillow. She undressed and joined him. He rolled into her arms and cried silently.

She had her answer; Hank loved her. Yes, in the beginning, their relationship was physical. However, the love she felt for him was also in his heart for her. She held him while he cried and fell asleep.

They slept until his mother cried for him just before dawn. Henry heard his mother, but he could not get up. He nudged Brandy while he struggled to gain his senses. Finally, she sprang to her feet and bounded out of his room. He could not find his pants and was stumbling when Brandy returned to his room.

"Hank, hurry. I just called the hospital. Your mother's water broke. Get moving, Hank!"

"I can't find my pants!" he said.

Brandy remembered she threw them in the laundry.

"Wear something else, Hank." Henry went through his drawers and found some old shorts.

At the hospital, Henry called Bobby and Barby. Benjamin Henry Rotyn came into the world weighing ten pounds and eleven ounces. He had a full head of thick dark hair and was a beautiful baby with green eyes and huge hands.

Brandy left Barneyville four days later.

Henry left Barneyville a week later.

CHAPTER 35

Brandy's Boston

*B*oston was very green in July; the immense juniper, oak, maple, and mix of evergreens shaded nearly every square foot of the suburbs. Massachusetts enjoyed the same dense tree growth as Michigan.

"Hank, let's go out for breakfast. Afterward, I want to take you over to my Boutique."

Brandy was delighted to have him in New England. He was tired from the long trip. He jumped out and took her in his arms. She kissed him tenderly but abruptly pulled away in a wisp. She asked playfully, "So, have you had your way with my little sister?"

Brandy was wearing blue jeans and a sweatshirt. He put his finger in a belt loop on her pants and asked her, "Is that the sort of thing women buy in your boutique?" Henry inquired.

Brandy punched him in the stomach.

"Hank, I want you to sleep in the guestroom tonight. Is that all right with you?"

"Is this any way to greet an old lover? You jumped me in the river."

"It's a bad time of the month for me. One more day, please?" She put her arms around his neck, "If you behave yourself, you might get lucky."

They slept in separate rooms the first night. Brandy had breakfast ready before she woke Henry. When he came to the table, he felt tough. "You need coffee, a bath, then a nice rubdown," she said. He nodded without saying a word. He picked up the coffee cup, held it under his nose, and let the aroma soak in.

Henry sipped it and woke up just a little more. "How did you sleep?" she asked, wrapping her arms around him. Brandy pushed his hair to the side and kissed his cheek. Then, she whispered, "I have not been with a man since my divorce. Well, other than the river, but that did not count."

Henry assured her, "I'm here to help you in any way I can. If that includes no sex, you must know that you mean much more to me than just a jump in the sack."

"Are you saying our lovemaking is just a jump in the sack?" she teased.

Henry smiled and remembered one of the lines his mother used to tell him: "Silence is golden."

Brandy served the meal and sat with him as they discussed everything they needed to catch up on.

"Hank, do you still run in the mornings in California?"

"No, not every morning," he said.

"Well, I could tell in Barneyville. Barby beat you, Henry. I run at least two miles every morning. I'll cut you some slack today, but we'll be out the door at sunrise tomorrow." When she smiled, her pearly white teeth enhanced the brightness of her beauty.

"Do you have any idea how much I love you?" He said in the most severe tone he could manage. Her green eyes brightened, and he reached out and touched her cheek.

After breakfast, Henry and Brandy ran a mile and a half. Afterward, he took a long shower, caring for his much-needed personal hygiene.

Brandy took him into town and gave him a grand tour of her Boutique. She introduced him to her employees.

Late that afternoon, they returned to Brandy's house. She was still smoking pot, and she had some dynamite Acapulco gold. They listened to some music and drank way too much wine. They laughed late into the night, retired, and slept together, but there was no sex. Henry wanted to be patient with her. She needed to spend some time with a gentleman, and he intended to give her that opportunity.

At sunrise, they were out the door. The morning run took Brandy and Henry into a public park along a small creek. The Park was already busy with runners of all ages. Flowerbeds lined the trail's edge while thick, well-trimmed grass grew to the water's edge on the Creekside. Every so often, flat granite boulders or limestone outcroppings stood in place of the grass.

She set a furious pace, and Henry struggled to keep up.

Later in the morning, she made him breakfast, and they ate outside on her patio. She made a bacon omelet with fresh rye toast and grapefruit wedges.

After consuming the meal, Henry asked, "What happened to the two-mile run?"

She smiled and said, "I know it was more like three this morning. I need to get you in shape. You'll need all the energy you can muster, buddy!"

She grabbed his hand and led him into the bedroom. They undressed while she filled her garden tub. Then, after a long bath, they returned to bed.

She was timid initially, but she took him on a trip to fantasy land.

Brandy took him to a bit of dinner at the country club. They played eighteen holes and made reservations for a tee time the following day.

Brandy drove around the city, pointed out the landmarks, and showed Henry her favorite places. Brandy and Henry spent hours talking about old times. They drank French wine, grilled T-bone steaks, and ate fresh corn on the cob.

The two lovers went to bed early. Brandy wore a silk nightgown. Henry had never enjoyed such soft, passionate love with Brandy until this week, and he fell deeply in love. The changes he noticed in her in Florida had become even more pronounced as she made love to him like an artist. Brandy cried in his arms after making love. Henry held her quietly for almost an hour.

On Sunday morning, after their run and shower, Brandy drove Henry north in the country to a little outdoor restaurant overlooking the ocean.

After they ordered their meals, Brandy asked, "Hank, can you get used to living in this part of the country?"

Henry did not know what to say. His silence instantly ruined the moment. He looked at her, and she tried to hide the tears in her eyes. Her statement caught him off guard. His awkwardness condemned his love for her.

Henry sat looking at his glass, and he still did not know what he wanted to say to Brandy. Henry wanted his opportunity to tell her that, yes, he would live here with her, but he blew it. Finally, he admitted, "Brandy, I love you very much. My life right now is in San Diego. I need to finish my education." Why did he say that? It was not what he meant! His inability to say what he meant tore at his heart.

Brandy yearned for him to express his love for her. But, as always, Barby watered down her love for him. She wanted him to address his feelings without her involvement. Brandy waited for him to say something, but he sat quietly. Finally, she turned away from him and cried silently.

"I'm not sure how I could break this to Barby." He rambled on, stumbling for the right words.

"Hank, Barby knows everything. I have never hidden anything from her. She knows where you are now!"

When she spoke about her sister, Henry sensed some hostility in Brandy's voice.

"I talked to Barby this morning. I asked her if she would understand if I proposed to you. She gave me her blessing, Hank."

Henry stood up, trying to clear his head. Memories flashed across his mind; he thought about his uncle's house on Coronado, and he saw Barby in the hot tub in Berkeley.

The waiter came over-interpreting his standing up to mean he was leaving the table. He moved his chair to the side, allowing Henry to walk away more. Henry decided to sit back down just as another patron motioned to the waiter. The waiter looked away from Henry just as Henry leaned back into his chair. Brandy saw what was happening but could not react quickly enough to prevent his fall. When Henry missed the chair, the waiter tried to catch him, but his efforts served to trip Henry even further. Henry went backward and hit his head on the table's edge behind him.

The next thing Henry remembered was that his head was in Brandy's lap. He had knocked himself out cold. Brandy helped him out to her car and took him home. "Hank, did Barby ask you to live in Berkeley?"

"No, why would she? She does not have her own home. She lives in a sorority house."

"Barby loves you but doesn't think you understand her world. I didn't think it would make you fall head over heels!" Instead, she smiled and wondered how much he loved her sister.

They stopped and bought some groceries on the way home. After putting them away, she entered the living room and sat on his lap.

Brandy had an old cat-like look in her eye. Henry tipped her back and cradled her, "Brandy, I would love to spend the rest of my life with you in any town, state, country, or planet."

Henry slipped from under her and knelt on one knee while holding her hands. Brandy pulled her hands loose and buried them in his hair. "Isn't this just a little chivalrous?" she asked, smiling brightly.

He looked deeply into her emerald eyes. "Brandy Sue Kraneger, would you do me the honor, fulfill my dreams, marry me, mother our children, become my wife, be my companion for as long as we both shall live?"

Henry pulled the ring out of the pocket his mother gave him. The crew had been in his family for over fifty years. It belonged to his great-great-grandmother, who came to America from Italy. His mother gave it to him and told him to keep it in the family.

"This ring has been in my family for over fifty years. I want you to wear this as a symbol of my love and the whole-hearted love from my family toward your family.

She started crying. "Do you feel this way? Aren't you still in love with Barby?"

"Yes. I will always love your sister, but not how I love you. The law says I can only marry one of you. Barby is not ready to get married. But, brandy, I don't want to wait until I am thirty to have children."

"Henry, I want to have a child right away. Can you handle being a daddy? I have always wanted to have your children, Honey. Yes, I will marry you, darling."

Brandy was more beautiful at that moment than at any time Henry could remember. Henry carried her to bed and tenderly made love to her.

She cried in his arms afterward. But, Hank, I don't want you to do something you'd regret."

"My beautiful Brandy darling. I carried your engagement ring with me soon after your Marriage ended. I have been waiting for the most opportunistic time. I have been waiting for our love to blossom like a beautiful flower."

They agreed to marry in Barneyville at the Inn in the morning. However, Brandy wanted to have an August wedding. That way, Henry could return to school somewhere in Boston.

Brandy told him she could pull some strings since she still had essential contacts at the University.

When they called the following day, Bobby was stunned at hearing the announcement.

Henry and Brandy both talked with Barby. She clarified that while supporting their decision, she still reserved the right to have a baby, Henry. Brandy agreed. Of course, this would remain their secret. Bobby did not care which of his sisters Henry married; he wanted him to marry only one.

CHAPTER 36

Mrs. Brandy Rotyn

Henry and Brandy became man and wife on a bright, warm day in August. The ceremony occurred in the outdoor lounge at the Flying Saucer Inn at sundown. Brandy was radiant. The twenty-five-year-old woman was basking in a glow of pure joy. Barby was the bridesmaid, and Bobby was the best man. The marriage ceremony was semi-private. However, the reception that followed was crowded, loud, and drunk. Well-wishers from Barneyville returned to the tiny village from all over the country, including Gary from Los Angeles. Tom is from Miami—and Terry is from San Jose. Brandy took Henry to Bermuda for seven days on their honeymoon. They stayed in a honeymoon suite at the Royal Princess Hotel. The plush accommodations and ocean view added a pleasant flair to the romantic occasion.

Henry and Brandy divided their time between sightseeing, golfing, swimming, tennis, and dancing. Every morning began with a long run on the beach. Then, we returned to the room, showering, making love, and showering again. Every evening, they enjoyed an excellent full-body massage. After dinner, they danced to the music of the island's steel drum bands. The meals were elaborate seven-course productions of exquisite British cuisine.

Henry rented a small boat, which they motored onto the coral heads. He dropped anchor, and they skin-dived under and around coral. Coral was a living organism; some were thirty feet across and looked like giant mushrooms. They could stand on top of many of them or dive under the umbrella-like structures, peering into an underwater world alive with fish. The colors were brilliant red, green, blue, and ivory shades. Long, sleek barracudas with fierce white teeth swam in schools around them but did not get too close. Tiny fish bit the short body hair on their arms and neck. The nipping was playful most of the time, but occasionally, the nip was a bite.

Henry and Brandy dove under the coral, hiding from the sun and watching the underwater world around them. The visibility was incredible. The water was as warm as a bathtub, and they often played in it all day. There was so much to see. So many intimate hidden parks and beaches provide hours of energetic fun. The colorful shops displayed bright linens. Brandy wanted to order some for her boutique. The nightlife became enchanting because the island music was always uplifting and charming. They spoke as they danced. "Henry, I think I'm pregnant." She looked at his facial expression. He looked like a daddy.

"Wow, now that's something to brag about, Brandy. I am really into you, Honey, simply crazy. You are positively glamorous tonight. The lights sparkle in your eyes and reflect off your silky dark hair. I love your lips; they turn up and down so lovely, and your perfume has always captivated my senses. We are going to be parents. Mom and Dad. Mother and father."

"I love your eyes, Hank. They paralyze me at times. You have me caught up in this indescribable feeling of total domination. I love you. "If you want me to rip your clothes off in public, just keep talking," he said.

She smiled, leaned on his shoulder, and followed his lead as they danced to the captivating music. He pulled her closer, and she cuddled into his tender embrace. "Brandy, we need to be certain."

She looked at his eyes, smiling brightly. "About what, Hank?"

"Our child, we need to be certain."

She screwed her facial expression into a contorted question. "What do you mean?"

He focused his eyes on hers. "I want to be certain you're pregnant."

She kissed him curtly. "Be patient, Hank. I am going to give you something special tonight." She had a cat-like look in her eye.

"I can't wait. Pinch me, gorgeous." She pinched his butt.

"Ouch. Hey, that hurt."

She put her chin on his chest and looked up into his eyes. "You told me to pinch you."

He smiled but then stuck out his bottom lip. "You need to rub the sore spot." He scolded.

She slowly swayed her head no. Finally, Brandy asked, "Why?"

"Why what, Brandy?"

"Why did you want me to pinch you?"

Henry grinned, "I thought I was in a fairy tale. I wanted to be sure this was real."

Brandy bit his neck, "I'm real, darling, and I'm going to make you come four times tonight."

Henry pulled her closer, "My eyeballs almost popped out of my head when I first saw your boobs."

She put her chin on his chest again, "I remember, but you couldn't keep your hands off of them either."

Henry smiled, "Look, Lady, I enjoyed touching them, but my intentions were an innocent touch."

"Bullshit. You were never innocent!"

Later that night in bed, Brandy kept her promise, and Henry could not keep up with her erotic appetite. She made him think he was about to lose his wits.

The next day, they went to Somerset and spent the day on a private beach. They had French wine, Italian bread, Portuguese lunch meat, and Wisconsin cheese. Brandy lay on the beach and clung to Henry all day, "Henry, I loved you before I got married. I didn't want you at my wedding because I knew if you were there, I would not have gone through with it."

"Brandy, you're my epitome of a fulfilled dream. I was captivated by you starting in the sixth grade. Then, on the Au Sable River, I began to experience the thrill of sharing your world. In Muskegon, this teenage boy ascended into manhood in the tender arms of Aphrodite's daughter. I will always cherish the gift I received on that moonlit beach. Then there was the city by the bay and the summer of love."

"Many friends questioned my devotion and love for you, Henry. But you know what? All of them are eating their hearts out now. You make me so happy; I feel much better in your arms." She stopped short of saying Quinn's name. She did not want to spoil the moment. "I love you, Henry."

"Why did you fall in love with me? You could have picked from the rich, powerful, educated, or sophisticated. I could go on for hours describing men with much more to offer than me."

"Henry, you never tried to be someone other than yourself. I love your cerulean blue eyes, I love your hair, I love your gentleness, and I love how smart you are. You have a beautiful mother; your babies should be beautiful. You have a great sense of humor and are wonderful in bed. What else could a lady ask for?"

"Did you know you're using my name, not my nickname?"

She smiled and kissed him. "Which do you prefer, darling?"

Henry looked down at her blouse; she readjusted herself to give him a better view. "I like them both." She pushed his chin up and snapped her fingers.

"Go on, Henry, but you must talk about two boobs or two names. Maybe this is too much for you, darling," Brandy giggled.

"Well, Henry is formal and proper. Whereas Hank is distinctive in that you are the only person using it that I acknowledge. You have been the only person who called me Hank all my life. Do you remember how long you have called me by my nickname?"

"Yes, Hank, I do. I was six, and you were two years old. I can still remember the fist you used to throw. The only thing that would bring you out of them was when I called you Hank. The name worked like magic. Your Mom and Dad tried using it, but you didn't respond to anyone but me."

"Brandy, do you think we can always talk like this?" She nodded, and he laid his head in her lap.

The high coral cliff over them blocked the sun, and the pink sandy beach was cooling in the shade. Brandy felt a cool breeze on her back and shivered.

"Are you getting cold, Honey?" Henry asked.

"A little. But, Henry, when we return to Boston, we must decide where we will live. I want to get a fresh start somewhere far away from New England. I have a very generous inheritance. So, we can live wherever we choose."

"Do you have anywhere in mind, Brandy?"

"San Francisco, I want to be near my sister. We need to wait a couple of years, though. I can sell my business for a profit by then, and I won't take a loss on my lease."

"I can go to school anywhere, Brandy."

"I want to go back to our room, Hank."

Henry precisely understood the kindness she needed.

In September, Henry started classes at Boston City College. The newlyweds fell into a busy routine. They ran two miles every day and five miles on Saturday mornings.

Henry was in school all day while she was at the boutique. Henry studied hard every evening, and Brandy was always there to push him.

Sunday was their day to do unique things together. They took long drives in the country. She loved to revel through the endless antique shops, looking for rare finds to enhance her home and, occasionally, her business.

Brandy took piano lessons through high school and college. She was an accomplished artist. Every Saturday morning, Henry woke up to beautiful music accompanied by her lovely voice. The intimate performances varied each week. One Saturday was a medley of Beatles songs. The following week, he may awaken to the Blue Danube.

Henry's love for Brandy matured immensely in just a few months, and she was bonkers for him. She had been that way since Florida.

Brandy discovered she was pregnant in September and was showing up for Thanksgiving. The morning sickness era passed, and their sex lives renewed. Henry did not know a woman could be so beautiful; Brandy was gorgeous.

Brandy worried about Henry because his draft deferment lottery number was in the low sixties. She did not want him to go to war and leave her with a baby. Unfortunately, Henry did not carry enough credits necessary to keep a college deferment, and Brandy constantly nagged him about it. She wished President Nixon would end the war once and for all.

Henry and Brandy shared beautiful expressions of love every morning.

The entire family traveled to Boston for Christmas. Bobby and Sherry arrived Saturday afternoon, Barby flew out Tuesday night, and Jessica and baby Ben arrived Wednesday night.

On Thursday morning, the smell of fresh pumpkin pies baking in the oven and a wonderful, cheerful sonata, "The Cave of the Ice King," lightly wove its way through the home.

Jessica came into Henry's bedroom and talked with her son.

"How are you kids doing, Honey?" She sat on the side of his bed. Baby Ben was feeding. Jessica had a light towel covering the baby as she fed the baby. She looked her oldest son in the eye.

Henry whined, "Mom?"

"I fed you this way. Why are you complaining now?" Jessica asked.

Henry threw his hands in the air. "We're fine, Mom, and I have a wonderful life and a beautiful wife. Brandy is going to be a wonderful mother."

"Are you happy, dear?"

"Mom, I'm going to be a daddy. I know it must be difficult for you, Brandy, and not Barby, but we have incredible chemistry. I feel like I have been married all my life. I am happy, comfortable, and spoiled.

"Mom, are you seeing anyone?"

"Nope, just taking care of my baby."

"Mom, you're still a lovely woman. Surely, men call on you; I know all of my coaches and teachers drooled all over themselves whenever you came up in conversation."

"Henry, why are you just now telling me these things?"

He smiled and said, "I guess I was a prude. I felt your grieving period should last ten years or something," he said.

Barby called them to breakfast.

Barby and Sherry were beautiful. Jessica, however, felt her years, but her beauty, like Brandy's, added a class flair to the gathering. Barby and Sherry knew it, but both were mature enough to bathe in it rather than compete.

When it came time to enjoy the meal, Henry asked everyone to say a few words, starting with his mother. Jessica stood at the end of the table.

"We have known each other for eons, but this may be our first Christmas together. Thanks to Henry and Brandy, we are all related now. Sadly, our numbers have reduced, but we must hang tough and support one another. We have Ben, and I believe I overheard the name Sarah?" Jessica smiled at the young audience.

Barby stood up next. "Well, Brandy. Can we live any further apart? You are on one coast, and I am on the other. I miss you; I am happy for you. Envious but happy. I wish you joy, contentment, love, and future fertility. Sherry, I am so sorry for *you. No, I feel so sorry. Call me. I can tell you more about him than he can. Jessica, how do you do it? You are the most beautiful woman I know. I will be ecstatic if I can retain your youthful look. Baby Ben, we are all going to spoil you. Bobby, I love Sherry; I do. Henry. Oh, Henry. Just breathe. Get up every morning and breathe." Barby sat down quickly.*

Brandy rose out of her seat. "My turn, Jessica; you're our only parent now. But I do not think parents are supposed to look this good. Baby Ben is a sweet, lovely baby. Sherry, I am sorry. I am sorry, but I am sorry. Call me. I know you need support. Bobby, Pudge, you got more than you deserve. I hope you make her happy, but I want you to be happy too. Barby, my kindred spirit, Sweetie, you know how I feel. You know what is on my mind. I love you. Please pay attention; Barby, Hank, and I have decided to move to Berkeley. We both love you and yearn to be your neighbor. Hank, you make me so happy." Brandy put both of her palms over her tummy. She looked down at her swollen belly. "Sarah, this is your family. These lovely people will be there for you. Respect them, honor them, love them, and believe in them. I do."

Barby started to clap lightly, and everyone joined her in recognizing a class act.

Bobby got up and said, "Ditto." Then he sat back down. Barby slugged his shoulder and contorted her face. Bobby got the message but has yet to get back up.

Sherry stood up, "Brandy, I love your brother. Barby, I love your brother. Jessica, I love Bobby. Henry, I love your hair."

Bobby bellowed, "Hey?"

Sherry put her fingers over his mouth, and he immediately quieted and mellowed out. "Bobby, I would have married you even if I had known you when you were younger!" She removed her fingers from his mouth, kissed him, and sat down.

Everyone looked at Henry. He looked at his mother and whispered, "Ditto?" She raised her eyebrows, pursed her lips, and shook her head now. He looked at Barby; she motioned for him to get back up. When he turned his attention to the others, they all smiled at him. Henry had been thinking about what he could say. He wrote a poem about his life so far. He was going to give it to Brandy on their anniversary.

Henry rose from his chair slowly. "Mother, best friend, best friends, my beautiful wife, Barby; I grew up loving you." Henry was still trying to remember all the words.

"This is for my wife, whom I adore."

Brandy sat up in her chair; she looked at Barby with surprising anxiety building on her face. But her smile was in full blossom. Barby gave her a giddy dip-the-shoulders, tip-the-head-back, aren't-you-special look.

Henry began,

"We are each on the road we did not foresee.

We yearned for and cherished love.

We aspire for freedom, yet we're afraid to be free.

We struggled for maturity, as our passions controlled the direction of our dreams."

All the women gazed at him, stunned and silent. Henry sat down quietly.

Jessica spoke first, "Henry, that was incredible."

Barby looked at Brandy. She silently lipped, "I want him back." Brandy smiled at her sister, fighting back the tears in her eyes. She hugged and kissed her husband.

"Thank you, Hank. You are full of surprises." Brandy said.

Sherry looked at Bobby; she was disappointed in him.

He saw the pain in her eyes. She asked, "Ditto?"

After the meal, Bobby announced a profit-sharing plan. His sisters would receive funds quarterly, starting with the New Year.

Later, Brandy secretly met Jessica. "I'm setting up an account for you to draw on. Now, I want you to take advantage of this, Jessica. If my father were alive, he would have been helping you long before this. I know that look, and this is not an optional arrangement. You need some assistance raising my brother. I set up a college fund. Do not worry; everything has confidentiality."

"Brandy, you kids need everything you can get your hands on. Please, baby Ben and I will be fine?"

"No, this is the final. You will be receiving papers in the mail from our attorney. You can have your attorney look them over. Have him send me a bill; I'll pay his fee."

"Thank you, dear." The two women embraced.

The next day, all the holiday guests left.

Brandy stayed in bed while Henry ran. Brandy took long walks with her husband, but her doctor told her she should not run. He also told her to think seriously about having a C-section. Brandy's doctor explained that her pelvis was too narrow. Brandy emphatically refused such nonsense but never told Henry what the doctor advised.

Henry and Brandy turned one of the bedrooms into a nursery. Brandy shopped for and bought all the typical baby amenities. Pink was the day's color because the baby would be a girl. So, they started spoiling Sarah before she was ever born.

When the snowmelt finished, Brandy was happy to see spring. A new life was blossoming. She and Henry were making a new life together; the baby was their crowning glory.

Henry often spoke with Brandy about how many children he wanted her to mother. She decided on six, three girls and three boys. Henry was happy with that number. He remembered Barby said she wanted four. He asked Brandy if she knew about Barby's four kids after thirty plans. Brandy told Henry that Barby might not have children because she loved to party too much. Brandy's negative expression was only the second time Henry heard Brandy disparage her younger sister.

Henry was so excited that the big day finally came, but he could tell Brandy was scared. She was intent on natural childbirth. Henry sensed her anxiety but did not know her doctor's advice.

Henry's Mom flew up. Barby came in from the coast, and Bobby and Sherry were in town.

CHAPTER 37

Brandy's Gift

*H*enry was with Brandy in the delivery room. She was in labor for more than fourteen hours. Finally, at about four in the morning, Sarah Fawn Rotyn came into the world. Brandy experienced an incredible amount of pain, and complications surfaced right after giving birth. She is hemorrhaging, and the nurses told Henry he had better leave. Brandy asked him to stay with the baby.

Henry kissed her, "I'll see you in a little while. Try not to worry," he said.

Brandy looked very worried, though, and Henry was uncomfortable. He felt helpless. Brandy did not want to leave her baby; she cried to Henry, "Stay with Sarah."

Then the doctor rushed her up to surgery.

Brandy was hemorrhaging before they arrived in the operating room. She insisted on talking with her sister before the anesthesiologist put her under. The doctors warned her that she needed immediate surgery. Brandy told them to wait.

Barby knew it was bad news. She had to put on operating garb before entering. When Barby saw all the blood, her heart almost stopped. "Brandy!" she cried.

When Brandy saw Barby's face, she forced a smile.

"Brandy, I love you. I love you." Barby cried helplessly. A tremulous fear swept over her body.

Brandy was weak and tired. "Barby, come closer. Honey, I know how bad it is." Tears streamed down Brandy's face. "I need to tell you two things."

"Brandy, you're going to be fine." Barby looked up at the doctor, and he did not express any kind of signal, no facial expression, no smile, and no hint of hope.

Barby was suddenly panic-stricken. "Yes, Brandy, you need to tell me two things?"

"I'm worried, Barby. If the worst—." Brandy could not face her fear. "Hank is my husband. He married me. I love him more than you ever did. You are my sister Barbara; sisters do not do the things we do.

We are selfish and treated Hank horribly. I feel very weak. Barbara, it is over. Our little scheme is finished. You could have married Hank, but you did not; I did. Hank is my husband. You cannot have him. You cannot ever have him. It would not be right. We need to make things right. If something happens to me, I want you to raise Sarah. Do it with some dignity?"

Brandy's voice was barely a whisper. Barby held her hand and moved closer.

"You cannot marry Hank. That is how I feel; that is my plea. You must honor—." Brandy could not see her sister and lunged out for her. She went unconscious.

Barby was there by her sister's side.

She squeezed her sister's hand until it was lifeless. She backed away, panic-stricken and saddened with grief. She could not remember her sister ever speaking so harshly. Were those going to be the last words she would remember? Barby was devastated. She mumbled incoherently. "No, Brandy. Do not do this to us. Brandy, please, I love you."

Brandy lost too much blood in a short time. She could not hear her sister's pleading cries.

The interns worked feverishly to bring the bleeding under control, but they were losing the battle badly, and they knew it. The attending physician who had left when Barby came in suddenly reappeared upon Barby's exit. No one would question his short absence because they all feared him. The interns had performed admirably but lacked the experience necessary to overcome the odds they were up against. Dr. Quinn Cunningham did not touch the woman who lay dying on his watch, but he insisted on allowing the most novice intern to stop the bleeding. Comments were passed from one intern to another about the seriousness of their plight and the life that lay before them. But no one would challenge Dr. Cunningham.

The surgery seemed to take forever. The patient suffered a complete loss of heart rhythm five times. Each time the attending physician talked his interns through the process of restarting life.

After two hours, an intern came and told Henry that Brandy was losing blood faster than they could transfuse her. He said he would get back to him later. Henry's Mom and Sherry were with Sarah Fawn. Bobby was just down the hall.

Henry informed everyone about the bad news. They reassured each other that the doctors would take good care of Brandy.

Finally, Henry was called to go into the recovery room. Brandy was not awake. The nurse quickly told him, "Just talk to her." She ignored him after that.

Henry looked at his wife. She was wearing a respirator. There were tubes hanging from her everywhere. He started talking, "Darling, we have a beautiful daughter. She has your nose and eyes. I love you, Brandy. Can you hear me, Honey?" He didn't know if she could hear him or not.

The same intern came in. "Your wife has lost a lot of blood. Her hemoglobin count is below two. The bleeding lasted too long, and well; you should prepare for the worst. I'm sorry." He did not say anything further and walked to the side of the room.

Henry's whole body went numb. Brandy was just weak; she was not conscious because of the drugs. These things seemed the only plausible explanation. The doctor was wrong, he told himself.

Henry felt so helpless. "What do you mean?" Henry asked. "She looks okay. What do you mean?" The doctor had no expression on his face; he looked like a mortician.

"I'm sorry," he repeated.

Henry cradled his arms around Brandy. "She's not dead. She's breathing."

The doctor said, "She's on a life support system; it's breathing for her. The part of her brain that controls breathing is still alive, but the rest of her brain is dead."

Henry thought Brandy squeezed his hand just a little, "She squeezed my hand, I felt it." Henry's heart was coming apart.

"We have a daughter. She needs her mother. Please don't tell me." Henry could not say it. He started crying.

The doctor stood there, helpless. He did not know what to say.

Barby was hiding around the corner; she knew how bad the outcome would affect Henry. Barby seemed to rush in out of nowhere. She grabbed Henry and held him in her arms.

A few moments later, Bobby and Jessica joined them.

Henry could not understand. It all happened so fast. He did not know if there was a God, but he asked him, "Please, spare my daughter's mother."

Another brain scan was done, and Brandy was pronounced brain dead at seven twenty-two a.m.

The family was ushered in again to see Brandy before unplugging the life support system. Barby was standing next to Henry when the doctor delivered the bad news.

"Oh, God, no," she said. "Oh, Henry." She clung to him.

Henry could not say a word. He looked at his beautiful wife and wept.

Bobby bent over and kissed his older sister and fell apart. "Brandy, God no, don't let this happen. Dad and Mom and now Brandy," he cried.

Sherry was with Sarah and Baby Ben.

Jessica was standing off to the side of her son. Her hands were clinging to her hair. She walked up behind her son, leaned against his back, and cried. "Brandy, I loved you as if you were my own daughter," she said.

Henry did not remember much after that. They arrived back in Barneyville a couple of days later. Henry's Mom and Barby helped Sarah. Henry was in a constant daze.

Jessica breast-fed Sarah right away. She knew this baby was going to need all the help she could get to survive. Some babies reject surrogate mothers, but not Sarah; she had a healthy appetite, and Jessica often fed both babies at the same time. Over the years, people would refer to this experience to explain why the two children were so close.

The Episcopal priest gave a nice sermon. Henry enjoyed the way he eulogized Brandy. He reminded everyone how she was the force behind the Millpond Park restoration. She had a fire burning inside her to bring sweeping changes to society, and mankind would have to wait for another lady to lift the torch of liberty in Barneyville.

When he concluded, he asked for friends and loved ones to please say a few words to encourage each other.

Bobby was the first person to take the podium. Many members of his football team were present, including a man who would eventually become the most loved coach of all time in the state of Michigan.

"As most of you are aware, I am not a skilled speaker, but please listen to what I have to say today. I think it is especially important.

"Siblings often find themselves at odds while growing up. This was the case with my sister and me. I do not remember ever telling her, 'I love you.' But I did love Brandy," he smiled. "Brandy had a way of bringing out the worst in me; she knew what buttons to push to aggravate me. I pretended not to know, but I did, and I loved the attention she showed me. I would suffer the awful indignity to gain her interest. I am a better person today because of my sister.

"I remember one day my father tried to make light of a particularly difficult occasion. To lessen my suffering, he mentioned to me. 'Did you let those trollops get the best of you again?' I laughed so hard I peed my pants. Of course, my father knew my sister was not a trollop. Everyone knew Brandy was a lady. She was so beautiful. I will miss the lady I called Stretch."

Bobby could not go on. He had more he wanted to say, but his emotional pain choked his voice. He silently walked away and sat with his wife, hanging his head and weeping.

Schoolmates, teachers, and friends took turns saying their goodbyes.

Barby looked at Henry. He motioned for her to go ahead. She wore a long black dress, and a dark veil covered her face. She walked up to the podium and took a deep breath.

"On behalf of the family, I want to take this opportunity to thank all of you for being here. There is standing room only inside, and there must be two hundred or more people outside.

"Brandy was, of course, my sister. She was my kindred spirit. We shared so many things in our lives. Most of all, Brandy shared herself. She had a zeal for life like I have never seen, nor do I ever expect to see again. We had a wonderful relationship. She taught me how to be a girl and a woman, a lady, a friend, a student, an artist, and, well, many things. There are some things I was hoping to learn from her that I will miss; how to be a good mother, among others. Like my brother, I, too, am proud to be her sibling. I love you, Brandy; I'll see you in my dreams."

Barby fainted into a black pillow of silk. Henry and Bobby rushed to extract her from the floor, but she was alert before they could assist her. Henry, always the noble servant, insisted on carrying her. She submitted to his wishes and relaxed in his arms. He carried her to his seat and put her in his chair next to his mother.

Henry walked back up to the podium. He looked out at the vast company of friends and relatives. "Friends, family, neighbors, and guests. It means so much to us in the family to see your warm, kind faces. Thank you once again for being here today. Brandy, my wife, was an incredibly special lady. She had the ability to put on a thousand different faces. It did not matter which face she wore; she could never hide her beauty. She had an inner beauty that spawned her physical attractiveness. She also had a lot of class, charm, wit, and style. I have a short poem I would like to share with you. I wrote it this morning over a cup of coffee and a glass of tears."

Henry fumbled with the paper.

> "Don't go chasing dreams.
> Pick the right one when it comes along.
> Dreams can be illusive.
> Hang on.
> Once in every lifetime, a dream comes true."

Henry walked over to the coffin and kissed his wife goodbye. Then he fairly fell into a seated position on the floor beside the coffin, crying. Barby got up and went to him and knelt between him and the crowd, trying to provide some privacy. She gave the funeral director a stern look, and he asked the attendants to dismiss the guests.

The funeral was the largest little Barneyville had ever seen. People came from all over America. Brandy was buried next to her mom. It was a warm April day with lots of sunshine. Henry was grateful for this small favor from Mother Nature.

Henry sold all the assets in Boston and spent the summer with his mother in Barneyville. Late in the fall, Henry, Sarah, Jessica, and baby Ben moved to Northern California. Henry opened his own heating and air conditioning business in the East Bay. He had a new lady in his life; she was fair skinned like her mother. She had his blonde hair and her mother's beautiful features.

Barby bought a house high in the Berkeley hills. Henry bought one on the street two blocks away. Barby visited nearly every night. Henry's mother lived with Henry, and they spent their weekends together raising Sarah and baby Ben.

Henry registered with the local draft board. He was given a special deferment because he was a single parent. It was a big load off his shoulders. He wanted to care for his daughter himself. Both his mother and Barby could have filled his shoes, but Henry felt a special responsibility on Brandy's behalf.

Barby and Henry did not have intimate relations; she said he was her brother-in-law. She said she needed to have things stay. It was her way of honoring her sister.

CHAPTER 38

Barby's Bullet

*B*arby uncovered an alarming detail regarding Brandy's death certificate. The signature on it was Dr. Quinn Cunningham. She called Bobby and asked him if it could be a mistake. Together, they hired a private investigator. Two months later, they were sickened to learn the signature was authentic. They hired a medical investigator to review the medical records. To their chagrin, many unexplained and confusing medical procedures were aborted or altered.

Bobby's attorney got involved and uncovered actionable deletions in a medical procedure. However, the district attorney in Boston refused to prosecute. Quinn had been committed to a reputable Mental Institution, and his internment was permanent.

Bobby wanted to drop everything at that point. Barby refused. She continued using the private investigator. Finally, after spending thousands of dollars, she gave up.

On the anniversary of Brandy's passing, Barby flew to Boston. She was supposedly on a business trip. She was speaking at a seminar on human fertilization, but it was just a cover.

It was a dark, moonless night when she arrived at her hotel on April 9. Barby drove to the sanitarium the following day. She was escorted to the office when she reached out and filled out the necessary papers. An hour later, she stood in Quinn's room waiting for the orderly to leave.

Quinn Cunningham sat restrained in a chair. He looked much older with a dull, featureless face. His eyes were in a dead stare. His shoulders drooped, and he did not attempt to adjust to the seemingly uncomfortable position.

Barby stood motionless, monitoring his posture and eye movement. She examined his face for some form of expression; Barby saw nothing.

Barby learned from the P.I. that many of the rooms in the institution would have microphones and hidden cameras.

She pulled a chair over and sat directly in front of him. She whispered, "You're a miserable prick. I know you can hear me, you son-of-a-bitch. Today is the first anniversary of my sister's death. Today is the day you will die. I have a loaded gun in my purse and will blow your brains out. But first, I want to tell you all about Brandy's daughter. Her name is Sarah. She is a beautiful blonde; she looks like her mother. She has her mother's intelligence and beauty. Brandy told me how you hated her because she was smarter than you. Look at you now; you are pathetic."

Quinn had not even flinched, but Barby was not satisfied yet.

"Hey, you weak ass, I'm talking to you. I thought you were something. Brandy did, too, but what a jerk you proved to be. Do you like fire? I hope so because this is how you will be a cloud of crispy dust." Barby was about to play her trump card and wanted to ensure he had the opportunity to react. "Hey, jerk. Do you remember the good-looking man with long blonde hair? His name is Henry, but Brandy called him Hank. Guess who the father of Brandy's baby is? You got it, creep; it is Hank. Henry is a wonderful father; unlike you, he knows how to treat a lady. He's wonderful in bed, too, not the dud Brandy told me you were!" Barby was highly disappointed; she wanted this evil monster to flinch slightly. But he did not react to any of her goads.

"Hey, stupid. Did you know I have cancer? I do. My doctor has given me two months to live. I want to accomplish something with my life before I die. I don't particularly appreciate looking at you anymore. First, you'll feel cold steel in the back of your head; then, you'll hear a click."

Barby did not have cancer. It was part of the ruse. She stood up and walked around behind him. She did have her gun. It was one Henry had given her two years ago. She placed her scarf over her purse and pulled out the weapon, hiding it under the scarf. Barby put it in the back of his skull and held it against his head. After making contact, she counted down from five and pulled the trigger.

The gun was not loaded.

Barby was watching closely, but Quinn did not flinch a muscle.

"If you ever leave here, my brother will kill you, asshole."

She could not look at his face again and suddenly became ill. Her chest hurt, and she ached all over. Barby was distraught with anger and fear. She had no bullets; she did not trust her emotional courage. Barby was shaking profoundly, and her legs felt wobbly. Finally, she left his room quietly in tears and sick from depression. She did not bother to close the door.

She did not tell a soul about visiting Quinn when she returned home.

CHAPTER 39

Loving Henry

*B*arby went on to graduate school; she lived by herself close to Henry. Bobby graduated in 1972 with a degree in business and continued to run the car dealership in Battle Creek.

Henry never went back to college; he was a single parent and needed to pay attention to the young lady in his life. Work was slow initially, but it took little time for business to pick up. He had two part-time technicians and made them both full-time employees.

Jessica lived with Henry. Ben and Sarah thought they were brother and sister. Henry's house, like many of the homes in his area, had four levels. The first was the garage; the second was the family room. The third level had four bedrooms; the top story was the kitchen and dining room. There was also a large veranda in the kitchen. The patio had a fantastic view overlooking the city by the Bay.

When Sarah was five years old, Henry enrolled her in kindergarten. She had been part of his life continuously for five years, and he thought he would go nuts having to be away from her for four hours a day.

Barby lived two blocks from Henry, and together, they raised Sarah, although not as husband and wife. In fact, for five long years, they had not had physical contact except for the briefest greetings. Nevertheless, their love for each other was apparent. Any man dating Barby understood the esoteric relationship. As for women dating Henry—it did not happen. Anyone who knew them thought they were secretly married and would not admit it for some unknown reason.

Sarah was becoming more beautiful every day. Her thick, long blonde hair was hanging to her waist by her fifth birthday.

Jessica cared for the children during the day. She took them both to preschool and the park and loved riding on the ferries. However, her heart ached for Henry and Barby. She saw their love for each other and could not understand their silly pact. Brandy had been dead for five years, and Sarah, for one, certainly thought Barby was her mother. Barby continued with it but insisted she would have a family when she turned thirty. Mrs. Rotyn tried to make some sense of their reasoning but gave up; her interest now lay in the needs of her granddaughter and son.

Henry was in constant turmoil over what to tell Sarah about her mother. He did not want her to suffer, thinking she was the reason her mother was dead.

Henry's mother met a man at a coffee shop. She saw him there every morning and began saying hello, and then they shared some conversation. Then he took her out for dinner. Jessica dated Preston Penapicali for several months. Preston took a shine to Henry's mother. He proposed, and they were married in two months. He lived in San Francisco in the Marina District. Jessica and young Ben moved to the city. Preston was five years older than Jessica, and he made her happy. Preston came into Henry's business as general manager. Preston freed Henry to spend more time with his daughter.

Barby took a job teaching reproductive biology at the University. She continued taking classes, eventually receiving her Doctorate in obstetrics and gynecology. She opened her own business specializing in artificial insemination.

Sarah was eight when Henry and Barby took her to Disneyland for the first time. They had a suite at the Hilton in Anaheim.

They spent five days in Los Angeles. After an exhaustive day with Sarah on the first night, the couple put Sarah to bed in the second bedroom and sat and talked.

"How long will we wait until we tell Sarah the truth, Henry?" Barby took a long drink of her margarita.

"Barby, what does it matter? She is a normal little girl and is incredibly happy. We need to wait until she's a teenager." Henry got up to get another beer. "How hot did it get today?" he asked. He looked over where she was sitting. She was taking off her bra without removing her blouse. His feelings for her suddenly peaked: his breathing increased, and he felt the old tense sense in his abdomen.

"You still hot?" She asked. She smiled and threw the bra at him, all wadded up.

Barby sat on the couch with both feet tucked under her. Henry wondered if she sat that way to make herself feel taller. But then he dismissed the idea because Barby was never paranoid about her physical stature.

"I feel like getting plastered, Henry," she said.

He grinned at her; she needed to unwind. Maybe getting shit-faced would do her some good. "Sure, sounds good to me. Do we need to order some more liquor?" he said.

She looked at him tenderly with amorous eyes. "I want to sleep in your bed tonight, but I want to be drunk."

"Barby, you know how I feel about you. Please don't be a tease." He saw something in her eyes that surprised him; he did not believe what he saw. It had been eight years since her eyes revealed the love; he knew she was absconding.

"Drunk and only drunk—that's my proposal." He does not believe me, she thought. She buried her love for Henry when Brandy died. Why should she continue to punish herself because of a promise? Quinn was the problem; however, Barby just received a letter from the Mental Institution that Quinn died. Barby promised not to marry Henry, but Brandy needed him. Barby recalled that awful day. Barby did not have the opportunity to answer her sister. Why did their relationship have to end on such a sour note? It did not matter; she could never marry Henry. How could she ever live with herself?

Barby never shared her conversation with her sister on that awful day with Henry. She knew she needed to but did not have the emotional courage yet.

Henry sat beside her and spoke without looking at her. "You're noticeably quiet, Barby. When you're ready, I want to listen to whatever haunts you." Barby smiled affectionately. "I know, and someday, I promise I'll share it with you." Henry had a right to know what happened the night Brandy died, and he couldn't go to jail. She smiled; no one could blame him now.

"Henry, I want to sleep with you. I want to sleep with you tonight, tomorrow, and the night after."

Henry thought she was ill; he was sure of it. "Let me look at you." Barby leaned against him; she turned over on her back and looked up at him with her head in his lap. "I love you, Henry." Barby had a sudden surge of irrational anguish.

Henry was not surprised at her hysterical outburst. He knew she was suppressing a traumatic injury. Sherry, the Psychologist, told him that exactly.

Henry held her tenderly and allowed her to cry until she fell asleep. Henry carried her into the bedroom and took off her blouse and skirt. He tucked her into bed, undressed, and climbed in next to her. She rolled over next to him and laid her head on his shoulder. She snuggled close, and her bare breast lay lightly against his chest. She slept soundly for the first time in eight years.

Henry lay awake until one is thinking about many things. Most of his reveries included the fond memories of the brown beauty who lay in his arms. Henry's virtue withstood the test, but her scent and perfume flooded his senses with fond memories. The reveries danced in his head while he slept.

Sarah woke them in the morning. "Why are you two in the same bed together?"

Barby realized she was practically naked, pulled the sheet over herself, and looked at Henry. "Hello! What are you doing in my bed? Where are my clothes, and who took my clothes off?"

Henry winked at Sarah. She winked back. "I want to watch TV. May I, Daddy?"

Sarah opened the door and said, "Would you like some privacy?" Henry and Barby started laughing.

Barby said, "No, dear. Come over here!" She sat up in bed and kept the sheet tucked in around her.

Sarah shook her head no. "Nope, I am going to watch Sesame Street. When it is over, I want to take a bath. Then you two are taking me to breakfast. I won't bother you again until I am ready for breakfast." Sarah closed the door.

Barby looked at Henry. "I have hardly any clothes on, and I hope you behaved yourself last night."

She broke the silence, "How's your heart, Honey?" and kissed him.

The kiss started innocently but quickly became amorous. Henry was already naked, and Barby was unaware of his lack of prudence until now. She continued the kiss when her hands found what her mind could not see.

Her panties quickly disappeared at the foot of the bed, and then she rolled over on top of him.

Barby cried, "Darling, I miss how you make me feel."

Neither had they had relations with anyone for eight long years. The reunited lovers slept with arms and legs tangled until a knock came on their door.

"Hey, Daddy and Mommy, I'm hungry." Sarah insisted.

Later, they showered and dressed quietly. Barby bumped into him on purpose as they prepared for the day. After they wrapped up, Sarah came in and joined them. Henry combed Barby's hair, Sarah combed his hair, and then Barby and Henry took turns searching for Sarah's.

It was a wonderful day. The unique family shared quality and memorable times, the times they would never forget, concern and love packaged into a quiet esoteric understanding.

Later that evening, the noise was so loud Sarah had to put a pillow over her ears.

On Friday, Henry woke up early. Barby was still asleep, so he got up and showered. Henry ordered coffee and made a few phone calls to his stepfather in Berkeley. Barby exited the bedroom and sat beside him on the couch discussing business. Henry's business flourished because his father-in-law was a terrific salesman and manager.

Henry hung up the phone and smiled. "Good morning, beautiful!" He kissed her neck.

She wrapped herself around him and whispered, "I'm pregnant."

He looked at her in total surprise. "How?"

She dropped her mouth open with a dumbfounded gesture. "Henry. How do you think, silly boy?" She loved his little teases, but sometimes she wondered if he was teasing or naïve.

"How could you possibly know?" he asked.

She turned around sideways. Barby gazed into the mirror and fluttered her eyes at him. "I can feel it."

He smiled, put his arms around her, and held her breasts with his palms. "I make a pretty good bra, huh?"

She giggled; it was the first time he remembered her real girl laugh since Brandy died.

"I love you, Barby. I have always loved you. Will you marry me now?"

Barby turned around and put her palms on his dimples. "No!" She got up and went in to take a bath before he could react.

Henry sat stunned. Had the past five days meant so little to her? He fell back into a sullen mood. He went out and flopped down on the couch until Sarah came out and jumped on him.

"Daddy, I'm hungry. When are we going to eat? I need a special breakfast. Something strawberry would do."

He smiled at his daughter. "You don't talk like an eight-year-old girl."

Sarah rested on her father and put her ear to his chest. "You have a good heartbeat. Do you love Mommy?"

Henry nodded his head yes.

"Why doesn't Mommy live with us?" Sarah grabbed hold of his dimples.

"Do you want her to live with us?" he asked.

Sarah kissed her father on the cheek. "Does Mommy want to live with us?"

"Sarah, when we get home, we'll ask your mommy that question."

Sarah lost interest and ran into her room and leaped on her bed. Then she ran back and hopped onto her father's belly.

On the long drive home, Henry and Barby talked while Sarah slept. The Cadillac was incredibly quiet. Barby loved her new car, but Henry did not share her enthusiasm.

"Okay, Mommy. Will you explain why if you're having my, I mean our baby, why won't you let me make an honest woman out of you?"

She shook her head no. "I remember a conversation I had with Brandy. She came into my room one night and told me to stay away from you. She said you wanted her to tell you about free sex. Every man's dream." She smiled and winked at him.

"Henry, this is your free sex!" She gave him one wifely look that a husband knows he is better off not answering.

"What will we tell Sarah?" he asked with a sad grimace. Henry was trying to convince himself that marrying Barby was the right thing to do. But deep down in his heart, he did not see it happening. Henry disagreed with his heart, but the fact remained that some other power bigger than both would prevent their union. If he could not understand the aberrant force at work, how could he make a defense against it?

Barby and Henry never discussed their ambivalent relationship after Brandy died.

Sarah was sleeping in the back seat. Barby was dozing. Henry's mind was racing faster than the large sedan. It whizzed past the fields of green vegetables on one side of the road and an orchard of orange trees on the other. Barby was keeping something from him; she as much as much. Henry often spoke with his therapist, the one Sherry recommended, about the deep feelings he still held for Barby. Time will heal all wounds, both real and imagined. Time was the result of four years of therapy. How much time was needed, certainly not enough in his lifetime? Henry terminated the expensive interludes over a year earlier. His relationship with Barby leaped ahead light-years in the past week.

Barby sat with her back to the door. She had been looking at the man tattooed in her heart since childhood. Was there any other man on earth she could ever love? No, the short time humans share would not allow her enough time to find another soul mate. However much she wished, dreamed, or fantasized, Barby knew no one except Henry could touch her heart like Henry.

Especially now, with a child on the way, Barby knew Henry would act with nobility and great virtue. She needed to create a life they could live with and remain close to without getting married. But Barby wanted so much to have children with Henry. Every time she looked at Sarah, her heart yearned for one of her own.

Sarah—how she loved her sister's only child. Barby remembered the love she had for her sister. Brandy was the most beautiful woman she had ever known, even to this day.

Barby glowed like a spring flower because she was close to motherhood herself.

Brandy spent hours teaching Barby about life, men, women, and truisms of many sorts. The love Barby held for her sister had migrated into the powerful dynamic maternal love she exuded for her niece.

Barby knew she needed to tell Sarah the truth about her birth mother. She knew two hearts would break on that fateful day, but she also knew if she did not tell Sarah and found out on her own from someone else—well, Barby was not going down that road, not now, not in the future. No, Henry was wrong. Sarah needed the truth quickly.

"Henry, I want to talk with you."

He thought she was still dozing and smiled at her awareness because he was bored. "I'm listening, dear."

It was late afternoon, and a long shadow fell alongside the road on Barby's side of the car.

"We need to talk, and then we both need to talk with Sarah."

He knew what she meant about the second point, but the first point worried him.

CHAPTER 40

Revealing Secrets

"Henry, I need several strong drinks. I am sorry, but I feel we must stop for the night. I know there is some reason why you want to get back tonight, but can it wait?"

They found lodging and a good restaurant that satisfied their needs.

Sarah was in bed in an adjoining room.

After four double margaritas, Barby started to cry. Henry was beside himself. He tried to comfort her, but she was incoherent and despondent. She wanted a bottle of whiskey, but Henry would not allow it.

"Barby, what's happening? Please talk to me, and we can get through it together." Henry held her on the side of the bed.

"Henry, I need to talk for a while. Please do not interrupt me; I can only say this once."

"Barby, you have my unequivocal promise."

Barby dried her eyes and blew her nose. Henry had never loved Barby more than he did at this very moment. But he worried about her enigmatic disposition.

"Henry, I love you. I love you so much it hurts. It hurts me emotionally, physically, and metaphysically."

Barby put her fingers across Henry's lips. "Please let me finish, no matter how much it hurts."

Henry bit down on his bottom lip and nodded yes.

"The night Brandy died, one of the interns found me looking in on Sarah. He told me I was to come alone to the operating room immediately. On the way to the operating room, the intern informed me of Brandy's condition. The area where the placenta breaks away from the uterine is hemorrhaging. The tear is not closing and is critical, and not very many women survive that sort of trauma. When I finally was allowed in to see Brandy, there was blood everywhere. She was barely conscious, but she was steadfast. She told me to tell you she loved you and that I was to help you raise Sarah. She said, "Tell Hank I love him." The second thing you now know. The first thing was this. Brandy told me I could never marry you. She said our agreement about sharing with you was off. She said I could not have you. That was her dying wish. How can I not honor her last wish?"

"It hurt to have her say that to me. You know very well what we shared with you. I remember you suffered unimaginable ambivalence, especially the morning in Florida. You remember Henry. Brandy and I created an esoteric, ambiguous relationship with you. Even when she married you, I told her I wanted your children. Brandy agreed. I do not know if she ever told you about that. You never mentioned it to me, so I avoided mentioning the subject. But I can never marry you, Henry. I could never live by myself. It has taken me eight years to gather the courage to speak about that night. It has also taken me eight years to develop the strength to have your children. But I will have them if you permit it. I can't marry you, though." Barby was struggling physically and emotionally, but the liquor was helping to shield her pain.

Henry wanted to smile, too, but she had to drop a bomb on him now. She did not want to, but she owed it to him.

"Henry, I left the operating room after Brandy lost consciousness. I had to. The doctors were about to operate to try to save her life. They were giving her blood, a lot of blood. But she bled to death right in front of them. I thought the doctors were doing all they could to save my sister. A month later, while paying the bills, I noticed something that has given me nightmares ever since. The attending physician who signed the death certificate was Dr. Quinn Cunningham."

Barby saw Henry's reaction—the disparity, the pain, the depression. She put her fingers over her lips when she saw the first tear fall down his cheek. She recognized the questioning expression forming on his face. "Henry, I didn't even know Quinn had access to that hospital."

Henry knew the truth. He recalled Quinn's hateful, horrible look on that fateful day in Florida.

"Henry, I hired a private investigator who uncovered all the details. He provided me with a lot of evidence against Quinn. It seems common practice for doctors to work with multiple hospitals. I had evidence proving Quinn delayed treating Brandy properly. Before I could act on any of this, he was committed to a mental institution. He was still in the same institution until three days ago. He died. In agreement with his father, he was to stay in that institution for life. I receive a notice from the institution quarterly about his death. He had been catatonic now for eight years."

She stopped because Henry broke down. Barby touched his shoulder. He was holding his head in his hands. "Henry, dear sweet Henry."

Henry's anguish ripped irreparable holes in his heart. He could have been more aggressive toward Quinn in Florida.

"Henry, if I had told you about this, you would have killed him. Hell, I almost killed him. When I saw his condition, I only thought about what Brandy told me about raising Sarah. I had to put my sister's child first. I could not kill him, darling."

Barby wept openly, tears streamed down her cheeks unabated, and Henry tried to gather her in his arms, but she pushed him away. She looked at him and silently lipped, "I'm sorry. I'm so sorry."

Henry was not mad any longer. He had been furious and had felt rage well up inside him. Barby trapped all of this inside herself for eight years. He could not imagine how difficult it must have been for her to endure the pain and torment.

"Why would you say you're not my Mommy?"

The tender, inquisitive voice sent chills up Barby's and Henry's backs.

Barby was stunned; her whole world turned upside down.

Henry's heart was breaking; he could not stand it any longer.

"Come here, precious." Sarah walked over to her father but kept her eyes on Barby. Henry picked her up and sat her on his knee.

"Sarah, please." She held out her arms, but Sarah leaned against her father. Barby pleaded, "Sarah, darling."

"Daddy, is that why Mommy (Sarah pointed to Barby) doesn't live with us?"

For the first time since sitting on her father's lap, Sarah took her eyes from Barby and looked imploringly into her father's eyes.

Henry spoke tenderly to the eyes and ears that studied him. Then, with a broken, emotionally taxed voice, Henry said, "Sarah, do you remember our conversation about courage and bravery?"

Sarah looked at Barby again and silently nodded her head.

"Yes, Daddy. I do."

Barby was beside herself with grief. Henry held up his index finger for Barby to see.

"Tell us dearly, what is the difference between courage and bravery."

"Okay, Daddy. Courage is the strength inside you. Bravery is similar, but the brave use their strength inside them to do things."

Barby's heart leaped when she understood what Henry was doing.

"Sarah, Barby was brave for eight years. Unfortunately, Barby is not your Mommy. Your Mommy died when you were born. Your Mommy was Barby's sister."

Sarah started to cry. "Why did Mommy die?" Sarah took her eyes from Barby, whom she studied, and looked at her father again. Then she quickly looked back at Barby and held out her arms. Barby came over and gathered Sarah into her arms.

"Sarah, my love, my little girl, my sweet." Barby Hen,ry, and Sarah cried together. They stroked each other, touching and bonding. Barby looked at Henry and kissed him tenderly.

Sarah looked into her aunt's eyes. "What do I call you?"

Barby looked at Henry. "I'm your aunt Barby, but you can still call me Mommy if you want to, Honey."

"Sarah, it is up to you. You can call Barby or Mommy if you want. We can keep this a secret, too. You let us know what you want to do. Okay?" Henry said.

Sarah gazed at her father, pressed her lips together, and nodded deeply. Then, she looked at the two adults, and tears welled up in her eyes. "I love you both, but will you tell me about my Mommy?"

Later that evening, they put Sarah to bed. They said their prayers together, and Barby read a book. Dr. Seuss is the CAT in the HAT. When she was asleep, the two parents went to their room.

"There is one more thing we must discuss, Henry."

Henry sat on the couch. Barby sat next to him. "Henry, I know I'm pregnant, Honey."

"I know Barby, and I see the glow of a woman bearing a child. I saw it in my mother and around Brandy."

"You're happy, Henry?" she asked.

"We can get married. We can, can't we?" He asked because her expression was not happy.

"I cannot do that, Henry. Nothing has changed, I am sorry, but I need to respect Brandy's last wish. I have to carry this to my grave."

Henry sat quietly and put his arm around her.

"Do you hate me, darling?" she asked.

"No, Barby, but can we please keep this dream as an option?" He asked.

"Of course, Ozaawindib."

CHAPTER 41

Barby's Burden

Barby struggled with her feelings for Henry. She wanted to wake up in his bed every morning and raise Sarah under the same roof.

Every night, she suffered the same dreams. First, Brandy tells her she cannot marry Henry. Then, she saw herself living with him, but the plans always ended tragically. Either she died, or he died, or Sarah died. The message the dreams painted in her mind and heart was unmistakable. She could not live with Henry. She must not marry him. For the sake of her sanity, she had no choice.

Henry would not rest until he broke her will. She knew he would win her; her willpower could not withstand his love. However, Barby knew the only way to preserve her peace of mind was not to marry Henry.

Barby had a beautiful baby boy in March. She did not have any trouble at all with the birth. However, Henry was apprehensive and sick. He was holding Barby's hand through delivery.

Barby named the baby Bartholomew Benjamin Kraneger Rotyn.

Bobby, Sherry, Jessica, Benjamin, Pepper, and Sarah were all at the hospital.

The child had a full head of bright yellow hair. His mother would only cut his hair once he was five years old, and then it was just a trim. Henry dubbed his golden-brown eyes.

Almost a year later, Barby had another baby, again a boy. His given name was William Henry Kraneger Rotyn. This lad was born bald and did not have much hair until he was almost three years old. His mother cut it short with reverence.

Sarah took an active interest in the boys. She was close to her brothers and spoiled every chance she got.

Henry adored the children from birth.

Sarah enjoyed her life as a big sister. Her love for Barby only expanded with time.

Barby buried her feelings for Henry and her life in her work and as a mother. The dreams faded over time, and Barby enjoyed a measure of happiness. The insulation Pepper provided between her heart and

Henry was working. Barby could breathe easier when she thought about him—every morning, Barby tended to her children even if the children reminded her of Henry.

CHAPTER 42

Sarah the Teen

*W*hen Sarah turned thirteen, her birthday party was an extravaganza supreme. She received many presents; Sarah's father bought her a bicycle and ten new outfits. Sarah went with her aunt to buy them. In addition, Henry gave her a new bedroom suite with her bureau and a canopy bed. Henry took his daughter to Barneyville for their summer vacation. Therefore, for the first time, Sarah could grieve for her mother.

Henry and Sarah stood together at Brandy's gravesite. Henry and Sarah placed large bouquets over the grave; Henry had his arms around Sarah, more for his support than hers. Sarah read the headstone out loud. "Brandy Sue Kraneger Rotyn was born July 7, 1946, and died April 10, 1970. Beloved Daughter, Sister, Wife, Mother of Sarah."

"Daddy," Sarah cried. "Daddy, says Sarah's mother. Daddy, my Mom?" When she looked into her father's eyes. She saw his pained expression and hugged him.

"Daddy, why did mom have to die?" Henry shrugged his shoulders and tipped his head. He opened his mouth, but the innocent, tender question opened the old gash in his heart. He wanted to say something to comfort her, but the words failed him.

She recognized his trauma and whispered, "Daddy, thank you for bringing me here; I can see how much you loved Mom. Let us talk to her, Daddy. It will make us feel better. I'll go first."

"Hello, my wonderous Mom; I'm thirteen years old now, Mommy. Daddy misses you, and so do I. Daddy has been a good father; I know you would be proud of him. I hug and kiss Daddy daily, Mom, because I know you cannot be there for him. I spoil him rotten. I wish I could have known you. We would have been close. Aunt Barby is there for me. Mom, I love you, and now Daddy needs to say a few things to you. I will come back again, I promise."

Henry's face was wet with tears. He did not know what to say, but for Sarah's sake, he needed to try.

"Brandy, it's been thirteen years. I still miss you terribly. Is this the life I need to live? Our daughter is beautiful. She is the only other woman who truly measures up to your beauty. I am still in love with you,

Brandy. I remember your face, the smell of your hair, and the color of your eyes; I remember your lips, the taste of your kiss, and your intimacy. But, brandy, something is missing in my heart."

Henry broke down and lost his voice. Sarah was practically holding him up. "Daddy, I had no idea."

Sarah was already five feet seven inches tall; she looked more like her mother every year. Then, they went to Battle Creek to visit Bobby and Sherry.

Bobby and his family took Henry and Sarah swimming at Lake Michigan on a warm, late July day. The waves were huge, and the two families wore themselves out in the surf.

Henry promised to take Sarah to dance at the infamous Flying Saucer Inn. Later that night, they visited the famous old structure.

Sarah wore white slacks and a hot pink blouse. Henry danced with his daughter most of the night. Finally, close to midnight, the teenager wore down. They had been goofing around, dancing to every song for over an hour.

"Daddy, this has been a wonderful day. I will never forget it. Thank you." She leaned her head on her father's shoulder.

"Barby and I used to dance here like this. We could dance for hours." He fondly recalled those summer nights.

She looked at him, mesmerized by his story. "Daddy, why didn't you and mom dance here?"

He smiled at her. "Well, sweetie." He remembered how Brandy used to call Barby sweetie. "Your Mom was four years older than me. Barby was my high school sweetheart."

Sarah's eyes got big, and her mouth dropped open. "Daddy, why didn't you tell me? I knew you and Aunt Barby shared something special, but I had no idea. Daddy, you're just full of surprises."

Henry's eyes filled full to the brink, and he suffered a sudden attack of melancholy.

"Daddy, don't cry. Please, Daddy."

He tried to smile at his daughter, but it was no good. It was pitch black, however, and he was surprised she could see his emotional weakness. "I'm all right, dear. I'm just an old sentimental fool."

She hugged him and kissed his cheek. "I'm here for you, Daddy."

"I love you, Sarah. You bring me so much pleasure."

The music stopped, and the lights came on.

"Time to turn in, Honey."

Sarah wanted to talk with her father. "Daddy, can we go down to the restaurant and talk?" She suddenly seemed formal. "You can buy me more of that peach cobbler ala mode."

Henry studied his daughter's face; she was so beautiful. He enjoyed how her facial gestures varied like her mother's. She pressed him for an answer, and he noticed she wore the business face of her mother. She had the same emerald green eyes shrouded by thick eyelashes, just like her mother. Her face was red from the sun, but her long blonde hair spilled gently over her shoulders. Her hair did not have the thick course strands like his but instead her mother's delicate, sheer, sleekness. She had her mother's long, thin, gentle nose, too. Her cheeks were his, light freckles, especially around the nose and under the eyes. Like her mother, her mouth was complete and comprehensive, with full lips and a flawless chin. She had one dimple on the right side when she smiled.

They sat together in the restaurant. "Daddy, I'm so surprised by what you told me tonight. I want to know everything. I want all the details, everything, but not tonight.

"Daddy, I want you to marry Aunt Barby. She loves you, Daddy. I want you to remind Barby that she used to be your girlfriend. You are still incredibly young. You are very handsome, Daddy. Many of my friends think you are gorgeous. I can tell Aunt Barby that you still love her. I know you two have been fooling around, too. That is right, I am not deaf and dumb, Daddy."

Henry looked at his daughter in a new light. "Sarah, you don't understand."

She pursed her lips and prepared to stand her ground. "Daddy, I'm serious."

Henry smiled and said, "You're thirteen years old. How serious can you be?" He immediately saw the pain in her expression. However, she did not retreat into depression as he had anticipated.

"Daddy, I'm much older than you think. I remember vividly the night you and Aunt Barby, well, the night when you made Bart, you know?"

Henry beamed. He could not hold it in or contain his pleasure. "I guess we can't put anything over on you, huh!"

Now it was her turn to beam, and she tipped her head over curtly. Or at least she told herself she was not.

They finished their treat, and he sat back. "Can we get some sleep now, princess?" She smiled contentedly, followed him to their room, and went to bed.

On the flight back to San Francisco, Henry shared his life history with his much older daughter. She realized her father had been flirting. No, worse—a womanizer. She immensely enjoyed the story and fully intended to cross-examine her aunt for further clarification and more details.

CHAPTER 43

Henry's Enigma

$\mathscr{B}$arby met Henry and Sarah at the airport. They were all going to Henry's mother's house for dinner. Sarah wanted to talk to her aunt about her father.

"Aunt Barby, Daddy took me dancing in the moonlight. He told me a secret, and you and I must have a long talk. Just girl talk, you know." Barby looked at Henry. She whispered into Sarah's ear. "He mesmerized his dates there on that dance floor. But, of course, you didn't fall for any of that, did you?"

Sarah rolled her eyes at her aunt. Then, she whispered in Barby's ear, "How can a woman resist his charm? I fell into his arms." Sarah threw her arms up, pretending to fall away.

Barby looked at her with a pained expression. "Silly girl!" she said.

Henry and Preston sat on the veranda overlooking San Francisco Bay. The late afternoon breeze was mixed with a swathing mixture of warm air for a few seconds, followed by an excellent heavy draft that washed the heat from the body. A happy, cheerful mood filled the home. Preston's humorous stories entertained the families as they shared precious moments.

Henry was happy for his mother. How could anyone dislike such a kind, animated, imaginative, courteous, and mirthful man?

Sarah was becoming a lady. She sat with Benjamin, talking about her trip to Barneyville. Henry loved his daughter and brother, who reminded him of Mr. Kraneger.

He studied with his daughter. While wholesome, virtuous, and joyous, his love for her lacked the love a man shares with his wife. That evening, Henry saw and felt the love he had for Barby and Preston had for his mother. He also saw his wife in his daughter, but Henry did not have a wife. He began to feel that loss acutely.

Henry excused himself; he informed his mother he was exhausted and needed a short nap. She saw the pained and tired expression on his face. She called Barby, and they escorted him into the guest room. He fell asleep quickly.

Jessica asked Barby to come into her bedroom. They sat and discussed Henry's condition. She then changed the subject.

"I never pry into your private affairs, but I always thought you would be my daughter-in-law. When Henry married Brandy, I did not have a good feeling about that and did not take that wrong because I genuinely loved your sister. Brandy made Henry happy in so many ways." Jessica sat and thought about what she was going to say next.

"Barby, I'm getting that horrid sickening feeling. I am afraid for my son. To be a mother."

Barby loved this kind, gentlewoman. She saw the weariness of a mother's love. She understood the heart-wrenching love a mother has for her son.

"Barby, I was extremely disappointed when you didn't marry Henry. I guess I have never let go of that hope. I am beginning to harbor ill feelings toward you. Henry is not happy. I am sorry to say this, but I think you're why he is so unhappy. I do not get it. Why didn't you marry Henry? I know he asked you. He told me so. I'm so mad at you!"

Barby did not know Jessica was still in the dark regarding Brandy. She knew Jessica was not mean; she was a mother, and her reaction was the reaction of a mother. But Barby still felt a cold chill run up her back.

"Jessica, I love Henry. I have always loved Henry. I will always love Henry. Before my sister died, she insisted I could not marry Henry. Her last words were, 'You can't have him.' That was her deathbed wish. I cannot allow myself to violate that wish. I can't do it."

Barby was crying; she was hurting all over, too. Finally, she fell on the bed, shaking and weeping.

Jessica put her hand over her mouth. "Barby, please forgive me. My God, I had no idea. Oh, you are poor, dear. Look what I have done. Barby, I am so ashamed. Oh, Honey, please do not cry. I was sad about this but should have kept my mouth shut. I do not mean to be vicious or cruel. I let my feelings come out and should have suppressed them."

Barby sat up and hugged Jessica. Jessica gave her some tissues. "Go in the bathroom, Honey, and freshen up a bit. It'll make you feel better."

When Barby came back, she was smiling. "You're the grandmother of my children. That makes me your daughter. Those are not just words. When I gave birth to my children, you were there. You have become my mother, and I have come to think of you that way now for many years. I love you, Jessica."

"Barby, what else is going on? You seem to be carrying some other burden as well. I'll listen if you would like to talk about it."

Barby loved Henry's mother almost as much as she loved her mother. "I wanted to go with Henry and Sarah when they went to Barneyville. But I told you, I still love Henry. I love him so much." She started crying again as the surrogate mother cradled her in her arms.

Barby told Jessica about the history she and Brandy shared with Henry. First, she told her about Quinn and the gun. Then, Barby told her about the deep, honorable, virtuous love Barby held in her heart for Henry. Barby spilled her guts completely; she did not hold anything back.

The two women embraced and kissed each other with the love a mother has for her daughter and the love a daughter has for her mother.

Sarah looked in on her father an hour later. He was still sleeping. She crawled in beside him and went to sleep.

A thick, cold fog covered the city in the morning. Barby went home after midnight, but Henry and Sarah slept over.

CHAPTER 44

Illusive Innocence

*S*arah was a freshman in middle school. Henry helped her athletically. She was on the basketball team. She was a scrappy point guard with terrific ball control.

"True, but so is your handicap; remember my handicap when I enjoy thirty-three degrees, Henry."

"Keep your head down and follow through, Henry. See you Wednesday."

Everyone tried to find a mate for Henry.

Henry would take a date to dinner occasionally and sometimes to a movie but would not let anyone get close to him again for a long time. He buried his heart in his work and his children.

Henry received several phone calls from a young girl who wanted to have him take a test to see if he was her father. She would not reveal her identity or where she lived. Barby wished to avoid meeting him. She would make all the arrangements and pay for the tests. Barby assured him in any way. She just wanted to find her biological father and implored him to cooperate, but he assured her he was not a candidate. Henry had only slept with three women in his life. He had led what was, in his estimation, a very conservative lifestyle. The young girl pleaded with him, calling him at work and home for over a month. He believed she was sincere, but after a month of haggling, he insisted she never call his residence or work again, or he would pursue a legal recourse.

Henry and Barby talked for some time about visiting Barneyville over the holidays. Henry arranged for everyone to travel to Battle Creek. Bobby and Sherry were preparing a memorable holiday for the family. On Christmas Eve, everyone went to Barneyville. The ice was good on the Millpond, and everyone wanted to go ice skating.

A light snow was falling. The air was still, and the fluffy flakes slipped back and forth, dancing slowly to the ground.

Henry helped Sarah get her skates on. Barby was already on the ice with Bart. Bart was a natural. He skated as if he were born on the ice. Sarah, on the other hand, was in big trouble. She was surprisingly good at inline skating, but this was much different.

Henry was a surprisingly good skater. Jessica circled the cabin with Benjamin in tow. He did very well independently but got a kick from his mother's surprising agility and skill.

Henry finally kept Sarah on her feet, and she began to feel the ice. Henry skated backward, holding her and gently instructing her how to use her skates properly. They talked as she glided confidently.

"Your mother was an extraordinarily talented skater. Your Grandma taught us all how to skate. Mom and Dad were ice dancers. They won a lot of contests back in the forties."

"Daddy, this is fun. It is freezing, though. My feet are freezing. Will I get frostbite?" She looked distraught, and Henry almost laughed at her seriousness but then caught himself.

"No, dear. It is not cold enough. It must be twenty degrees or less. You can go in and warm up in a few minutes." They caught up with Barby and Bart.

"Henry, Sarah, you make a beautiful couple on the ice," Barby said.

Bart yelled, "Dad, Mom says you two danced together on the ice. How about strutting your stuff?"

"Bart, I'm too old for what we did out here."

"Daddy, you're not too old," Sarah whined.

Henry looked at Barby, and she flashed her eyes at him. "You game, pretty girl?" Barby's smile was all he needed.

"Bart, take your cousin. You seem to be doing well enough."

"Grandma, Daddy, and Aunt Barby will skate together," Sarah yelled.

The other family members slipped off to the edge of the clean ice. Other skaters on the ice began murmuring among themselves.

Even the ice fishermen left their holes and came running when they saw the crowd gathering.

Henry and Barby watched all the commotion and were amazed by the crowd forming.

"Well, you can still draw a crowd, Barby," Henry said.

She looked at him with her mouth hanging open. "Henry, we haven't danced on the ice for over twelve years. Just what do you have in mind?"

Henry gulped, "Come on Barby, we'll wing it."

He took her hand and glided to the middle of the ice. A loud commotion started on the edge of the ice. Men were whistling and yelling. Henry knew Ben, Bart, and Sarah. However, the others joined them, and suddenly, a roaring crowd was clapping and thundering. People came running from the park and cottages on the edge of the Millpond.

Henry was laughing now, and Barby was dumbfounded. The crowd kept getting noisier. "We better do something, or I think we could get tarred and feathered," she yelled.

She took his hand, and they started around the back of the cabin. They built up their speed until she began slipping. He increased his grip, and she swung out in front of him, and he pushed her faster. Barby was always better at going backward than Henry. They reached their starting point, and the crowd was going wild.

Henry pulled her into his embrace and nearly dropped her; she came into him with a thud, but his strength kept them upright.

"Oh, Henry. Do you remember how it used to be? The way we felt. You're very handsome tonight, silly boy."

He grinned as she slipped again. He caught her, and she began to get a feel for the ice.

"Are you ready, Henry? Slow stuff, no jumps, just dancing."

"I'm tired already, Barby. Let us go, sweetie."

The two skaters dazzled the crowd with their footwork. She slipped around him and under him. He lifted her once, but she was terrified, so he gently put her down. They slithered back and forth, spinning and spraying ice into the crowd. He pulled her into his embrace as they circled the cabin.

"It feels good to be in your arms, Henry," she said.

He thought seriously about asking her to spend the night with him, but he lost his nerve. "I remember, pretty girl. You're in my dreams every night."

She looked at him with a new reverence. She wanted to spend the night in his arms. She was going to tell him, but she lost her nerve.

"Double camel, can you do it, old girl?"

She pushed away from his grasp. "Watch me, you old fart!"

They circled the cabin hand in hand, building speed, and when they came around, she sprayed the crowd, stayed on her feet, and spun into a perfect camel. Henry caught an edge, went down, and slid into the group.

The audience went wild over Barby's performance—the loudest yelling from a man lying on the ice.

When she finished, Barby curtsied, slipped off the ice and jumped on Henry.

A snowball fight started, and snow flew everywhere. Down on the ice, though, where it was safe, two lovers were kissing, hiding themselves under the flailing snow.

"Old girl, my ass. You sleep with me tonight, fellow, and see if this is an old girl." Barby could not believe what she said, but somehow, it felt right and wonderful.

That evening after midnight, Barby sneaked into Henry's room. He had been waiting for her. He threw on his robe, and they went downstairs and out the back door.

"Where are we going, Henry?" He pointed to the barn.

"My feet are freezing, Honey." Henry picked her up and carried her to the horse barn.

They went to the far end and found an empty stall. Henry went up into the loft and threw down two bales of straw. He busted them up in the empty booth, creating a soft bed. He took off his robe and lay her on it. She took off her robe and draped it over him.

It was hot in the barn. Six horses watched Henry sow his oats. She shuddered under him, climbing peaks of splendor and falling off the edges, only to be caught up again, rising higher until she reached the summit only to lose her grip and fall into his embrace.

He wanted to make up for years of lost love. He tried to give impetus to the subdued glances they shared every day. He recalled her perky body bouncing about him, but he was unable to touch her, feel her, or taste her kiss. He was bottling and packaging these memories, not wanting the esteemed experience ever to leave his heart.

Barby clawed at him and wanted more. Barby was whimpering loudly. The filly was crossing her bridge into wonderland. She unlocked her special vault of memories. Her body was releasing exuberant waves of delight. She relaxed and felt his love for her as he touched her in her most tender places. Her lust mellowed, and she knew she was harnessed and saddled. She let him ride her for all she was worth.

They nestled together, falling off into a tranquil, mindless sleep.

Barby was startled awake sometime later when the barn door opened. She pushed at Henry until he opened his eyes. Henry sat up and looked through the slats. It was Sherry.

Sherry heard strange noises coming from the barn. She was very protective of her horses. She turned on a light by the door. The horses, startled by the light, shook their stalls.

Henry grabbed his robe, put it on, shoved Barby into the corner, and covered her with straw.

"Who's there? Speak up, I have a gun." Henry saw the shotgun now. He stepped out where she could see him.

"Sherry, don't shoot me!" he said.

Sherry could not believe her eyes. "Henry, what the hell are you doing out here? It's two-thirty in the morning?"

"I couldn't sleep. All the memories, you know." He hoped she would not come closer, but she walked toward him. He tightened his robe and noticed Barby's robe sticking out just a bit; Barby must have seen him look because she pulled it under the pile of straw.

Henry walked out of the stall toward Sherry. She was at the far end of the barn, and Henry walked briskly toward her, trying to act nonchalant. He was not wearing any shoes and suddenly felt naked.

"Where are your shoes? Did you walk across the snow barefoot? I thought I saw two footprints coming out here, but there was only one. Are you alright? Damn, Henry. Have you been lying in the straw? There's a bunch of it in your hair."

Sherry came closer, "What are you doing out here?"

"I couldn't sleep. I came out to see the horses, but after I got there, I realized my feet were too cold to return. So, I was waiting for the morning. I did not want to wake anyone. Brandy used to walk in the snow barefoot. I did it to feel what it was like. Stupid huh? All of this stuff started at the graveyard today."

"Want me to carry you piggyback?" She giggled.

He smiled. "You couldn't carry me, Sherry."

She looked at him tenderly. "You poor baby. You loved Brandy too much, Henry. You must keep a safe barrier around your heart. How long has it been since you were with a woman, sugar?"

Henry looked down at the ground, trying to look pathetic. "I lost track, don't think about it much."

She approached him, touched his face, and asked, "Way too long?"

He nodded without saying a word.

She took off her coat and put it around his shoulders. "You are taking a chill, Henry. We need to warm you up."

Sherry wore a bright blue chemise, and after taking her coat off, her taught nipples showed through. Henry wished he had not seen them, but he had. She walked toward the stall he came from looking, trying to see something.

Henry panicked. He grabbed her and pulled her into his embrace. She was startled but did not fight him.

"Well, I suppose this is one way to warm up." She said with an unimpressed whisky voice.

He kissed her, but she did not kiss him back.

"That's another way to warm up." She replied aloofly.

Henry did not want to become aroused, but it was happening just the same.

Her face became red, and she pulled herself out of his grasp. She looked up at him suspiciously. "Henry, I'm your best friend's wife, for God's sake."

She tried to turn toward the stall where Barby was hiding. Henry pulled her back into his embrace. He was letting her feel him, and the gesture mesmerized her.

His action repulsed her, but she was too embarrassed to push away from him. She could not believe he was putting a move on her.

He was hoping Barby would sneak out the back, but there was no motion he could detect from the far stall. He guided Sherry toward the front of the barn, but she turned again, and he pulled her back.

Henry thought that if he kissed her, Barby could sneak away. He held her cheeks and kissed her tenderly.

Sherry was curious now; she measured him up. She never felt a man so large. She wondered how far he was willing to go. Her chemise slipped off her shoulder, exposing one of her breasts.

When he saw her white breast and dark brown nipple, he shuddered.

She felt his reaction, and the gravity of what he was doing hit her. "No, Henry."

He held her, wondering what to do.

She struggled trying to free herself, and her chemise dropped off completely.

Sherry stood in front of him, dropping her hands at her side.

Henry had no idea she was that beautiful. Her short, slender body was immaculate. Her thin waist and shapely hips were well concealed by how she dressed.

Sherry watched him stare at her body as she reached down, picked up her chemise, and covered herself. The garment had quick-release straps, and he had accidentally opened them when he hugged her.

"Well, you've seen mine, Henry. I hope you are happy, and I hope you got an eyeful. Why? Why are you acting like this?"

He still did not see any movement from the far end of the barn. He wondered why Barby would not leave. His heart was not in this, and he could not continue the ruse.

"What's wrong, darling? You can't do this, can you?" Sherry whined, almost crying.

He shook his head, hanging it low. "No. I'm sorry, Sherry, I'm very sorry."

She pulled him close and kissed him hard. He did not kiss her back at first, but when she pulled herself against him, rubbing against his arousal, he responded. When he did, she pulled her lips away from his and bit his neck hard. She pushed him away violently and began sobbing.

"You jerk. I thought you were different, Henry. I thought you were a true gentleman. You are no different than any other man. You, pitiful fool, I will put you in an unmarked grave." She picked up her coat and ran out of the barn, choking on her tears.

Henry walked half-naked and confused toward the other end of the barn. Barby was rustling out of the straw. She came around the corner and walked up to him. The glaring look she had on her face pierced his heart. The shame Henry felt was unimaginable. He held his head down, unable to look at her directly.

"I don't suppose you could have handled that differently. Damn you, Henry." She reached up and slapped him hard across his face, busting his bottom lip. She walked past him and headed for the house, covering her face with her hands. She was cursing and crying while she walked and did not look back.

When Barby came out of the barn, Sherry was waiting to see who came. "I knew someone was in there. What are you up to, Barby?" Sherry asked.

"Sherry, I'm so sorry. Henry was trying to keep our secret. Henry and I have not done anything crazy for years. Pretty dumb, huh?" she replied and dried her eyes.

"Henry was trying to hide you from me. My god, when are you going to grow up?"

Henry walked out into the snow. "She's right, Barby. I'm so sorry, Sherry." Henry said.

"Both of you are unbelievable!" Sherry cried.

"Henry took this way too far. We are deeply sorry, Sherry." Barby replied.

"Henry, how can you do this to me? You saw me naked, for crying out loud. I hate you now. How can I ever forgive you?" Sherry cried.

Henry hung his head in shame.

"Look at you, blood dripping all over your face.

"I walloped him pretty good." Barby laughed.

"You two amaze me. Get in the house before you freeze to death. Stop putting on heirs, too. Everybody knows you love each other. Come on, you two." Sherry laughed.

Henry lay in his bed later, wondering how he could have worsened things.

When Henry saw Sherry the following day, she was still terribly angry. His guilty disposition did not help his grief.

"Sherry, please. I'll never tell Bobby if that is what you wish, or I will face his wrath if you desire."

"He can never learn about what happened last night, Henry. I am pregnant again. Bobby does not know yet. I was going to tell him today. About my pregnancy, I mean." She saw the panic in Henry's face and kind of enjoyed it. He was afraid of Bobby, and she liked that—she liked that a lot.

Barby would not even look at Henry at breakfast. She had dreamed of someday moving in with Henry. How could he embarrass himself and her and Sherry so much? It broke her heart.

For the next four years, she seemed to evaporate. Benjamin and Sarah were graduating from high school. Barby still avoided Henry privately, but she did speak to him around other people. She was careful never to let her emotional disappointment display itself around their children. Barby never spoke to Sherry again that fretful evening. The shame and indignity were too much for her.

As the years passed, Barby reasoned over the event, time and again. She convinced herself over time that Henry's groping of Sherry was a mistake. There was not much to it. She saw a little humor in it, too. Neither of them could have gone through with it. Plus, it was all brought on by him trying to protect her. Barby's heart construed wrong and not-so-wrong interpretations over the years. In time, she slowly began to accept his innocence. However, she secretly decided never to let him know how she felt.

CHAPTER 45

Jennifer the Woman

*B*arby watched Henry's loneliness and private despair; Henry had become particularly sad over the past two years. He put a lot of time into his business, but he was home every night.

Sarah confided in her aunt that her father often cried in his sleep. When Barby saw Sarah's tears falling on her lovely face, she knew things had gotten out of control.

Barby, Sarah, and Henry's mother cornered Henry in his house. He was sitting in his living room reading the paper when the three ladies converged around him.

"Hello, ladies. Mom, Barby, Sarah. What are the three of you up to?" Henry knew he was in for a hard time. These three females he dearly loved were smiling and seemed happy, but he knew they were conspiring to perform some imagined goodness. He remembered how many times in his life things like that had caused much more suffering than joy. However, it was refreshing to see Barby's smile.

Henry's mother spoke first. "Henry, you're not happy. You need to find a good woman, but you will not even try anymore, and we are all worried about you. You won't go to your therapist anymore, so we forced you to tell us what you will do about this."

He thought carefully before answering. "My heart isn't in it. I do not want emotional baggage. I do not feel I can manage a relationship. I'm happy; I have three beautiful women in my life."

"Daddy, I hear you sometimes cry at night, breaking my heart." Sarah was unable to say another word because the emotional pain smothered her.

Henry got up and went to his daughter. He sat beside her, and she flung herself into his embrace, sobbing enormously and babbling about her fears. Henry looked at his mother, not knowing what to say.

Barby sat patiently beside Sarah on the long sofa. She caressed Sarah's back and shoulders. Sarah was as much her daughter as Henry's, and her fragile heart struggled to maintain a healthy rhythm. Barby waited for a surge of emotion to pass and then said, "Henry, we love you so very much, and it is tearing our hearts out to see you unhappy. When

Sarah came to us, we had no choice. We must do something to help you. I love you so much it hurts it—physically hurts. Not a day goes by that I don't fight the urge to move in with you and end the pain." Barby could not go on as her crushing grief and sorrow choked her words.

She reached over, clasped his free hand, and buried her face.

Jessica stood up. "Stand up, Barby and Sarah. Our lives cannot go on this way. Henry, it would help if you began dating again. The entire family has felt your pain for years, Honey. We have lives we need to live, but you are making us all sick. That is the way families are, though. If one member is sick, we're all sick."

"I'll flirt a little and maybe even date someone, but my heart belongs to all of you. So now I'll take you all out for lunch if you promise not to cry anymore." He smiled at his daughter and his lifelong sweetheart.

Briefly, Henry was able to speak with Barby. "Did you mean what you said earlier?"

She looked into his eyes. She reached out and touched his cheek. "Of course I did, silly boy." Barby still loved him immensely.

"Please, Barby, about Sherry." Henry couldn't continue because Barby put her fingers over his lips.

"No, please." She closed her eyes and recalled the heart-rending event. Then, she reopened her eyes and focused on the present. She put the other event out of her mind and concentrated on her love for him. She gathered up all her strength and smiled at him.

Henry knew things would be all right. Barby still loved him. He could not have survived if she did not love him.

Henry made a phone call the next day. He phoned a private investigator to learn where Jennifer Jenkins lived.

Jennifer was still in Bremerton, Washington. A week later, Henry was on a plane for Seattle. When he arrived, he rented a car and drove to the address he received from the private eye. It was in an affluent residential neighborhood with large mansion-size lots and huge three- and four-story homes. He found the address and sat in the car across the street from the main entrance. It was just past three pm. He knew nothing about her except that she had not changed her name. He sat back in the seat and waited.

He listened to some music while he studied in the neighborhood. Teenagers carrying stuffed backpacks and kids walked past on skateboards and bicycles.

Just after four pm, a black Mercedes with tinted windows pulled into the long-curved driveway and disappeared into a garage attached to the house. He could not see who was driving but was sure the silhouette was feminine.

Henry waited ten more minutes, got out, and walked up the long sidewalk onto the grand entry. He rang the doorbell. It was an intercom, and a familiar voice he recognized immediately asked, "Who is it?"

Henry stood, embarrassed, wanting to run back to the car to avoid the ambivalence he suffered. But, instead, the familiar voice asked again, "Who is it?"

"It's an old friend. You may need to remember. It's Henry, Henry Rotyn of Michigan."

The door opened, and a thirty-seven-year-old Jennifer stood in front of him. "Oh, my God! Henry. Oh no. I must look frightful. No, I must look terrible. Henry, wow, how long has it been? What are you doing in Washington? You look fabulous, darling."

"Hello, Jennifer. It's good to see you after all these years."

She was gorgeous; her long, light blonde hair spilled softly across her shoulders. She wore a bright blue pantsuit with a white fringe along her collar and sleeves. Henry forgot how tall she was. When she hugged and kissed him on the cheek, she stared at him almost eye to eye. She was not as thin, but what she had was in all the right places.

"Won't you come in, Henry, please?"

She walked into a bright yellow great room with marble floors. The place reeked of money and reminded Henry of the Kraneger mansion.

An older man dressed in a black uniform approached.

"Gibbs, I got the door, but could you see to Mr. Rotyn's car, please."

Henry gave him the keys. A woman in a white uniform walked into the room with a tray of glasses and some brandy.

"Henry, please sit here while I meet a few necessary obligations. Marie, will you please make the gentleman comfortable? I shall return in a moment."

The young lady in white asked, "How do you like your brandy?"

"I guess on the rocks is fine, thank you," Henry replied.

Henry sat on a white leather sofa and sipped his drink. The high ceilings were enormous. Fine wooden furniture lined the walls, and the couch sat in the center with some easy chairs in a semi-circle. A black granite coffee table sat in the center of the assembled futons, sofas, and lounges.

Jennifer entered the room wearing a low-cut, dark blue evening dress. She came over to Henry and sat beside him. She smelled like a million bucks.

"You are the most beautiful woman I've seen in many years." He was smiling, and she did not glean even a hint of depression from his demeanor.

"I want to learn all about you. You're doing very well!" Henry turned his head and motioned to the elaborate surroundings.

"Oh, I don't know where to start. After finishing school, I spent four wonderful years at the University of Washington. I majored in Bio-kinetics. I got a great job overseeing some state-of-the-art computer models in their developmental stages. I received thousands of shares in my company, and when we went public, I was an instant millionaire. I married a wonderful man, the father of two of my three children. My husband is an airline pilot, and I hardly ever see him. I have three beautiful girls. Rachel is nineteen; she is a freshman at Stanford. Celeste is fourteen, and Christy is twelve. Celeste and Christy live here with their father and me. They are abroad with their grandparents in Europe somewhere."

She looked sensuous. Henry remembered the night they spent making love in the thunderstorm. "I'm incredibly happy for you, but I have to ask. I have wondered all through the years. Are you happy?"

She had a long drink but kept her blue eyes fixed on him. "Yes. I am delighted. But I must tell you, seeing you could end all of that. Oh, Henry. Do you remember the times we had together? I have never had another lover who, well, you know." She spoke the last few words so softly he could barely hear her.

The servant appeared with a shawl.

Jennifer spoke with her servant privately and then walked up to Henry. "Henry, would you be my guest for dinner this evening?"

Henry was surprised at her willingness to accompany him privately with so little introduction.

They walked to the garage, and she put the keys in his hand and smiled when he accepted them.

They drove off and were finally alone. Jennifer leaned over and kissed him on his cheek. "Oh, Henry. It is so exciting to see you again.

Now tell me about yourself, please." She remembered his eyes and his long, thick, fabulous hair.

Henry shared his life's course, the wonders, and the disappointments. Sometimes, he became sullen and quite emotional, and she was amazed at his openness in expressing his deep feelings.

She enjoyed being with a tender, masculine man. But, unfortunately, even her husband of fourteen years had become withdrawn, losing his amiable personality.

She took him to a quaint, dark, quiet restaurant. They were in a private corner and had become completely engrossed with each other.

Jennifer was divorced once, but her current marriage was working out, and she was delighted. That is until she saw Henry again.

"We should have had children, Henry." Her unabashed statement struck him merrily at first, but then he saw the eager, radiant look on her face. "I have a picture of Rachel, and she's my oldest. Look how beautiful she has become."

Henry examined the photo and the date placed a few years ago. Rachel was blonde like her mother. However, Henry was alarmed to see her eyes were cerulean blue, unlike her mother's navy blue eyes. The young girl stood beside a fountain, and Henry recognized it as Ghirardelli Square in San Francisco. She wore one of the fashionable blue and white school uniforms so standard in the city's many private schools.

"She is beautiful, absolutely gorgeous, Jennifer." They sat in a round booth, and Jennifer slid over awfully close to him.

"I was in San Francisco three weeks ago. I've been there often; Rachel attended high school in the Bay Area."

Henry became unsettled and amorous. Finally, he put his arm around her, and she snuggled into his side.

"Henry, please try to understand what I am about to tell you. In April of 1968, I gave birth to a beautiful daughter. Unfortunately, she has never met her real father, but I have always hoped she might have that opportunity someday."

Henry broke out in a cold sweat. He recalled the phone calls he had had several years ago from a young lady who claimed he might have been her father.

Jennifer sensed his ambivalent reaction and knew he was wondering if perhaps he was her father. "I was pretty wild back then, Henry, and I don't know who her father is." She saw that the condescending remark did not relieve his anguish.

A wave of emotion rewashed over her, and she worried that her eyes betrayed her lack of composure. However, she relaxed when she realized she was in the company of an old friend. She did not know what his reaction would be. When she observed his calmness, she asked, "Do you think you might be Rachel's father?" she asked.

Henry came to Seattle seeking happiness, perhaps even matrimony. Now, Henry saw himself on the opposite end of that scale. He suffered an altruistic reverie toward the young girl who had called him. He studied the photo. Henry knew deep in his heart Rachel had been the anonymous caller.

"Jennifer, I may be her father. She has my eyes and my hair and looks at the dimples. When can I meet her?"

"I always wondered if you could have been Rachel's father. But look, Henry, I don't want to create a headache for you. I'll never ask for support. I don't need it, darling." Jennifer was reluctant to contact him because she felt he might be penniless. Plus, she needed proof. And then there was always the 2200 miles.

"Thank you, Jennifer, but I have four children, no marriage, and three boys from the lady next door. My daughter is from the lady next door's sister. Unfortunately, Brandy died giving birth to Sarah. I'm afraid I still haven't been able to keep my eyes dry, too, darling."

"Jennifer and a neighbor boy were caught together. The boy's parents acted quickly and enrolled him in a private school back east." However, my parents insisted on keeping the baby and cared for her until she was six. By then, I was in my second marriage, had a good job, and matured into a responsible person. Rachel finally lived with her birth mother.

Henry noticed Jennifer's eyes weeping and could only imagine how her feminine emotions were tearing at her heart.

Jennifer used her napkin to dry her eyes but could not stop the source from regenerating more tears. Finally, she covered her face with both hands and the napkin and began sobbing uncontrollably.

Ever the gentleman, Henry pulled her against his shoulder and consoled her as best he could.

Jennifer reminded Henry of Mrs. Kraneger. Everything about her was high class. Not even Brandy carried herself with such dignity. Jennifer's every word was well thought out and spoken with perfect grammar. Her clothes and jewelry were the finest money could buy. She drove an expensive dollar automobile and lived in a mansion worth five times the Kraneger's. However, the woman had feelings and cried the same as any other woman had ever called into his arms.

He wanted to carry her away from all her high society responsibilities, but he knew that would never happen, so he did the next best thing. Henry was kind and virtuous.

After they arrived back at Jennifer's home, she regained her composure.

"Henry, there is an ongoing problem between Rachel and me. She insisted on leaving home. We had a terrible fight, and I am afraid I stated some things I should not have said. I think Rachel hates me now. When she was fourteen, I told her Dan was not her birth father. Dan is my husband. She did not seem to upset about it at first, but she became obsessed with locating her biological father as time passed. Her efforts became a source of irritation for her stepfather and me. She became tormented by the failures she experienced. I tried to persuade her to go slower and not let it dominate her every waking hour. We tried therapy, but it did not help. We bought her expensive gifts and granted her freedom beyond her age. Everything we tried drove her further away from us. She is in San Francisco now. She would have gone further away if my husband had not intervened. Rachel used the issue as a ruse, but I was terrified to do anything because I love my daughter and didn't want to lose her. I don't know what to do anymore."

Jennifer broke down again, crying softly in his arms. Henry felt like an immigrant in the expensive surroundings. It was past midnight, and he told Jennifer to get some sleep and that he would fix everything. Gibbs showed him to the guestroom.

Jennifer could not get Henry off her mind. He was so very handsome and masculine. She wanted to tear his clothes off when they returned from the restaurant, but she suppressed her yearnings. She looked at her clock. It was two-twenty. She sat up, thinking about going into his room. She would go in and jump him. Can he please? He seemed like a gentleman but looked at her amorously several times. Didn't he? Yes, she was pretty sure. She dangled her legs off the side of the bed and let her feet find the floor. Just do it! She did not care about the consequences. Were there consequences? Her husband was not a saint. She knew he was not keeping it in his pants. There was that time she found the condoms in his travel bag. She never even confronted him about that one. There had been other signs, but she ignored them because she did not care. Yes, she loved him, but she hated the fights;

avoiding those issues and maintaining a happy family life was better. Her daughters, after all, thought the world of him. She did step out on occasion, too. However, those rare adventures were not in her business, not even in Washington, certainly not in her home. Henry was different; Henry was virile, dreamy, so damn good-looking.

She was on her feet and out the door, dismissing further debate. She slipped into bed. She was delighted to discover Henry was sleeping nude when she rolled on top. He opened his eyes, and she kissed him. She did not say a word.

"Hello, beautiful." He was acutely aware of his vulnerability.

Jennifer disregarded his attempt at modesty. Instead, she greedily took all he offered.

Later that day, Jennifer bought Henry a new Mercedes convertible. Henry left for San Francisco with Jennifer next to him the following day.

They stopped in Salem that night in the middle of an explosive thunderstorm. She directed him to a remote park along a river. They left the car and took a blanket she had brought for such an occasion. They found a secluded grassy knoll under a large oak tree at the park's far end.

The romantic reenactment of their union while teenagers was a considerable success and delighted them merrily. They laughed and cried as they caressed each other. It was a hot night, and the hard rain did little to cool the muggy night air. Jennifer bathed in Henry's arms, giving and taking of herself without restraint. The stamina he expounded fed her unlimited strengths, allowing her to meet his intensity with an unbroken will to gratify her every need.

Jennifer reserved a suite at the Sheraton. They arrived soaked to the bone. They retired for the night and slept soundly.

They awoke late in the morning, taking their time and enjoying their day together.

Before nightfall, they were at Henry's, where Sarah met Jennifer for the first time. They became immediate friends.

Barby came downstairs; she heard a voice that was not familiar.

"Hello, she stated."

"Jennifer, this is the mother of our children. Barby, this is Jennifer; Jennifer is an old friend of mine, Barby. She lives in Bremerton, Washington. She is visiting her daughter, who is in college at Stanford."

"I am pleased to meet you, Barby. Henry, you seem to be in a household of beautiful women."

"Henry, I need to speak to you in private for a moment. Sarah, could you show Jennifer around while I speak with your father."

"Yes, Mom, of course."

"Excuse us for a moment, Jennifer," Barby replied kindly.

Barby looked at Henry and motioned for him to follow her. She walked out on the veranda. "An old friend? You better start explaining yourself, Mister! You have been gone for four days, and I did not know. You snuck out of here like a thief. How long have you been with this woman, Hank?"

"You look pretty mad, Barby. Please try to understand. Everything you learn about me is new to me, too. Listen, Barby, to the information I shared about my relationship with another girl long ago. Well, the story was real. You took the story as if it was a prank. I let it be because you seemed alright with me dating another girl. As far as I was concerned, Barby, the concise relationship was over. End of story."

"Henry, you don't get it, do you? You have an affair with another girl, a total stranger. You admitted the prank and thought it was over. Henry, I am so disappointed in you."

"I have some more explaining to do. The affair is going to produce, well, another young lady. Do you remember the prank phone calls I received earlier this year?"

"Oh, my God. Henry, do not tell me you have another daughter!"

"I have a sample of her DNA. Here is Jennifer's daughter's toothbrush and my toothbrush. Can you have it tested ASAP?"

"I can have it tested in less than an hour. I will be back in a few minutes. You better hope the DNA test is negative. I'll cut your balls off, Hank."

Barby took Jennifer with her.

Barby recalled Henry's inappropriate activity in her brother's barn. She could read him like a book, and when she realized he was having an affair with the woman sitting next to her now, it made Barby furious.

"What do you do for a living, Jennifer?" Barby asked.

"I have my own business. I am the CEO of a large Kinetics firm."

"Impressive business. The medical industry relies heavily on the publications your business creates. Now, that is impressive. A woman in a man's world, huh?" Barby smiled.

"You hit the nail on the head, lady; I face ridicule and harassment weekly." Jennifer said."

"How long have you been practicing medicine, Barby?"

"I started at Berkeley. I worked up to medical degrees until I started my business six years ago. I practice OB/GYN and Specialize in artificial insemination. I have three children. Sarah is my sister's daughter. Her mom passed away giving birth."

"Wow, I'm so sorry. Is this why you practice medicine?"

"Mostly, I guess. But Henry is Sarah's father; he is also the father of my three boys."

Sarah, please keep your father in the house. I don't want to chase him all over America. Jennifer is going with me over to my lab."

"Mom, Daddy won't get away from me, I promise." Sarah giggled.

On the way home, Barby handed me the envelope containing the DNA test results. "I haven't looked at the results. It goes into an envelope automatically. So, you get to do the honor, Jennifer. If Henry is the father, I told him I would castrate him. I was dating him during that period. How my sister married him is a long story. Someday, I'll share it with you, but not today."

Jennifer opened the envelope. She studied the results and wondered how Barby would react. They were climbing the Berkeley hills from the east side, swaying back and forth toward Henry's house. "How many of your children are Henry's?

"All of them. We refuse to live together, and we refuse to fool around very much. However, we fool around enough to make the family grow.

"You're not going to shoot me, are you, Barby."

"No, I'm starting to like you, Jennifer."

"Henry is my daughter's father."

Jennifer held up both hands to prevent Barby's attack.

"Now that is funny, Jennifer. Put down the defense. Did you go to school at Stanford? Tell me the truth, darling. Did you know Henry went to school at San Diego State while you attended Stanford University?"

"Barby, I haven't seen Henry in over twenty years."

Barby saw Henry dart into the downstairs bathroom.

"Excuse me for a moment, Jennifer."

Barby crept in behind him.

"Barby, I have to take a leak."

She flashed one of her most evil looks at him. "Don't let me stop you. Your modesty is not an issue. Jennifer is a married woman, Henry. What virtue is there in pursuing her now, Henry? By the way, how many other young women will come strutting into your life? I will tell you what; this is one for the books. Aren't you done yet?"

"No, I've been holding it long, Barby." Henry turned to face her.

"I still got my gun loaded. I cannot believe you, Henry!"

"Thank you for caring; I mean it. Thank you." He was sad and sincere.

Her heart could not resist him, although her mind fought a good fight. He held out his arms. "Wash your hands first, Henry."

After Henry washed his hands, she walked into his embrace. "Henry, I love you. I'm not too fond of it when you are with other women. I hate you, Henry!"

He held her close. He was always amazed at her ability to come on to him at the most awkward times.

"How long can we go on kidding each other, Barby?"

She kissed him lightly and walked out without answering his question.

"Barby, where is Jennifer?"

"In the Mercedes, she bought for you."

"What did you find out, Barby?"

"Jennifer has the results. Go now; you need to beat the traffic to Stanford."

Jennifer jumped out of the car. Good, you have the flowers and card Sarah delivered to the house. I am not going with you, Henry. You do know how to get to Stanford?"

"I know how to get to Stanford, but I need to know my way around the campus.

"Call me, and I can help you. Good luck talking to your daughter." She turned away and walked into the house.

Henry never slept with Jennifer again. But they had beautiful memories of their tender affair.

CHAPTER 46

Rachel

Barby watched Henry's loneliness and private despair; Henry had become particularly sad over the past two years. He put a lot of time into his business, but he was home every night.

Sarah confided in her aunt that her father often cried in his sleep. When Barby saw Sarah's tears falling on her lovely face, she knew things had gotten out of control.

Barby, Sarah, and Henry's mother cornered Henry in his house. He was sitting in his living room reading the paper when the three ladies converged around him.

"Hello, ladies. Mom, Barby, Sarah. What are the three of you up to?" Henry knew he was in for a hard time. These three females he dearly loved were smiling and seemed happy, but he knew they were conspiring to perform some imagined goodness. He remembered how many times in his life things like that had caused much more suffering than joy. However, it was refreshing to see Barby's smile.

Henry's mother spoke first. "Henry, you're not happy. You need to find a good woman, but you will not even try anymore, and we are all worried about you. You won't go to your therapist anymore, so we forced you to tell us what you will do about this."

He thought carefully before answering. "My heart isn't in it. I do not want emotional baggage. I do not feel I can manage a relationship. I'm happy; I have three beautiful women in my life."

"Daddy, I hear you sometimes cry at night, breaking my heart." Sarah was unable to say another word because the emotional pain smothered her.

Henry got up and went to his daughter. He sat beside her, and she flung herself into his embrace, sobbing enormously and babbling about her fears. Henry looked at his mother, not knowing what to say.

Barby sat patiently beside Sarah on the long sofa. She caressed Sarah's back and shoulders. Sarah was as much her daughter as Henry's, and her fragile heart struggled to maintain a healthy rhythm. Barby waited for a surge of emotion to pass and then said, "Henry, we love you so very much, and it is tearing our hearts out to see you unhappy. When

Sarah came to us, we had no choice. We must do something to help you. I love you so much it hurts it—physically hurts. Not a day goes by that I don't fight the urge to move in with you and end the pain." Barby could not go on as her crushing grief and sorrow choked her words.

She reached over, clasped his free hand, and buried her face.

Jessica stood up. "Stand up, Barby and Sarah. Our lives cannot go on this way. Henry, it would help if you began dating again. The entire family has felt your pain for years, Honey. We have lives we need to live, but you are making us all sick. That is the way families are, though. If one member is sick, we're all sick."

"I'll flirt a little and maybe even date someone, but my heart belongs to all of you. So now I'll take you all out for lunch if you promise not to cry anymore." He smiled at his daughter and his lifelong sweetheart.

Briefly, Henry was able to speak with Barby. "Did you mean what you said earlier?"

She looked into his eyes. She reached out and touched his cheek. "Of course I did, silly boy." Barby still loved him immensely.

"Please, Barby, about Sherry." Henry couldn't continue because Barby put her fingers over his lips.

"No, please." She closed her eyes and recalled the heart-rending event. Then, she reopened her eyes and focused on the present. She put the other event out of her mind and concentrated on her love for him. She gathered up all her strength and smiled at him.

Henry knew things would be all right. Barby still loved him. He could not have survived if she did not love him.

Henry made a phone call the next day. He phoned a private investigator to learn where Jennifer Jenkins lived.

Jennifer was still in Bremerton, Washington. A week later, Henry was on a plane for Seattle. When he arrived, he rented a car and drove to the address he received from the private eye. It was in an affluent residential neighborhood with large mansion-size lots and huge three- and four-story homes. He found the address and sat in the car across the street from the main entrance. It was just past three pm. He knew nothing about her except that she had not changed her name. He sat back in the seat and waited.

He listened to some music while he studied in the neighborhood. Teenagers carrying stuffed backpacks and kids walked past on skateboards and bicycles.

Just after four pm, a black Mercedes with tinted windows pulled into the long-curved driveway and disappeared into a garage attached to the house. He could not see who was driving but was sure the silhouette was feminine.

Henry waited ten more minutes, got out, and walked up the long sidewalk onto the grand entry. He rang the doorbell. It was an intercom, and a familiar voice he recognized immediately asked, "Who is it?"

Henry stood, embarrassed, wanting to run back to the car to avoid the ambivalence he suffered. But, instead, the familiar voice asked again, "Who is it?"

"It's an old friend. You may need to remember. It's Henry, Henry Rotyn of Michigan."

The door opened, and a thirty-seven-year-old Jennifer stood in front of him. "Oh, my God! Henry. Oh no. I must look frightful. No, I must look terrible. Henry, wow, how long has it been? What are you doing in Washington? You look fabulous, darling."

"Hello, Jennifer. It's good to see you after all these years."

She was gorgeous; her long, light blonde hair spilled softly across her shoulders. She wore a bright blue pantsuit with a white fringe along her collar and sleeves. Henry forgot how tall she was. When she hugged and kissed him on the cheek, she stared at him almost eye to eye. She was not as thin, but what she had was in all the right places.

"Won't you come in, Henry, please?"

She walked into a bright yellow great room with marble floors. The place reeked of money and reminded Henry of the Kraneger mansion.

An older man dressed in a black uniform approached.

"Gibbs, I got the door, but could you see to Mr. Rotyn's car, please."

Henry gave him the keys. A woman in a white uniform walked into the room with a tray of glasses and some brandy.

"Henry, please sit here while I meet a few necessary obligations. Marie, will you please make the gentleman comfortable? I shall return in a moment."

The young lady in white asked, "How do you like your brandy?"

"I guess on the rocks is fine, thank you," Henry replied.

Henry sat on a white leather sofa and sipped his drink. The high ceilings were enormous. Fine wooden furniture lined the walls, and the couch sat in the center with some easy chairs in a semi-circle. A black granite coffee table sat in the center of the assembled futons, sofas, and lounges.

Jennifer entered the room wearing a low-cut, dark blue evening dress. She came over to Henry and sat beside him. She smelled like a million bucks.

"You are the most beautiful woman I've seen in many years." He was smiling, and she did not glean even a hint of depression from his demeanor.

"I want to learn all about you. You're doing very well!" Henry turned his head and motioned to the elaborate surroundings.

"Oh, I don't know where to start. After finishing school, I spent four wonderful years at the University of Washington. I majored in Bio-kinetics. I got a great job overseeing some state-of-the-art computer models in their developmental stages. I received thousands of shares in my company, and when we went public, I was an instant millionaire. I married a wonderful man, the father of two of my three children. My husband is an airline pilot, and I hardly ever see him. I have three beautiful girls. Rachel is nineteen; she is a freshman at Stanford. Celeste is fourteen, and Christy is twelve. Celeste and Christy live here with their father and me. They are abroad with their grandparents in Europe somewhere."

She looked sensuous. Henry remembered the night they spent making love in the thunderstorm. "I'm incredibly happy for you, but I have to ask. I have wondered all through the years. Are you happy?"

She had a long drink but kept her blue eyes fixed on him. "Yes. I am delighted. But I must tell you, seeing you could end all of that. Oh, Henry. Do you remember the times we had together? I have never had another lover who, well, you know." She spoke the last few words so softly he could barely hear her.

The servant appeared with a shawl.

Jennifer spoke with her servant privately and then walked up to Henry. "Henry, would you be my guest for dinner this evening?"

Henry was surprised at her willingness to accompany him privately with so little introduction.

They walked to the garage, and she put the keys in his hand and smiled when he accepted them.

They drove off and were finally alone. Jennifer leaned over and kissed him on his cheek. "Oh, Henry. It is so exciting to see you again.

Now tell me about yourself, please." She remembered his eyes and his long, thick, fabulous hair.

Henry shared his life's course, the wonders, and the disappointments. Sometimes, he became sullen and quite emotional, and she was amazed at his openness in expressing his deep feelings.

She enjoyed being with a tender, masculine man. But, unfortunately, even her husband of fourteen years had become withdrawn, losing his amiable personality.

She took him to a quaint, dark, quiet restaurant. They were in a private corner and had become completely engrossed with each other.

Jennifer was divorced once, but her current marriage was working out, and she was delighted. That is until she saw Henry again.

"We should have had children, Henry." Her unabashed statement struck him merrily at first, but then he saw the eager, radiant look on her face. "I have a picture of Rachel, and she's my oldest. Look how beautiful she has become."

Henry examined the photo and the date placed a few years ago. Rachel was blonde like her mother. However, Henry was alarmed to see her eyes were cerulean blue, unlike her mother's navy blue eyes. The young girl stood beside a fountain, and Henry recognized it as Ghirardelli Square in San Francisco. She wore one of the fashionable blue and white school uniforms so standard in the city's many private schools.

"She is beautiful, absolutely gorgeous, Jennifer." They sat in a round booth, and Jennifer slid over awfully close to him.

"I was in San Francisco three weeks ago. I've been there often; Rachel attended high school in the Bay Area."

Henry became unsettled and amorous. Finally, he put his arm around her, and she snuggled into his side.

"Henry, please try to understand what I am about to tell you. In April of 1968, I gave birth to a beautiful daughter. Unfortunately, she has never met her real father, but I have always hoped she might have that opportunity someday."

Henry broke out in a cold sweat. He recalled the phone calls he had had several years ago from a young lady who claimed he might have been her father.

Jennifer sensed his ambivalent reaction and knew he was wondering if perhaps he was her father. "I was pretty wild back then, Henry, and I don't know who her father is." She saw that the condescending remark did not relieve his anguish.

A wave of emotion rewashed over her, and she worried that her eyes betrayed her lack of composure. However, she relaxed when she realized she was in the company of an old friend. She did not know what his reaction would be. When she observed his calmness, she asked, "Do you think you might be Rachel's father?" she asked.

Henry came to Seattle seeking happiness, perhaps even matrimony. Now, Henry saw himself on the opposite end of that scale. He suffered an altruistic reverie toward the young girl who had called him. He studied the photo. Henry knew deep in his heart Rachel had been the anonymous caller.

"Jennifer, I may be her father. She has my eyes and my hair and looks at the dimples. When can I meet her?"

"I always wondered if you could have been Rachel's father. But look, Henry, I don't want to create a headache for you. I'll never ask for support. I don't need it, darling." Jennifer was reluctant to contact him because she felt he might be penniless. Plus, she needed proof. And then there was always the 2200 miles.

"Thank you, Jennifer, but I have four children, no marriage, and three boys from the lady next door. My daughter is from the lady next door's sister. Unfortunately, Brandy died giving birth to Sarah. I'm afraid I still haven't been able to keep my eyes dry, too, darling."

"Jennifer and a neighbor boy were caught together. The boy's parents acted quickly and enrolled him in a private school back east." However, my parents insisted on keeping the baby and cared for her until she was six. By then, I was in my second marriage, had a good job, and matured into a responsible person. Rachel finally lived with her birth mother.

Henry noticed Jennifer's eyes weeping and could only imagine how her feminine emotions were tearing at her heart.

Jennifer used her napkin to dry her eyes but could not stop the source from regenerating more tears. Finally, she covered her face with both hands and the napkin and began sobbing uncontrollably.

Ever the gentleman, Henry pulled her against his shoulder and consoled her as best he could.

Jennifer reminded Henry of Mrs. Kraneger. Everything about her was high class. Not even Brandy carried herself with such dignity. Jennifer's every word was well thought out and spoken with perfect grammar. Her clothes and jewelry were the finest money could buy. She drove an expensive dollar automobile and lived in a mansion worth five times the Kraneger's. However, the woman had feelings and cried the same as any other woman had ever called into his arms.

He wanted to carry her away from all her high society responsibilities, but he knew that would never happen, so he did the next best thing. Henry was kind and virtuous.

After they arrived back at Jennifer's home, she regained her composure.

"Henry, there is an ongoing problem between Rachel and me. She insisted on leaving home. We had a terrible fight, and I am afraid I stated some things I should not have said. I think Rachel hates me now. When she was fourteen, I told her Dan was not her birth father. Dan is my husband. She did not seem to upset about it at first, but she became obsessed with locating her biological father as time passed. Her efforts became a source of irritation for her stepfather and me. She became tormented by the failures she experienced. I tried to persuade her to go slower and not let it dominate her every waking hour. We tried therapy, but it did not help. We bought her expensive gifts and granted her freedom beyond her age. Everything we tried drove her further away from us. She is in San Francisco now. She would have gone further away if my husband had not intervened. Rachel used the issue as a ruse, but I was terrified to do anything because I love my daughter and didn't want to lose her. I don't know what to do anymore."

Jennifer broke down again, crying softly in his arms. Henry felt like an immigrant in the expensive surroundings. It was past midnight, and he told Jennifer to get some sleep and that he would fix everything. Gibbs showed him to the guestroom.

Jennifer could not get Henry off her mind. He was so very handsome and masculine. She wanted to tear his clothes off when they returned from the restaurant, but she suppressed her yearnings. She looked at her clock. It was two-twenty. She sat up, thinking about going into his room. She would go in and jump him. Can he please? He seemed like a gentleman but looked at her amorously several times. Didn't he? Yes, she was pretty sure. She dangled her legs off the side of the bed and let her feet find the floor. Just do it! She did not care about the consequences. Were there consequences? Her husband was not a saint. She knew he was not keeping it in his pants. There was that time she found the condoms in his travel bag. She never even confronted him about that one. There had been other signs, but she ignored them because she did not care. Yes, she loved him, but she hated the fights;

avoiding those issues and maintaining a happy family life was better. Her daughters, after all, thought the world of him. She did step out on occasion, too. However, those rare adventures were not in her business, not even in Washington, certainly not in her home. Henry was different; Henry was virile, dreamy, so damn good-looking.

She was on her feet and out the door, dismissing further debate. She slipped into bed. She was delighted to discover Henry was sleeping nude when she rolled on top. He opened his eyes, and she kissed him. She did not say a word.

"Hello, beautiful." He was acutely aware of his vulnerability.

Jennifer disregarded his attempt at modesty. Instead, she greedily took all he offered.

Later that day, Jennifer bought Henry a new Mercedes convertible. Henry left for San Francisco with Jennifer next to him the following day.

They stopped in Salem that night in the middle of an explosive thunderstorm. She directed him to a remote park along a river. They left the car and took a blanket she had brought for such an occasion. They found a secluded grassy knoll under a large oak tree at the park's far end. The romantic reenactment of their union while teenagers was a considerable success and delighted them merrily. They laughed and cried as they caressed each other. It was a hot night, and the hard rain did little to cool the muggy night air. Jennifer bathed in Henry's arms, giving and taking of herself without restraint. The stamina he expounded fed her unlimited strengths, allowing her to meet his intensity with an unbroken will to gratify her every need.

Jennifer reserved a suite at the Sheraton. They arrived soaked to the bone. They retired for the night and slept soundly.

They awoke late in the morning, taking their time and enjoying their day together.

Before nightfall, they were at Henry's, where Sarah met Jennifer for the first time. They became immediate friends.

Barby came downstairs; she heard a voice that was not familiar.

"Hello, she stated."

"Jennifer, this is the mother of our children. Barby, this is Jennifer; Jennifer is an old friend of mine, Barby. She lives in Bremerton, Washington. She is visiting her daughter, who is in college at Stanford."

"I am pleased to meet you, Barby. Henry, you seem to be in a household of beautiful women."

"Henry, I need to speak to you in private for a moment. Sarah, could you show Jennifer around while I speak with your father."

"Yes, Mom, of course."

"Excuse us for a moment, Jennifer," Barby replied kindly.

Barby looked at Henry and motioned for him to follow her. She walked out on the veranda. "An old friend? You better start explaining yourself, Mister! You have been gone for four days, and I did not know. You snuck out of here like a thief. How long have you been with this woman, Hank?"

"You look pretty mad, Barby. Please try to understand. Everything you learn about me is new to me, too. Listen, Barby, to the information I shared about my relationship with another girl long ago. Well, the story was real. You took the story as if it was a prank. I let it be because you seemed alright with me dating another girl. As far as I was concerned, Barby, the concise relationship was over. End of story."

"Henry, you don't get it, do you? You have an affair with another girl, a total stranger. You admitted the prank and thought it was over. Henry, I am so disappointed in you."

"I have some more explaining to do. The affair is going to produce, well, another young lady. Do you remember the prank phone calls I received earlier this year?"

"Oh, my God. Henry, do not tell me you have another daughter!"

"I have a sample of her DNA. Here is Jennifer's daughter's toothbrush and my toothbrush. Can you have it tested ASAP?"

"I can have it tested in less than an hour. I will be back in a few minutes. You better hope the DNA test is negative. I'll cut your balls off, Hank."

Barby took Jennifer with her.

Barby recalled Henry's inappropriate activity in her brother's barn. She could read him like a book, and when she realized he was having an affair with the woman sitting next to her now, it made Barby furious.

"What do you do for a living, Jennifer?" Barby asked.

"I have my own business. I am the CEO of a large Kinetics firm."

"Impressive business. The medical industry relies heavily on the publications your business creates. Now, that is impressive. A woman in a man's world, huh?" Barby smiled.

"You hit the nail on the head, lady; I face ridicule and harassment weekly." Jennifer said."

"How long have you been practicing medicine, Barby?"

"I started at Berkeley. I worked up to medical degrees until I started my business six years ago. I practice OB/GYN and Specialize in artificial insemination. I have three children. Sarah is my sister's daughter. Her mom passed away giving birth."

"Wow, I'm so sorry. Is this why you practice medicine?"

"Mostly, I guess. But Henry is Sarah's father; he is also the father of my three boys."

Sarah, please keep your father in the house. I don't want to chase him all over America. Jennifer is going with me over to my lab."

"Mom, Daddy won't get away from me, I promise." Sarah giggled.

On the way home, Barby handed me the envelope containing the DNA test results. "I haven't looked at the results. It goes into an envelope automatically. So, you get to do the honor, Jennifer. If Henry is the father, I told him I would castrate him. I was dating him during that period. How my sister married him is a long story. Someday, I'll share it with you, but not today."

Jennifer opened the envelope. She studied the results and wondered how Barby would react. They were climbing the Berkeley hills from the east side, swaying back and forth toward Henry's house. "How many of your children are Henry's?

"All of them. We refuse to live together, and we refuse to fool around very much. However, we fool around enough to make the family grow.

"You're not going to shoot me, are you, Barby."

"No, I'm starting to like you, Jennifer."

"Henry is my daughter's father."

Jennifer held up both hands to prevent Barby's attack.

"Now that is funny, Jennifer. Put down the defense. Did you go to school at Stanford? Tell me the truth, darling. Did you know Henry went to school at San Diego State while you attended Stanford University?"

"Barby, I haven't seen Henry in over twenty years."

Barby saw Henry dart into the downstairs bathroom.

"Excuse me for a moment, Jennifer."

Barby crept in behind him.

"Barby, I have to take a leak."

She flashed one of her most evil looks at him. "Don't let me stop you. Your modesty is not an issue. Jennifer is a married woman, Henry. What virtue is there in pursuing her now, Henry? By the way, how many other young women will come strutting into your life? I will tell you what; this is one for the books. Aren't you done yet?"

"No, I've been holding it long, Barby." Henry turned to face her.

"I still got my gun loaded. I cannot believe you, Henry!"

"Thank you for caring; I mean it. Thank you." He was sad and sincere.

Her heart could not resist him, although her mind fought a good fight. He held out his arms. "Wash your hands first, Henry."

After Henry washed his hands, she walked into his embrace. "Henry, I love you. I'm not too fond of it when you are with other women. I hate you, Henry!"

He held her close. He was always amazed at her ability to come on to him at the most awkward times.

"How long can we go on kidding each other, Barby?"

She kissed him lightly and walked out without answering his question.

"Barby, where is Jennifer?"

"In the Mercedes, she bought for you."

"What did you find out, Barby?"

"Jennifer has the results. Go now; you need to beat the traffic to Stanford."

Jennifer jumped out of the car. Good, you have the flowers and card Sarah delivered to the house. I am not going with you, Henry. You do know how to get to Stanford?"

"I know how to get to Stanford, but I need to know my way around the campus.

"Call me, and I can help you. Good luck talking to your daughter." She turned away and walked into the house.

Henry never slept with Jennifer again. But they had beautiful memories of their tender affair.

CHAPTER 47

The Waitress

*H*enry's business flourished, and he began traveling more, promoting an online web page he designed for merchants. His latest trip was an across-the-country forty-five-day marathon. He was very lonely, and his daughters kept pestering him to find a girlfriend, but his heart was not in it.

Henry left his room and walked outside; thunder rumbled in the distance. He breathed deeply in the cool spring air, freshly washed from the overnight rain. While he filled his lungs, cobwebs cluttering his mind began to clear. The mild stinging sensation deep in his chest resurfaced boyhood memories. Even in early May, frigid spring mornings were typical in Michigan.

He stood stretching, soaking in the fresh air. He wondered what the weather was like in California. Sarah and Rachel would still be in bed, sound asleep. He needed to call his daughters today. He loved them both very much. However, Sarah was still in college, and her finals were this week.

Benjamin was in his fourth year of premed in Ann Arbor. Henry would see him later in the week.

Barby hated it when Ben decided to go to Michigan. Henry thought she secretly feared her boys would follow in Bobby's footsteps. Henry's mother was so mad at Ben. She understood Barby's concern, but Henry reminded Barby of a young girl who did exactly the opposite and went to Berkeley instead of an Ivy League college like her sister. Barby never dreamed Ben would light the candle to the Maize and Blue. Henry got the best of her, which was not usual. He remembered her reaction, but when Henry mentioned Jennifer, Barby pursed her lips and would not look at Henry."

Henry was happy to finally visit his old hometown. It would mean much more to have Sarah and Barby here with him.

He thought about Brandy. He would be close to her today, but every year, it was harder to remember the love he lost so many years ago. He made a mental note to get flowers when he visited her gravesite later.

He promised Sarah he would not forget the flowers whenever he visited Brandy's grave. Henry intended to keep this promise.

He wanted to catch an early breakfast. He entered the foyer of the Flying Saucer Restaurant, quickly climbing the staircase leading up to the outer wing of the restaurant. The physical exertion was exhilarating. It felt good to stretch his legs after all his driving.

He noticed the waitress when he came through the doorway. When he caught her eye, she motioned for him to sit. She was beautiful; her fair complexion and long raven-black hair struck a nerve. In addition, she was slender and graceful with noticeable feminine features; the combinations worked well.

Karen loved the early mornings. It was still before six, and she had time to visit the regulars before the crowds began around seven. Karen enjoyed working at the Inn. She started this job to help pay her way through college. That was nine years ago. Her degree in marketing had yet to do much for her, and it would only once she got out of Barneyville. The sleepy little community was in her blood. Karen questioned her resolve but took a deep breath and gazed through the panoramic view into the grey dawn. What has happened to my dreams? She lamented.

A familiar longing pulled at her heart, and she wanted to start her own life, but her mother died during her senior year in college. Karen gladly became a temporary parent to her two younger brothers. They had recently gone off their separate ways: one in the Navy, one in college. Karen was still in Barneyville, but nothing prevented her from leaving. However, Barneyville was home; it was safe and comfortable. She could not commit to going just yet, but soon, she promised herself, real soon.

The tall gentleman with long blonde hair was looking for her way. She needed to get to his table. She held up her hand, motioning with her index finger that she would be there instantly. There was something about him that bothered her. She looked out into the darkness, then put on her best smile as she relinquished her dreams for yet another day.

Henry studied her perky bounce as she walked around the narrow corridor. Her big smile seemed genuine and exciting. He kept a glancing eye her way as she delivered orders that came up from the dumb servers. The call lights kept flashing until she arrived at each one, removed the contents, and returned the empty shell to the kitchen. Henry remembered there was a dumbwaiter stationed at every six tables.

She was making progress, and he monitored her every move. Her short black skirt revealed her slender athletic legs. Her firm bust occupied the available space in her starched white blouse. She was vibrant and excited to watch, but he did not want to stare. She seemed sincerely happy.

Lightning flashed in the distant sky. The storm that kept Henry from a sound sleep was still visible to the east.

The local newspaper reported some relief from the rain.

The parking lot was filling up with all kinds of vehicles. Henry strained to make out objects in the gray dawn. He was eager to see some of the old neighborhood.

Karen just loved his long blonde hair. However, he wore it in an unusual style. His hair was in a long ponytail, but the sides were short. She tried to place its origin, maybe South America or Asia. It seemed out of place for Barneyville.

She wondered if he drove the Green Mercedes. She saw it in the parking lot coming in to work this morning. It had out-of-state plates but was too dark to determine which state.

Karen took an order from the couple at the table next to him.

Henry grinned as the big smile-on-legs came to take his order. He tried to duplicate her cheery disposition, but his weariness won out.

"Coffee?" she asked.

"Please," he said.

"Just passing through?" she asked as she filled his cup. His charming blue eyes appeared tranquil, but her sensory instincts issued warning signals. Pay attention and do not stare, silly. You are acting like a schoolgirl.

Henry took a sip of coffee and tried to clear his mind before he answered her. "No, I'm here for a few days. I did not sleep very well last night. I think the storm kept me awake." He held up his cup. "Coffee works every time."

"You must not be from around here; we have storms like that once a week this time of year." She tried to avoid contacting those eyes.

He looked at the menu, gave her his choice, and handed the menu back to her. She was charming, and the freckles on her cheeks over the fair complexion created a quality he had not seen in a long time.

Karen felt him staring and smiling, but she learned to accept how men looked at her. Karen sensed his observation lacked the degenerate, perverted attitude of many men. This gentleman was uniquely different.

He was handsome, his hands were clean, and his fingernails manicured. He looked as if someone was taking excellent care of him. In addition, he had a pleasant, cultured look about him. Karen reasoned he must be the kind of person people like being around. She smiled and left his table to send his order to the kitchen.

The aroma of fresh coffee is one of life's simple pleasures; Henry thought as he sipped from his cup. The night's rest served to invigorate his disposition to some extent. He hoped the hot coffee would stimulate his spirit. Unfortunately, Henry was exceptionally weary after traveling for thirty-two days—the latest excursion from Indianapolis to Calhoun County, Michigan.

He studied the design of the old Barneyville Inn, and he tried to remember what it looked like twenty years ago. Then, the building looked like a vast flying saucer with a raised top from the outside. Indoors, the large, exposed ceiling beams were barely visible, but their patterns seemed unchanged. The elevated outer wing or raised circular deck where Henry sat still had what appeared to be the original six-foot-high windows—the panoramic view wrapped around the entire building on the second floor. At first light, a vast ocean of green treetops smothered the southeastern end of what used to be the Millpond.

The carousel of windows illuminated the restaurant during daylight hours, but the darkness of night changed the whole mood. Looking into the interior, numerous tables, like tiny islands, were dimly visible at differing levels throughout the Inn's interior. Islands disconnected from each other as access stairs, landings, and walkways were not apparent, camouflaged by a maze of vines, plants, and trees.

The interior tables were for evening dining. The breakfast and lunch crowds only had access to the narrow outer wing that circled the entire building. Here, the dining tables were patrons who had an uninhibited view through the carousel of windows. There was just enough space in that narrow corridor from the windows to the inside railing for one table and some walking space. The string of tables wrapped around the raised deck as far as the eye could see, creating an unbroken circle.

The Inn changed its name. It was "The Flying Saucer Inn." The Barneyville Inn was its name now. The Inn was quiet—not empty, just slow. Some patrons gathered in small groups here and there. The place was taking on a sampling of the brisk, bustling crowds to follow. However, it was still too early for all that.

The big-smile-on-legs brought his order. "So, you don't live in the area?" Karen prodded lightly.

"No, I live in Northern California," Henry said.

"That explains the long hair." She wanted to tell him how nice his hair looked, and she caught a whiff of his cologne. She cultivated a swelling warmness for him.

"You don't like my long hair?" he asked. He felt a giddy nervousness come over him.

Karen said, "No, I mean yes. But, hey, I love your hair. It is incredible! I do not see many good-looking men with long hair. The few who do have long hair look like they need exterminators."

Henry chuckled. "Good looking, huh?" He flashed his best smile.

Karen smiled and realized she had allowed words to leave her tongue meant for her heart. "Like you don't know it." She could not believe she had done it again. What a dream to wake up to, but he is too old for you to be silly; she imagined he must be in his late thirties, married with seven kids.

He smiled because he could see she was flustered.

"California, huh?" she queried.

"Northern California," he responded.

"I've never been there. Maybe someday," Karen remarked.

"How about you; have you been here long?" he asked.

He had a kindness about him, she thought. "I grew up in Barneyville. My mother managed this Inn for seven years."

Henry wondered if he knew any of her family."

"I remember faces, but I don't remember seeing you here before," she stated. She knew she would not forget those blue eyes and that hair. She caught herself dreaming, almost drooling. Her reaction made her uncomfortable.

"Well, it has been quite a while since I was back this way. Why say, my name is Henry." He stood up, and she reached out to shake his hand.

"My name is Karen. Pleased to meet you, Henry."

A long-jagged bolt of lightning lit the countryside. Henry and Karen focused on the phenomenon while they stood together looking into the dawn.

"The pleasure's all mine," he added. Henry allowed himself a moment to savor the fragrance of her perfume. "You never tire of it, do you?" He remarked in a low whisper.

"No, there are times when I think I would, but when Mother Nature puts on a show like this. Well, it's breathtaking, isn't it?" she said.

Henry smiled at her, and they turned away from the panoramic view. "I don't get in here too often anymore; however, this Inn and I go back a long way. I came here a lot back when I was a kid in the sixties. He admired her pearl-white teeth.

"Did you go to school here?" she asked. Henry was taller up close, more so than she imagined. Still, he seemed very tender, and this touched her deeply.

"Yes, kindergarten through twelfth grade. You too?" He asked.

"Yes, second grade through twelve. Someday, I will leave, only come back for memories." Karen held her head high, making it plain she, too, would make her way out of Barneyville.

"May I say you're a lovely woman?" Henry was not the sort of fellow to blurt out his feelings. He was sure he was too forward.

His demeanor, although candid, came off as very elegant. "Well, thank you for the compliment."

"Handsome, charismatic, I love your hair! Have you always worn it long?" she asked.

"Whenever someone compliments my hair, I think of my mother. Although she never admitted as much, she wanted a girl and had let my hair grow long since infancy. She had it shortened when I entered the first grade, but it was still shouldering length. Then, starting sometime in the fifth grade, she decided she wanted me to wear it longer. I have had it trimmed since then but never shortened."

"Here in Barneyville?" she gasped.

"Yes, my mom worked in the principal's office at the school. I knew many faculty members didn't like how long my hair was, but most kept their opinions to themselves."

"This is such a conservative community. I can't recall the long hair, Henry," she said.

"Yes, well, I was a bit of a rebel, I guess." Henry leaned against the window frame.

"This school system would give you a hard time today," she said emphatically.

"Where did you live?" I wonder if I know any of his family, she pondered.

"Our house is at 312 Jefferson Avenue," he stated.

I live in Jefferson, she reflected. That is the large two-story brick house on the corner. She knew the people who lived there, and they had been there for many years.

"You're kidding. The big brick two-story?"

"Yes. Do you know where it is?" He asked.

"Yes, we live just across the street in the old Kraneger mansion."

Henry could not believe it. He studied her carefully now, and emotion crept over his chest. She had her hair, she had her eyes, Karen had her body, and she even had her smile. Why didn't he see it before? Twenty-year-old memories flooded his senses as he grappled for the bottom of the windowsill to regain stability.

"Hey, watch out," she grabbed his shoulder.

Her thoughts were racing. Who are you? She wondered again. Why are you here? She wanted to know more about him. She propped him up against her bosom and lowered him into his chair.

"Do you know him?" Another employee asked, thinking her action suggested she was a close friend.

"No, I do not know him, but I think I know who," she said.

Henry stared at the beautiful woman in white.

She smiled at him.

"Do you know Brandy?" he asked.

"Hush, you almost fell. Don't move until you regain your senses."

He leaned back into her bosom. She was beautiful.

"Who is Brandy?" she asked.

He looked at her closely as reality set in. "You look like Brandy, but you are not Brandy."

"My name is Karen," she said.

"Who is Brandy?" she asked again.

"My wife." Henry tried to smile but did not know how much success he had. He wanted to explain himself but could not manage the necessary emotional courage.

So, he was married. Karen knew he looked too nice to be a bachelor. She had an older cousin named Brandy, who had died for years.

Karen ordered a warm breakfast for him. Henry sat and ate while Karen waited on him continuously. She even took a short break and sat with him. "My aunt and her two children and I moved into the Kraneger Mansion almost thirteen years ago. My mother died when I was five, and I never met my dad. So here I am, Henry."

"Do you remember the Kraneger's, Henry?"

Where would I start, he asked himself. It seemed too much to consider all at once.

He seemed uncomfortable, and she suddenly realized he had tripped over his chair when she had last mentioned the Kraneger's. She studied him closely; his blue eyes had lost their charming glow. Karen wondered what secrets he hid in his past.

"I knew the Kranegers very well," he said.

She gave him a strange look. She felt a bit overwhelmed. "I'll be back in a moment," she said.

She had to take care of another customer. She wondered why bringing up the Kranegers threw him for a loop.

There must be some connection between Karen and the Kraneger; Henry thought while he finished his meal. The surreal experience he envisioned earlier still tore at him.

"I'm going to walk you down to your room, Henry."

She seemed distant after he told her he knew the Kranegers. He would not force the issue if she did not want to discuss it further. However, he did wonders.

When Henry stood up, he felt a little dizzy. He put his right hand on Karen's shoulder.

She grabbed him and pulled him into her bosom. "Hang on to me," she said quietly, not wanting to draw attention to his condition. He was not steady, and she needed to get him to his room. She considered calling for help, but he seemed to stabilize quickly.

He steadied himself, and she loosened her grip on him.

"Can you walk now?" she asked softly.

"Yeah, I think so. Thank you," Henry whispered. His lips brushed her neck, and the fragrance of her perfume trailed into his nostrils.

They separated and began walking toward the staircase that led to the lodging rooms.

"What time do you get off?" he asked. Karen was taller up close, and her beauty became more apparent.

"I work from five until one-thirty," she said. Karen hoped Henry was not coming on to her. He was married, and she did not fool around with married men. However, she enjoyed walking closely with him. He appeared stronger now, and she found herself thinking of him in an increasingly attractive way.

When they arrived at his room, she insisted on going in.

"You're going to get some rest, and then I'll check in on you later." She pulled out a pillow from under the bedspread and fluffed it up. Henry sat down on the bed, and she took off his shoes.

Henry noticed the room was spinning a bit.

"I have to go." she quibbled. "I'll check in on you later. Get some rest." Her words were calmer this time.

He was still experiencing vertigo.

"Thank you for being so kind," he said. Then, before Henry could say another word, she was gone.

His thoughts remained inquisitively on the young woman he had just met. How old was she? He wondered. Was she related to Brandy somehow? The resemblance was extraordinary. Henry knew almost everyone who had been there if she said she had.

He looked at his hands; the index finger on both hands constantly itched or ached. Henry wondered if it was because of the four years he spent topping onions as a teen. There were visible scars on both fingers even after all these years. He wondered if his onion-topping experience contributed to his being ambidextrous.

Memories of his old hometown flashed in his mind's eye. He could remember most of the landmarks.

The old Millpond did not have any water in it. Instead, a small stream weaved through the cat of nine tails. The tall growth camouflaged what used to be a massive body of water, more than a mile across and more than six miles long.

Closer to town, Trojan Park was between the highway and downtown. The statue of the Greek poet Homer, a massive World War I cannon, and the old clock tower on a stone pedestal were landmarks of the community.

Henry thought about his loved ones in Riverview, the old graveyard on the other side of the highway.

He needed to get a feel for things occasionally. His memory and inner picture of his old hometown sometimes required him to focus more. Barneyville still held so many memories. Happy ones, all good except the one he had on his mind that would never go away; Henry would not let it.

He recalled he was on his way to Baltimore. His business was so successful that someone in every major city was clamoring to get on board. These things were on his mind while he drifted off to sleep.

CHAPTER 48

Karen

*S*omeone was knocking on his door. Henry got up to see who it was. He had slept hard and was a little dizzy. When he opened the door, Bobby stood filling the doorway.

"Well, hello, stranger. How are you, Henry?"

"Hey, come on in, Rogue. How is life treating you, old friend?"

"Damn, man. Get some light in here. It looks like a morgue, Henry. When did you get in?" He opened the drapes while he talked.

"Yesterday," Henry said.

"Sarah called me last week and said you had been pushing yourself too hard. She is worried about you. You need to call your daughter more often. Man, it is hard to believe Sarah is a senior at Berkeley. Those college days—that was the life."

"Yes, I'm very proud of her, but she has this independent spirit like her mother," Henry said.

"I called Sarah after you called Sherry to tell us you were in town. Why didn't you come out to the house?" Bobby asked.

"Oh, I just ran out of gas, I guess," Henry said.

"You need to call Sarah, Henry."

"How are the boys?" Henry recalled Bobby had three boys. Brent, who had just graduated from the University of Michigan, joined his father in his business. Bruce was in his sophomore year at Central Michigan. Brandon was still in high school.

"Damn," Bobby said under his breath. "Brandon is driving me nuts. Were we girl crazy when we were teenagers?" Bobby asked.

"Yeah, I think we were," Henry said.

"I know you were. But, of course, if I had more than two sisters, you would have gotten in their shorts, too, huh?"

Henry smiled.

"Hey, that's great," Bobby said.

Henry wondered if he was referring to his smile or his sisters.

The two old friends drove around town, looking at the old neighborhood. They stopped and talked to people on the streets. Bobby knew everyone.

"It's hard to believe Barby has three boys. I thought she would never have any children for a long time." Bobby slapped his old friend on the back.

"Barby seems incredibly happy. She and Sarah are sure good friends. What is this stuff about another daughter? I have not met Rachel, but she is all Sarah would talk about when I spoke with her. How many more kids will pop up across the country with your name tattooed to their ass?"

"I remember a girl named Penelope." Henry smiled.

"Shit, Rogue, Sherry doesn't know anything about her."

Henry ignored his concern and pointed at the weedy valley that used to be the Millpond. "It isn't right, such a waste."

"Some fellows from Detroit bought up all the bottomland. I have heard rumors about farming the 160 acres. Nothing has happened. It is a wasteland." Bobby said.

"Looks like a swamp," Henry said.

Bobby shrugged his shoulders. "Barby told me she works with Rachel and Sarah. So that is nice, you know. It's nice."

"Barby thinks you've been a wonderful father—single parent. Then I heard you are the father of Barby's boys. They do not say much about having a mom and dad who are in love but not married. They all live in both homes. Do they think their lives are normal? What is up with you and my sister Rogue? Why didn't you two ever get together?"

Henry looked at Bobby, "I thought you knew?"

"Knew what? Hey, if I am too nosy."

After some moments, Henry broke the silence.

"Barby told me that on the day Brandy died, Brandy's dying wish was that Barby could not marry me. Barby argues that the spirit of Brandy's statement was more important than the actual outcome. Barby still loves me, and I hear matrimony mentioned, but that's all.

"Damn, Rogue, Barby never told me. Sherry can help her. Barby should not be carrying all that baggage by herself. I will make it a point to spend time with her and get her to see Sherry. When did you learn about this, Henry?" he asked quietly.

"Not very long ago, maybe two years," Henry said.

"Is Bartholomew your son, Henry?" Bobby asked respectfully.

"Yeah, he's quite a character. Did you know Barby calls him Hank?" Henry's aching head repressed his smile.

"Is Barby dating anyone?" Bobby asked.

"I don't think so," Henry said.

"Who is the father of Bill and Tom?" Bobby asked.

Henry grinned. "Who do you think, Bobby?"

"For crying out loud. I do not understand why you two are not married. Life is not a game, Henry. How do the boys feel about all of this? I don't understand, and it doesn't make any sense."

"Talk to your sister, Bobby."

Bobby's face twisted into a repulsive expression. "You know my father once called my sisters trollops. Of course, he didn't mean it in a nasty or vicious sense, but I can see how they had their claws in you, huh!"

Henry smiled, "No, I don't see my relationship with them that way. Of course, I loved Barby, but when Brandy and I started fooling around, our hearts got tangled, and we couldn't untie the knots."

"That's beautiful, Henry. Thank you for sharing that with me." Bobby said.

With a big grin, Henry said, " Where did that come from?"

Bobby ducked his shoulders; "Sherry has me going to these classes. I'm in a group therapy class, and I'm supposed to be more sensitive in how I look at other people's problems."

Henry continued to smile widely and was full of pleasure. "It made me feel pretty good, Bobby."

"Henry, there is one thing I feel we need to talk about, Rogue."

Henry noticed the sorrow in his eyes. He knew what was coming.

"You and Barby keep playing these games, and sometimes you create untenable results. Sherry told me all about the fucked-up game you played on her, you, and Barby. Shit, man, you saw my wife naked, Rogue. Life is not a game you can play, especially when you hurt others. Sherry was upset. She wanted me to talk to you a long time ago. I avoided this conversation because I knew it was part of the sick game you both imagined. Nobody cares, Henry. Marry my sister, Henry, please."

"I'm deeply sorry for my stupid behavior. I am truly ashamed of myself. Sherry taunted my recklessness. My life has been one illusive mess after another. Barby and I have looked at life from a broken, macabre disposition. I do not have an answer, Bobby. Our boys and Sarah laugh at our silliness. My oldest daughter, Rachel, is a millionaire. Jennifer, her mom, bought me my ride. You must have seen it."

"The Mercedes? I saw it had California plates. She bought that for you. How well did that go over with Barby?"

"Not very well, Rogue." Henry grinned.

"Henry, you need to get a grip on life. You're making a mess of things."

"I'm sorry. I'll apologize to Sherry the next time I see her," Henry said.

"Buckle your seatbelt, Rogue. You are having dinner with us tonight. Your opportunity is close at hand," Bobby advised.

It was nice to be back in Barneyville. They visited the graveyard. Henry's father was close to Brandy. Henry still could not compose himself even after all these years.

"You're never going to get over her, are you?" Bobby asked.

Bobby put a hand around his shoulder, "Henry, man, you need to get on with your life. You need to marry my sister."

Henry's eyes were watering. Finally, he told himself it was only the wind.

"I had a good woman, Bobby. Maybe you are only supposed to have just one. Why do you keep beating that drum of matrimony for us, Bobby?"

They drove back to the Inn in silence. They had a few drinks at the outdoor lounge, and Henry enjoyed spending time with Bobby. He had become a little pushy, but Henry supposed that came with the territory. Henry knew something about sales, although he had yet to pursue the art with Bobby's world's effusiveness required.

Bobby left about three. Henry decided to join Bobby's family for dinner the following night. Henry finished his whiskey sour and tried to recall all the beautiful memories in the old Inn. Finally, the night air became cool at dusk, and he went upstairs to have dinner.

He sat at a table with a view of the valley.

Henry slept hard for a few hours, then went to the bathroom. When he returned to his bed, he could not sleep. It was almost two. He picked up his phone and called Barby.

"Hello." Her voice sounded sleepy.

"Hey, pretty girl. How are you, Barby?" Henry asked.

"Henry, hi honey, where are you?"

"I'm in Barneyville. Did I wake you up?" he asked apologetically.

"Yes, you woke me up, but that's okay. What are you doing in Barneyville? We are worried about you, Henry. Are you coming home soon?" her voice was apprehensive.

"I don't know, maybe in a couple of weeks. Say, I need to get some information from you. Who's living in your house now?" he asked mysteriously.

Barby wondered what he was up to, and a spark of hope touched her heart. "Why do you ask, Henry?"

"Well, I met someone, and she says she lives in the old Kraneger mansion. Who is she, Barby?" He was nervous and felt a bit tenuous.

"I know, Honey. She looks a lot like her. Did you think you saw a ghost?" Barby held her breath, waiting for his reply.

"Yeah. Henry's voice was barely a whisper. Who is Karen, Barby?"

"Karen is my mother's youngest sister's only daughter. She is my cousin, Honey. I have been trying to get her to come to California. I knew if you met her, you would be impressed. I have told her all about you, Henry. She thought you were too old for her. Do you like her?"

"Yes, she's gorgeous. I cannot sleep. Do you think this is too weird? I do not find her interesting just because she looks like Brandy. I am not that naïve, am I? I do not know what to think, but I have not felt this way long. What do you think?" He wanted her approval. He needed to hear her say he was not insane or something worse.

"Henry, Karen is an adult. She will let you know if she is not interested. Be yourself, darling. I am pleased, tickled. But, Henry, call your daughter. What is wrong with you? Sarah is so upset. She asks me every night to see if I have heard from you."

"Thanks, Barby. I'll call her tomorrow, I promise." Finally, Henry felt a little better.

"Get some sleep, Henry. I love you."

"I love you too, Barby. Bye."

Barby felt sick. She wanted to tell Henry so many things.

CHAPTER 49

Serendipity?

*H*enry went to breakfast the following day, eager to see Karen again. Henry located her on the other side of the restaurant.

She saw him wave, and her smile quieted all his trepidation. She slowly made her way over to his side. "Good morning sunshine, I'm working the other side today. Please sneak over this way, sweety?"

"Good morning, Karen. I'll come that way right now." he felt lighthearted.

"Henry, I hope you got some rest. Or should I say, Hank? How are you feeling this morning?" Her face broke out in a wide grin.

"I'm fine, thank you," he replied.

"I know who you are!" she said playfully.

She was so direct it caught him off guard. "Who am I? Hell, I don't know who I am."

Karen sat at his table. "I talked to my Aunt. So, you are the guy my cousin Barby has been trying to get me to meet. Quite Don Juan, huh? You were in love with both of my cousins?"

Henry shrugged his shoulders. He took a deep breath and let it out.

"That was a long time ago," he said quietly.

"Barby told me you still haven't got over losing Brandy. Henry, for a Don Juan type not to remarry, that makes people talk, Honey."

"What are they talking about?" he asked.

She thought for a moment. "Bobby has told me all kinds of stories. But, of course, I will not discuss the stories Bobby tells." she raised her eyebrows and grinned.

"I sure wish Bobby would keep quiet regarding family matters."

"Be careful, mister; I happen to be family." Karen twisted her smile into a scowl.

"Wow, you just saw an idiot insult a lady. Karen, will you be so gracious and forget I said something stupid."

"Henry, you didn't seem disparaging yesterday. I want to stuff that into a heavy-duty box and bury it deep in the ground. I'm not very happy." Karen stood up and walked away.

Henry finished his breakfast and went down to his room. He remembered one flower shop in the tiny town; Henry grabbed his keys and drove down the road. Blooming Heartache, he always liked the name.

"Good morning, Lady. Boy, do I need a beautiful Bouquet?"

"Henry Rotyn, what kind of trouble are you in now?"

"Wow, I keep getting into trouble everywhere I go. I know your beautiful eyes, Cynthia." Henry grinned with a hopeful adjective.

"How's Barby and things in California, lover, boy." Cynthia grinned.
"Barby is doing well; she has three boys, and I have two girls. The boys are mine too, but Barby won't marry me." Henry looked down.

"Why are you dating Karen; she is a little young for you, old man."

"Cynthia, how do you know so much?" Henry tried to smile.

"Karen loves tulips, purple tulips, Henry." Cynthia stared at him.

"Cynthia, please help me find a beautiful don't hate card and a huge, expensive purple Tulip Bouquet?"

"Henry, I have just the thing, dear; I can spend some of your money too."

An hour later, Henry walked up the stairwell into the restaurant. He sat the bouquet in the middle of the table with the card leaned against the cut glass vase.

Henry dressed up for the occasion. He looked all over for Karen but didn't see her anywhere. So, Henry looked out at the landscape. Henry couldn't tell where the river was upstream. The area had so many trees and brush it was impossible to see any part of the river.

He turned, and Karen draped her arms around him and pinned him against the window frame.

"I need to apologize, Hank. May I call you Hank?" Karen said.

"I would like that very much, Karen."

"Will you forgive me for stepping out of line, Darling?" Karen whispered.

"You must like tulips?" Henry smiled.

"I love tulips, Honey. I loved the card too, Henry."

"Have you ever had dinner at Wynn Schuler's?" Henry asked.

"No, I cannot afford anything like Wynn Schuler's. I've never been there, Darling." Karen teased.

"Karen, you live in a mansion. How many people live there, Honey?"

"Bobby doesn't charge rent. He allows family only. My Aunt and her two boys, myself, Bobby's oldest boy, and Sherry's sister and her three children. Nine of us in all." Karen kissed him for a long time.

They drove the Mercedes Convertible the next night with the top down across country roads. They both had to wear ponytails to keep their hair under control.

"Henry, my goodness, the Mercedes is such a wonderful ride. Barby told me a girlfriend bought that for you, brand new. May I ask what kind of performance brought that car home?" she giggled.

"Alright, Karen, I'll step into this trap. We were both eighteen, and this was my first time. The car didn't come to light until eighteen years later, and she is a Billionaire today.

"Why didn't you marry Barby when Brandy died?" Do you still love her?" she asked.

"You should ask your cousin. We would have been man and wife long ago if I had my way. It is a complicated issue, Karen. I love Barby, and she loves me, and we had three boys together; we stop right there." He was getting too serious and tried to smile.

"Karen, can we please discuss our time together?" Henry implored.

"The wine is exquisite, Darling; do you enjoy a California wine every night?" Karen asked.

"Almost every night, but that sometimes depends on fish, meat, or poultry." Henry smiled.

"Brandy taught me everything about wines, fine food, cooking, caring for a lady, and acting like a gentleman. Brandy taught me everything about life: kindness, love never fails, patience, hope, and decency will win you many happy memories."

"You speak like a very charismatic man." Karen marveled at his remarks.

"Karen, have you ever visited California?"

"No, I've been to Florida," she replied.

"Do you have your college credentials? She asked.

"I never graduated from college. When Brandy died, I sold her house and business. I moved to Berkeley to be close to Barby. Brandy told her sister to help raise Sarah. California was the answer."

"Bobby told me the family helped each other until the lawyers finished with all the legal stuff. Then everybody left in the family became rich overnight." Karen said.

"It worked out like that, but I bought an HVAC business from my uncle. I am not, nor was I ever, a poor person."

"You have a very colorful reputation." Henry.

She looked at him like his mother did when she questioned his morals, but the philanderer in him abated years ago.

"Why didn't you ever remarry Henry?"

Henry smiled, "Who is this aunt of yours?"

"Aunt Elizabeth said you wouldn't know her, but she knows all about you. She's older than my Mom but younger than Aunt Eileen."

"Well, why didn't you remarry? Surely, in twenty years, you must have met a woman who caught your eye—and you are beautiful."

Henry's smile left; he sat thinking for a minute. He did not know why, but he felt a chill come over him, and he needed to stretch his legs.

"Hey, are you alright?" Karen requested.

Henry fought off the wave of emotion. "How long is a normal person supposed to grieve a loved one?"

Karen slid over next to him. "It's been a long time, Henry." She wanted to comfort him in some way but just sat quietly beside him. "Brandy's out at Riverview, isn't she?"

Henry looked at her curiously. "Yeah, I was there yesterday with Bobby." He tried to smile again.

"Come on," she said. You need some fresh air." Karen stopped by the kitchen and arranged for another waitress to assume her responsibilities.

Karen and Henry walked out to her car, and she drove to Riverview. He found the gravesite and sat down on a rock nearby.

Karen asked kindly but with convincing empathy, "Henry, tell me all about Brandy."

Henry thought for a minute. Then, he began telling her the story of his relationship with Barby and Brandy. Henry laughed and had some tearful moments several times. She sat and listened for more than two hours while he shared many memories of his life with Brandy and Barby.

Henry told Karen, "You look a lot like Brandy. She was athletic, fair-skinned, and beautiful."

She leaned over and kissed him gently.

Henry was feeling unfamiliar, clumsy emotions. The kiss lasted longer than intended, and Henry returned seated.

"That was very nice." She implied.

"I like being near her. She made me incredibly happy. Sarah is such a beautiful girl. Would you like to see her picture?"

"Of course!" Karen knelt near him.

Henry pulled out his favorite picture of Sarah. She was in her cheerleader uniform. "It was her junior year in high school. She is a senior at the University of California now."

"She is a darling. She looks a lot like her Mom," she returned the picture.

They sat and talked for a while longer.

They got back to the Inn, where they had lunch together.

"So, you've never married?" he asked.

"Nope, many guys have tried to bully me, but I don't want to live around here. So I'm content awaiting my prince to ride here and carry me off."

"So, you're into chivalry; how long are you willing to wait for such a meritorious monarch?" he asked.

"Why, do you think I'm getting too old?" She wanted to see him dodge this one.

He smiled but decided to be quiet.

They spent the rest of the day together; Henry met her Aunt later in the afternoon. He learned Karen's last name was Hanson.

They drove to Battle Creek and had dinner with Bobby and Sherry.

Karen wore a killer red dress. After dinner, they set up a stereo and danced late into the night. Henry was surprised when Sherry asked him to dance.

"You look very nice tonight, Sherry," Henry said.

"Henry, you look genuinely nice too. I need to get this off my chest. Bobby told me he spoke to you about your conduct many years ago. Do not think you are off my indiscreet list. You have been at the top of that memo for many years. I am going to spill my guts completely. You should have gone to Bobby the night you insulted me, saw me naked, rubbed yourself against me, kissed me, and I think you would have gone further. Instead, I followed your advances to discover who was with you. It turns out low and beholds, and it was Barby. I have been upset with both of you for too many years. There, I cleared the air. Do not ever pull that scumbag trick again. I love you. I will always love you. However, I love Bobby much more. We are family and need to be friends. I want to be your friend." Sherry held her head high and kissed him.

"Doesn't matter what I say, Sherry. I was wrong, and I admit this to you. However, I have always held you in high esteem. Bobby is still my best friend; you are a wonderful wife, mother, and friend. My last prayer before I die will be to ask for forgiveness regarding how I hurt you. I want to earn your respect and honor. However, if you feel I should remain at the top of your list, let it be just so. Now, may I clear something off my chest?" he asked.

"Henry, you have the floor."

"Sherry, how am I supposed to ignore your cleavage? I know I should not recognize your femininity." Henry grinned.

"Honey, looking at a woman's femininity is not what gets you in trouble. But thank you for the compliment." Sherry smiled.

"Listen, do you know what Brandy told Barby just before she died?"

"No, Henry, I don't know anything about this at all, Honey," Sherry implored.

"Brandy told Barby that she could never marry me. She died; those were her last words. I think Barby finally told Bobby. Barby takes these words literally. Barby won't marry me, but she will fool around and have our children. We sleep together several times yearly, but it is always a sneaky hide-in-the-hay thing. Sherry, can you help Barby? We live four houses away, and our children are confused, but I love Bar so much. I'm dating Karen, but I'm almost old enough to be her father. Sherry, can you help Barby, please?"

Yes, I will fly out to spend a few days with Barby. I'll do what I can; you know it's free. I l; behave yourself, mister." Sherry kissed him for longer than she expected and walked away.

Bobby walked up to him. "Henry, why are you kissing my wife?"

"I didn't kiss her; Sherry kissed me, Bobby."

"Well, I want to kiss someone too. But I cannot kiss my cousin." Bobby said.

"Go kiss your wife, Bobby." Henry laughed.

Henry stayed in one of the guestrooms at the Kraneger mansion that night. Sleeping in the old mansion brought back countless memories, and he floated fairly as the reveries danced in his mind all night.

In the morning, Henry and Karen went to the Inn together. They had breakfast and sat talking.

"Karen, this is a tiny town, and the neighbors will be talking soon." Her smile captivated him, and he liked her a lot, although he secretly did not think he could win her over.

"Should we give them something to talk about?" she teased.

Karen leaned over and kissed him.

Henry raised his eyebrows. "Wow, what a lallapaloosa Karen."

She laughed, "What is a lallapaloosa?" she giggled.

Henry stood up, pulled her into his arms, tipped her way back, and kissed her. Then, he brought her back to her feet. "Lallapaloosa!" he announced.

"My favorite kiss, darling." she smiled and stared. Then, she leaned over and kissed him. "You liked that, huh!" she said.

He nodded approvingly.

"Listen to me, mister. I like kissing you, but you belong to another woman. Barby is my cousin. I love her, and I know she loves me too," she said.

"My name is Henry Rotyn. I was raised and educated in this small town. I do not live here anymore, but it is still my home. So, I have small-town values. When I was growing up, I had this fixation on virtue and honesty. I am leaving Barneyville on Friday. I would like it if you could come out and visit California. I immensely enjoyed our time together. Just think about what I am saying. I am not asking you to make any decisions. Let us become friends."

Her face lit up, but she tried to repress her elation. "I don't know you," she said.

"I just introduced myself; my name is Henry Rotyn. Your Aunt knows me."

"I don't know you," she said. Her face reddened until it peaked, with her cheeks rosy and glowing.

"We have three more days. Can you take some time off and spend some time together?"

"Henry, you are quite a bit older than me. I like you, but we have too many years between us. I would like very much to become friends. Yes, I can take some time off. I would like that very much, Honey, but with some sense of reality. Please rationalize our opportunities. Friendship first and whatever later."

"We have already spent a night together." Oops, he realized he might have said a few words too many.

"In your dreams!" Her mouth fell open, and Karen could not believe he would publicly say such a thing.

"What do you dream about when you lay in bed?" he asked.

She did not answer his question, and she had a puzzled look on her face. "I'm not telling."

"I've had the same dream for many years. I dream I meet a beautiful woman, and we are happy together." Henry said.

"Now, just a minute; there is no use creating romantic love," she said.

"In my dreams, we are very romantically involved, and I make you very happy!" he took her hand.

She smiled but did not say a word for a few minutes. "Are you mentally challenged, Henry!" she laughed.

"Karen, please give me a chance. I know I can sweep you off your feet." He pulled her out of her chair and kissed her before she could resist.

She enjoyed his kiss. She put her arms around him, pulling herself closer than she should in public. Her sense of decency resurfaced, and she pushed out of his grasp. "So, you're a good kisser. I'm impressed." She said, moving away, trying to regain her senses.

"Karen, I can make you incredibly happy. I'm the prince that will carry you off to his castle."

He wrapped his arms around her waist. She leaned backward away from his lips with a sheepish grin.

"Oh, what the hell; where's your castle, Prince Henry?"

"A man's home is his castle. Mine is in Berkeley, fourteen hundred feet above the San Francisco Bay."

"Do we have to have sex?" she asked.

He smiled and whispered, "No, but we can make babies."

Everyone started clapping, and he kissed her again.

"I can take three days off but will not go to your castle. I'm staying in Barneyville."

Karen put her arms around him and uninhibitedly accepted his embrace.

"Did you ever meet Brandy?" Henry asked Karen.

"Yes, but I was so young, only four or five, I think, but I remember Aunt Eileen."

Thursday night, Henry and Karen had dinner with Bobby and Sherry. Sherry was very mature. Bobby was not surprised Henry had uncovered his beautiful cousin in Barneyville. However, he was thankful she had no sisters.

Henry canceled the remainder of his business appointments.

The following day, they drove up to Holland. Henry put the top down. "Did you know I'm about forty percent Chippewa?" he asked.

No, I had no idea, Henry," she said.

"I assume your mother and her two sisters had the same Father?" Henry asked.

"Yes, Henry, their fathers were the same, I believe."

"Then you too are Chippewa, at 20%, dear." Henry grinned.

"I had no idea, darling." Karen was stunned.

"My Father was eighty percent Chippewa. My mother is mostly Swedish."

"My mother is Italian. My father was a mixed-race, but he died in Vietnam."

"Oh Karen, I am sorry for your loss. How old were you when that happened?"

"I was an infant. I never knew him. My Mom was a nurse in Battle Creek. She never married again. However, I was an only child, and my Mom brought a nice income. I was happy."

"My dad was in Korea. He died when I was thirteen. Mom never married again until the past few years."

"Can you stay with me again tonight? I mean, be together. I trust you, Henry."

"I would love to stay with you tonight. Yes, you can trust me, Honey."

"We probably won't get home until well after dark too." She spoke.

"Karen, are you warm enough?"

"Yes, I love convertibles. I have never ridden in a Mercedes. It's a lovely ride, Henry."

"My Mom is from Holland. Karen, you look gorgeous this morning."

"How old are you, Henry?"

"I'm forty-three. That's old, huh?

"No, my goodness. You are sixteen years older, so what? Who will take care of you? Single men usually look nicer than married men, but someone takes good care of you.

"Sarah is my hygienist. She thinks I need forty-five minutes of a girl's touch every morning," he laughed.

"A good woman can make her man look very chic."

"Karen, do I look chic?"

"Yes, yes, yes!"

"I feel better," he smiled.

"Friendship, Henry. Don't get excited."

"I live in a social world, Karen. I will keep it that way until you tell me to take my foot off the brake pedal."

"I will remember Henry. You can tease, treat me like a woman, act like a gentleman, and smile."

"There is Lake Michigan; do you get over here very often?"

"Yes, in late July to the middle of August, Henry. Do you know how to body surf? She asked.

"Yeah, but I'm a pretty good surfer too."

"Can you teach me how to surf? I'll wear my bikini," she said.

"I would love to teach you, but don't get out this way often. It takes weeks to learn. I mean, a tight bikini is a solid option. But, Karen, I am puzzled. Well, I guess friendship can go a long way, huh," he said.

"We have two more days, mister. I am glad my bikini has some value. Especially if I keep it on."

"Oh my, Henry. Look at the colors. Look at the tulips. Darling, this is extraordinary."

"Darling?"

She looked at him and smiled.

"I have not been here for more than twenty years. Have you ever been here, Karen?"

"I was here a long time ago. Look at all the colors. Holland is a beautiful city, Henry."

"We need to talk," he said.

"What, Honey? I'm listening, dear," she said.

"Did you bring your bikini?"

"No, but you could stop and buy me a very nice one."

"Well, I wouldn't want you to think I was trying to take advantage of you, Karen."

"Look at the flowers, Henry. I'd love to have a bikini with these flowers."

Henry pulled into a wet burrito restaurant.

"Hey Karen, did you notice the ladies' apparel across the street?"

"Henry, I could kiss you."

"Henry, what beautiful ring hangs on your neck?"

"This ring is Brandy's marriage ring." Henry holds it in Karen's palm.

They walked back to the car with beautiful fruit-colored bikinis.

He opened the door for her. She turned and kissed him for a long time.

They walked through thousands of rows of flowers. Then, in mid-afternoon, they went to the state beach. He had a bathing suit in the trunk. They both changed clothes and took beach towels and flip-flops to the water. He put sunscreen on her shoulders, arms, chest, and belly. He told her he did not burn.

They swam out to the breakers and caught five-foot waves for two hours.

They stopped in waist-deep water and kissed.

"Hey, beautiful green eyes. Are you ready to change and hit the road?"

"I'm having a wonderful day, Henry."

"You, my dear, are making my day wonderful."

Henry called Bobby. "Hello, Rogue. Do you have an extra room, Bobby?"

"Yes, we do, Rogue. Will Karen need a room?"

"I honestly haven't asked her, and I'm a little hesitant regarding that subject." Henry didn't say much.

"Hey, don't worry about it, Rogue. We can let the women figure it out planned to spend the night there. Henry told Sherry they would not arrive until after eight. Sherry told him they only ate after eight most nights.

Karen slept at Battle Creek.

Karen took a shower when they arrived and came out with the most beautiful tropical V-neck and skirt. Henry wore Bermuda shorts and a sleeveless shirt.

"Would you like to be in a bedroom by yourself, Karen?" Sherry asked.

"I think Henry will behave himself. Won't you, Darling?"

"I don't have an excellent reputation around here, Karen. But look, I'm so tired I will probably fall asleep when my head hits my pillow."

Everyone turned in about midnight, and Karen slipped into bed while Henry was brushing his teeth. Henry turned out the lights and curled in next to her. She kissed him goodnight.

Henry slept in until ten.

Karen was talking to Sherry when Henry walked out in his boxers.

"No, no, no, mister. March right back into your room and put some clothes on." Sherry yelled.

"Karen, did he go to bed like that, too?" she asked.

"I think so, and I didn't frisk him. He was not horny; he kissed me goodnight and went to sleep.

"You are kidding me, Karen. So, you were bare-ass naked, and he did not make a move?"

"I still don't think he knows. Let us get some coffee and see if he remembers, Sherry."

Henry came out fully dressed. "I did not mean to come out here in my skivvies. I don't think I knew where I was, ladies."

"Have a nice hot cup of coffee. Cream but no sugar?" Sherry asked.

"Yes, thank you," Henry said.

"What time did you come to bed, sleepy boy?" Karen asked. She smiled at Sherry.

"Midnight. Why do you ask, dear?"

"You must have been very tired, slippery. What do you remember about last night, Henry?" Karen asked.

"Did I do something wrong? I know I do not walk in my sleep. Am I in trouble?" Henry asked.

"No, Henry, you are not in trouble. We wanted to know what you remembered about last night." Sherry asked.

"I don't remember anything. What is going on here? Is Barby hiding around the corner?" Henry asked.

"What did I wear to bet, Honey?" Karen asked.

"I don't know, something white?" he asked.

"Henry, I was bare-assed naked." Karen smiled.

"No, you were wearing something. I would have noticed. I remember you were hot." Henry smiled.

"My what, Henry? What do you remember?" Karen asked.

"I am sorry, but that is all I remember, and I ruined our night?"

"Maybe, kind of, just a little bit." Karen grinned.

"Any chance I could get a second opportunity?"

"Nope, don't think so. You are leaving in twenty-four hours. My period started this morning." Karen grinned again.

"You're not coming to California?" he asked.

"Not right away. Maybe before the snow flies."

"Sherry, is your phone turned on? Something funny is going on here." Henry asked.

"Hello, sweety. I heard everything you said. Do the horses jinx you, Darling? So, what would have happened last night if you were not dead tired?" Barby asked.

"I want to go home. I like all of you. I love all of you, but I want to go home. Damn it, Barby, I want to come home. I want you in my bed every night. I need you, Barby. You tell me to search worldwide for a woman I can love. Finally, I have a woman I can love and do not need anyone else. I lived a double life for so many years. I grew up believing in my innocence in everything, but that charisma was elusive. So, I'm leaving for California today. I love you, Barby." Henry held his head down.

Henry walked Karen to the Kraneger Mansion. He pulled Karen into his arms and kissed her goodbye.

"Please come to California, Darling. You can stay at my house. You're a smart woman, Karen. I need a lady in my office; the lady who runs the office is retiring. I'd love to see your beautiful face every morning."

CHAPTER 50

Barby & Henry

*H*enry's heart leaped when Sarah entered the restaurant; she looked much like her mother. "Hello, darling," he said.

Sarah didn't say a word. Instead, she looked at her Father without moving an inch. Then she crossed her arms and looked past her Father.

"I have been looking forward to seeing you, young lady."

She was dressed to the nines and happy to see her Father, but she wouldn't show weakness. Sarah Rotyn was upset with her Father, but she was hiding her emotions. He had been gone far too long, and she would let him have it with both barrels. She spent two hours getting her hair done, along with a facial and having her nails done, too. She wore her emerald green evening dress; it was her Father's favorite. Barby weaved a princess braid on the back of her head with her long blond hair. Her diamond earrings completed the glimmer in her eyes. Sarah loved her Father and missed his company terribly.

"Daddy, it is so good to see you." When Henry rose to help her into her chair, she embraced him tenderly but firmly. She whispered, "I love you." Sarah kissed her Father lightly on the lips, then on the left cheek and right cheek.

Henry guided her into her chair, and she sat ladylike, just like her mother would have done in public. Henry ached to tell her how much like her mother she had become, the mother she never knew.

"Daddy, what are you doing? Did you finally get tired of all the traveling? I mean, my God, how long has it been? I thought you forgot you had a daughter. Why don't you call me? I had to wait for a call from Uncle Bobby to find out where you were. Barneyville? Daddy, you promised we would go there together. I love you. I want you to be happy, and I want you to be safe, but I want you to be near me. I don't like it when you go off on these cross-country treks."

Henry leaned over the table and spoke. "Inhale."

Sarah hated it when he did that to her, but she was furious now because he dared to do it publicly. Her purse sat on the chair next to her, and she grabbed it by its long leather strap and flung it at his head. Henry's left hand took the brunt of the impact. He ducked and held at it with his right hand, catching the strap. He returned it to her but with hesitant reluctance.

"Hey! I thought you missed me. Is that any way to treat your Father?"

"No! I want you to be more responsible in our relationship!"

Henry smiled, "I suppose you still want me to get married too!"

"Yes, Daddy. It would be best if you had someone as a companion. You know how I feel about that, so do not joke around. I mean it." She still had a formidable grip on her handbag.

Rachel appeared from the crowd, and Sarah jumped up and caught her sister in stride. They embraced and kissed on both cheeks. They picked up European origin when they were in Paris. Rachel turned to face her Father, whom she had left sitting awkwardly. She wore the same dress as Sarah, except hers was cerulean blue, matching her eyes. The two young women could have passed for twins.

However, Rachel commanded a presence with her refinement and dignified posture that Sarah could not match. In addition, Rachel was more elegant, whereas Sarah was more athletic.

"Father, four weeks? Have you become irresponsible? We had a dinner engagement before you left; we had another last week, and you stood me up twice. I was humiliated. Do you know how a girl looks eating dinner alone?"

He sat staring at her, unable to move or comment. Henry felt like a little boy chastised by a parent. Then, finally, he looked at Sarah but received the cold shoulder. Her reaction was undoubtedly a direct result of her association with Rachel.

"I have been on my feet all day, Father. How long must a girl stand?" She tapped her fingernails on the table impatiently.

Henry jumped up. "Pardon me, dear, and I'm not myself tonight. However, it's obvious you two are on the same page."

Rachel put up her left hand before sitting down. "Father, my temperament is persnickety at best."

"Sarah, may I compliment you on your taste this evening? You look fabulous. I love what you have done with your hair, and your taste in apparel is impeccable." Rachel said, looking at her Father.

"Daddy, you have not said a word about how we look. Your bank account took a major hit, and your lack of appreciation for our intensive and exhaustive shopping only leaves us with one recourse."

"I can go into the city on Friday. How about you, Rachel?"

Henry held up his hands, "I give up. I am sorry, but please understand there is no doubt in my mind. There is not another father in America blessed with beauty; I am privileged to be in the company of this evening. I truly stand in awe."

Rachel looked at Sarah. She held up three fingers, and Sarah held up four. "Father, when only one hand is needed…I implore you; please express yourself using stronger superlatives!" Rachel's smile could have killed from one hundred feet away.

"Father, have you found your soul mate yet?" Rachel stared and waited for his reply.

Henry threw his hands in the air again, "How would it be if I just grabbed the first good-looking woman I see?"

"Daddy, don't be this, Way. I swear I will tickle you to death. Right here, right now!" Sarah pursed her lips tightly. Then she kicked Henry under the table.

"Ouch! Don't do that," he said.

"Daddy, you're embarrassing me," Sarah whined.

"Father, get a grip, please!" Rachel quipped.

Henry looked at his daughter and said, "Sarah, I'm not interested."

Rachel emptied her glass of water on his head.

Henry wiped his face and smiled at Rachel. "Is this a tag team match?" he asked.

"Daddy, why isn't Karen with you?" Sarah asked.

"How did you know about Karen?" he asked.

"I told her," Barby said.

Henry turned and smiled at Barby. He stood up quickly. "Barby, you startled me."

Barby looked tired and sad. She had dark circles under her eyes, and her clothes were frumpy.

"Where's Karen at Henry?" Barby asked.

Henry looked at the floor. He scratched his head and took a deep breath. "She stayed in Michigan," he mumbled.

"Daddy!" Sarah cried.

Barby felt a sliver of hope touch her heart. Then she remembered Sherry and the horse barn. A sullen and miserable mood filled her heart and ached clear to her bones. No, she would not allow herself to sink into that awful quagmire. She touched his face and said, "We don't have to discuss this in public." she said peacefully.

Rachel touched his shoulder. "You look so unhappy, Father."

Henry helped Barby into her seat beside him. Sarah was on his left, and Rachel sat across from him.

Barby looked into his eyes and said, "We need to talk, Henry."

Henry got a queasy, uneasy feeling in his gut. It had not surfaced in many years. However, the weak-kneed symptoms were unmistakable. It came to him first in Florida when Barby walked in on him in Brandy's bed; the sickness filled him with grief. What ignoble experience awaited him from this vixen he had loved so desperately all his life? What sordid scheme had the beautiful, brown-eyed Darling concocted? His gut feeling warned him of an immense collaboration about to unfold. He was pillowless this time and looked for a place to hide. But, of course, they would need to be found. After all, it was part of the plan and the conspiracy. Henry looked at the floor; he could not bring himself to look up. He tried, but he could not do it. The nausea got worse.

He stood up, thinking she wanted to talk privately. Instead, Barby got up and hugged him.

Barby hung her arms around his neck. She lifted his chin, and then she kissed him tenderly.

Henry liked it, and he liked it a lot. Suddenly, old memories like seeds that waited for rain burst forth: her taste, hair's smell, and perfume. He responded and returned her kiss. Henry wanted to consume her.

Sarah screamed, "Daddy!" Henry staggered back a little.

Rachel added, "Way to go, Father. Nothing like sowing wild oats. You might, however, assume some semblance of dignity."

After he regained his composure, he looked into her beautiful brown eyes. "Hello, pretty girl." Barby had a strange look in her eye. She pressed against him again; her belly was slightly bulged and rounded. He touched it with both hands as their lips met again.

Sarah yelled again, "Daddy, what the hell are you doing?"

"Please, Aunt Barby." Sarah pleaded.

Henry pulled away and asked, "Barby, are you pregnant again?"

"Hold still, you fool!" Barby's face broke out in a huge smile.

Henry looked at Rachel; she had a scornful look on her face. But then, he looked over at Sarah, and she was gleaming.

"Okay, what in the hell is going on here? Why did you do that to me, Barby?"

Barby whispered into his ear, "I remember an episode in a horse barn!" She explained sarcastically.

Henry intuitively knew. He felt the queasiness return.

Barby whispered, "I made you a promise years ago; I don't break promises. I asked you once before, and you had forgotten my promise. So, tell me my promise to you."

Henry got the same stupid look on his face, and she began to get mad. Henry whispered to her tenuously, "You promised to love me?" She bit his ear lobe hard.

"Ouch, why did you do that, Barby?"

She pursed her lips and turned her head but kept her eyes on him. She was beaming now.

Sarah was giggling like a teenager.

Rachel said, "Should we tell him or just let him flounder?"

Sarah yelled, "Let him flounder!"

Barby said, "Henry, do you remember last winter when I asked you to give us a sperm sample because our bank was in short supply?"

Henry sat down. He looked at Sarah; she shrugged her shoulders again. Finally, he looked at Rachel, but she snubbed him. "I'm not part of this, but I knew about it," Rachel said.

He looked into Barby's brown eyes and asked, "Are you telling me…" Henry could not say it. Barby moved her head up and down.

Henry said, "You mean...."

She moved her head up and down again. Finally, he stood up again and wrapped his arms around her in a tender embrace.

Henry's face broke out into a broad smile. The double dimples remained fixed and natural. "It would have been nice to have just a little more to do with this."

Barby said in a very seductive voice, "Oh, I don't doubt that for a moment. How the hell did you find my cousin? Are you a bloodhound? I mean, sniffing out my family like that!"

Henry recalled his history with Barby; warm memories flooded his mind with sweetness. He recalled the passionate evenings in the Berkeley hills so many years ago. Then there were those nights in Anaheim.

Rachel said, "You should see your face. It's beet red, Father."

Sarah chirped in, "Daddy?"

"Hey, come on, Barby. You told me that you tried to get Karen to come to California. You said you were going to introduce her to me. We met, and we did not know each other. I didn't even make a connection with your family."

"Yeah, right," Barby said. She looked at her niece for support, but by the look on her face, Barby could tell Sarah was buying his load of rotten potatoes.

"Isn't there something illegal about this?" he whined.

Barby drew herself close to him and whispered. "Do you want to press charges?" Barby bumped her belly against him at the same time.

"Funny," Henry said sarcastically.

Henry felt uncomfortable about the situation; Barby still had something up her sleeve, as if she were waiting to play a trump card.

Barby shoved him backward; he almost fell over his chair.

"Sherry flew out here for two days while you dragged your feet getting here. So, we talked for two full days. I'm sorry, Henry; I love you so much." Barby said.

Henry started to get mad, he turned to face Barby, and she thumped him in the chest.

"Hey, you dope, I have your baby! And it's a girl." Barby said.

"I know how all of this will thwart our lives." Henry looked at the floor.

Barby's eyes became sullen and sad. Her cheeks puffed up, and her eyes became watery.

Henry never intended to hurt this woman he had loved for so long. However, he sensed her love for him and knew she was in deep emotional pain.

Sarah said, "Daddy, we will all get up and leave here!"

Rachel added, "Father, I will hurt you, I promise. You will feel pain acutely."

Henry said, "I'm sorry, Barby, but this is a lot to lay on a guy. I have loved you my entire life."

"Do you want to know her name, silly boy?" Barby forced a smile but was still fighting off tears.

Henry bit his lip and nodded yes.

"Her name will be Brandy Eileen Rotyn."

Henry smiled. "While tears dripped down his cheeks. I don't know what to say, Honey."

"Henry, it's going to be all right," Barby said.

Barby kissed him tenderly. He responded, and her perfume and her taste overwhelmed him. Henry's knees became weak, and he fought off vertigo.

Barby looked into his eyes and said, "Sarah, how many children do we have sugar?"

Sarah said, "Three."

"Henry, how many children have I always told you I would have?"

Henry grinned. "You always told me four. Sarah is one of four."

"My fourth child is yours, just like the first three are ours. I do not have a problem with that. Do you?"

Barby displayed a spirit Henry had not seen since Brandy was in college. He loved this independent woman and fully intended to support her and their child.

Rachel and Sarah came and put their arms around the embracing couple.

Barby whispered into his ear, "You are my first love and my last love. Now, do you remember?"

Henry became very emotional, "It was the night on the school bus after Dad died?"

Barby beamed brightly. "We can raise this child together; it isn't our first. Silly boy!"

Henry replied, almost in tears, "I'm not sure my heart can take it."

Barby said, "Maybe not, but there are five hearts here, and I have always heard there is strength in numbers. Besides, I know Brandy would approve."

Henry was confused. "Barby, I love you; I have always loved you. I cannot live without you. I cannot do this anymore. I do not want to date another woman. I do not want to pretend I am looking at my soul mate. I found her years ago. I do not care how messy it gets or who gets mad about it. All I know is that I cannot do this anymore. I want to kiss you goodnight and feel you beside me in the morning."

Barby watched him drop to his knees. Henry pulled a ring out of his pants that he had for many years. Barby, it would be best if you were my wife. I know you love me. But, please, Darling, I am begging you," Henry said.

Barby placed her fingers over his mouth. She kissed him tenderly and wrapped herself around him. "I know you love me, Henry. I've always loved you too."

"I'd like you to drop one knee, Henry."

"Ask me, right now, right here. In front of your girls. Ask me, Henry?"

"Barby, will you marry me?"

Tears streamed down her face. "Yes, my love. Yes, my love." I will not torture you anymore. I want you to kiss me goodnight every night, and I want to wake up in your arms."

She kissed him for a long, long time. "Henry, our children can visit their parents in the same house. I will take your name, and we will be happy. I promise."

"Barby, I am removing this ring from around my neck. This Darling is Brandy's wedding ring. I would like you to wear it on special occasions. So, we can share it, and I want Sarah and Rachel to share it with you and me, Darling."

Henry felt a terrific weight lift off his shoulders. Brandy would approve; he was sure of it.

Barby wiped the single tear that had fallen and lingered on his cheek. Then, she kissed the spot where the incision had been.

"I dream about you every night, Henry," Barby said.

Sarah whined, "Oh, Daddy. You and Barby will be delighted."

Rachel put her left hand on Henry's cheek. "If you weren't my father, I'd marry you too."

Henry looked at Barby, and her beauty touched his heart as Brandy's beauty affected him. But she was not Brandy.

Henry kissed Barby. "Silly girl, are you sure about this?"

"I've always loved you, Henry. It is the best thing for our families. It is the best thing for us. We have two houses. You and I will live in one. The older children can live in the other house. Love is an easy word to say but a difficult word to learn," Barby said.

"Sherry was wonderful, Honey; we cried together for two long days. She helped me come to my senses. Sherry loves you, Henry." Barby kissed him again.

Henry looked at each of the women clinging to him and smiled contentedly. "You never know the direction of your dreams. I have four beautiful women in my life now, soon to be five. I have three wonderful men. I love this family. I truly do."

Barby touched her lips to his. Henry and Barby were happy. I am so thrilled.

We yearned for and cherished love.
We aspired to freedom yet were afraid to be free.
We struggled for maturity, as our passions controlled the direction of our dreams.

Michael Patrick Tryon 2023

ABOUT THE AUTHOR

*M*ICHAEL PATRICK TRYON was born and raised in Michigan. He was a Seabee Diver (NEC 5345) in the U.S. Navy. He was a P.A.D.I. scuba diving instructor and taught diving in California and Bermuda. He worked in the HVAC&R trade for forty-five years in California.

He was an avid sailor on his Islander 36, for many years.

He taught heating and air conditioning and refrigeration part time at IBT in Santa Clara, California for ten years and for Local 39 in San Francisco for four years.

Michael is retired. He still lives with his wife Janice of fifty years.

Michael lives in Shreveport, LA.

Michael other published books are "Seabee Diver" and "Spoof

*H*enry and Barby are neighbors, classmates, and more. Barby's family is affluent and well-to-do, while Henry's family leads a simple life on a small income. Feelings of ambivalence pervade young Henry's adolescence because he falls in love with both Barby and her sister. Brandy, Barby's older sister, seduces college bound Henry and their secret sexual escapades entrap them in a love they try to ignore. While Henry struggles to endure the love of two sisters, college, and careers span from coast to coast. Then tragedy strikes and the two families unite as they try to hold on to normalcy.

THESE WERE THE INNOCENT YEARS.

The two teenagers sat and talked and warmed themselves by the fire.

"Henry, I hate you."

Henry looked at Barby bewildered. "What did I do now?"

Barby reached out and pulled his hair over his head and covered his face. "Your hair looks nicer than mine. I refuse to associate with a boy who has hair like that. It's bad enough that it's longer but it looks nicer too!"

He looked at her and rolled his eyes back and forth. "So, wash it once in a while."

She slapped him across his shoulder with her open palm. "Ouch," she said. "Now you tried to hurt me." Her face broke into a repressed grin.

"Barby, you hit me, I didn't hit you."

She pouted and stuck out her bottom lip. "Do you think I'm pretty?"

Henry put his hands over his face to hide his response. "I think Brandy is pretty," he said in a low voice—almost a whisper.

www.ingramcontent.com/pod-product-compliance
Lightning Source LLC
Chambersburg PA
CBHW020918140626
46545CB00015B/102